EARL PEYROUX'S
"Gourmet Cooking"

EARL PEYROUX'S
"Gourmet Cooking"
By Earl Peyroux

PELICAN PUBLISHING COMPANY
Gretna 1999

*The word "Pelican" and the depiction of a pelican are
trademarks of Pelican Publishing Company, Inc., and are
registered in the U.S. Patent and Trademark Office*

Library of Congress Cataloging-in-Publication Data
Peyroux, Earl.
  Earl Peyroux's "Gourmet Cooking" / Earl Peyroux.
    p.   cm.
  Includes index.
  ISBN 1-56554-323-8 (hc : alk. paper)
  1. Cookery. 2. Cookery, Cajun. 3. Cookery, Creole. 4. Cookery, Mediterranean. 5. Gourmet cooking with Earl Peyroux
(Television program) I. Gourmet cooking with Earl Peyroux (Television program) II. Title.
TX714.P464 1998
641.5—dc21   98-3361
                                                         CIP

Manufactured in the United States of America
Published by Pelican Publishing Company, Inc.
1000 Burmaster Street, Gretna, Louisiana 70053

To
my late parents,
Alma Marie Guidry
and
John Alexander Peyroux, Jr.

Contents

Introduction

At an early age, I was exposed to a unique and magnificent style of cuisine peculiar to southern Louisiana, especially New Orleans, where I was born and reared. While living at home, my interest in food was as a consumer, and consume I did, with enthusiasm. My mother was an excellent Creole cook who learned her skills from her mother and my father's grandmother, and occasionally I would assist her in the preparation of various meals.

After school and a tour in the U.S. Navy, I found myself living on my own and having the need to entertain. It was then that I discovered how much I had learned from my mother when assisting her in food preparation. It was during this period of my life that I became interested in the art of the table and frequently shared cooking experiences with friends and relatives.

In 1963 I got "sand in my shoes" while visiting friends and the beaches, and I moved to Pensacola, Florida. It was here that my cooking interest and skills took on a new dimension. The Gulf of Mexico provided a fabulous source of fresh seafood, and the Spanish heritage of the area took me into new directions. I became known among friends as a good cook and was often asked to cook a meal or food for a cocktail party. A friend—the late Pat Lloyd, fashion editor of the *News Journal*—suggested to Dr. Peggy Morrison, head of the home-economics department at Pensacola Junior College, that I teach a course called "Gourmet Foods." Dr. Morrison asked, and I accepted. What fun I had! It was during this time that I decided to expand my knowledge of food and its preparation.

In 1976 I had the unique experience of attending the world's most prestigious cooking school, Le Cordon Bleu, Ecole de Cuisine et de Patisserie, in Paris, France. My first trip lasted for six weeks in the capital of good food, where I learned from the masters. I shared cooking instructions with other students from the United States, England, Japan, Holland, Mexico, Arabia, Canada, and Germany. It was an experience that changed my life, and I have returned to Le Cordon Bleu many times for varying lengths of time, from a few weeks to four months. Each trip has expanded my knowledge of French cuisine and added to my repertoire.

Upon my return from France, Dr. Morrison suggested that I do a cooking show on the Public Broadcasting System. Because the college owns the franchise for the PBS in Pensacola, it was a natural idea to transfer the teaching from the classroom to the TV screen, thereby reaching a larger audience. We taped thirteen shows in the summer of 1977 and started broadcasting them in October. Somehow, the show clicked. We immediately began to receive requests for recipes. The demand prompted more shows. We had produced 114 shows when the Southern Educational Communications Association (SECA), a consortium of the PBS stations in the Southeast, asked for fifty-two shows to make available to all PBS stations in the country via satellite. Suddenly, we became national. We hastily compiled a book of recipes from the 114 shows to accompany the broadcasts. After exhausting the first group of shows, the network asked for more. We compiled a second book, covering two years of shows that SECA had televised. Since then, we have produced 605 shows and have compiled six books.

In 1979 I had the pleasure of escorting a group of twenty-four cooking enthusiasts to cooking classes in the city of Angers in the Loire Valley of France. Our teacher was a young chef, Phillip Bezout, who introduced us to a rich but humble cuisine from the "Garden of France," as the Loire Valley is called. Since then, I have attended cooking instructions with Italian chefs Giuliano Bugialli of Florence Marcella Hazen of Venice; taken restaurant tours with Mari and Shoeman Tsunoda, restaurateurs in Tokyo, Yokahama, and Hayama, Japan; and visited Madrid and Barcelona as a guest of the Spanish government. In the United States, with advice from Paul Prudhomme, the late Lee Barnes, and the late Leon Soniat, I learned ways to improve my skills in Creole and Cajun cuisine.

In 1994, after surgery for a thyroid cancer that affected my vocal cords, I had to stop doing the TV shows that I loved so much. In the meantime, because I have been receiving so many letters from viewers asking for another book, I have gone though my files to gather recipes never before done on the show; I also have revisited some that have been very popular with viewers. Thus, we have produced this book from the files of "Gourmet Cooking."

I hope the collection of recipes I present here pleases you and encourages you to rush into the kitchen and get to work. Perhaps one or more recipes will become your favorites and you will include them in your permanent repertoire. I hope you will have as much fun and enjoyment in preparing and presenting these dishes as I have. Happy cooking!

ABBREVIATIONS

STANDARD

tsp.   =   teaspoon
tbsp. =   tablespoon
oz.   =   ounce
qt.   =   quart
lb.   =   pound

METRIC

ml.   =   milliliter
l.   =   liter
g.   =   gram
kg.   =   kilogram
mg.   =   milligram

STANDARD METRIC APPROXIMATIONS

⅛ teaspoon	=	.6 milliliter		
¼ teaspoon	=	1.2 milliliters		
½ teaspoon	=	2.5 milliliters		
1 teaspoon	=	5 milliliters		
1 tablespoon	=	15 milliliters		
4 tablespoons	=	¼ cup	=	60 milliliters
8 tablespoons	=	½ cup	=	118 milliliters
16 tablespoons	=	1 cup	=	236 milliliters
2 cups	=	473 milliliters		
2 ½ cups	=	563 milliliters		
4 cups	=	946 milliliters		
1 quart	=	4 cups	=	.94 liter

SOLID MEASUREMENTS

½ ounce	=	15 grams		
1 ounce	=	25 grams		
4 ounces	=	110 grams		
16 ounces	=	1 pound	=	454 grams

Earl Peyroux's "Gourmet Cooking"

Hors d'Oeuvres
and First Courses

Hors d'oeuvres is the French name for a variety of foods served before the main meal and means "outside the work." Almost every cuisine has a body of foods that are customarily served before a formal meal: Italian cuisine has *antipasto*, Spanish *entremesses*, Russian *zakuska*, Greek *mezedaki*, German *vorspeise*, and Mexican *antojitos*. This first course is intended to pique the appetite and set the stage for what is to follow.

In France, hors d'oeuvres, first courses, and a variety of salads are called *entrées* and are usually available from a side table, from which the diner chooses one or more of the offerings. These include a variety of salads, raw vegetable *(crudités)* with dressings, fish, crustaceans, shellfish, pâtés, cheeses, eggs, and prepared meats of all kinds.

The Italians, on the other hand, usually serve an *antipasto* ("before the pasta"), a variety of vegetables, seafood, pork products, and olive-oil, garlic-flavored breads, artfully arranged on serving dishes, while *i primi,* the "first courses," almost always are pasta, flavored rice, or soup.

Tapas ("appetizers") accompany the Spanish custom of gathering together for a drink of beer or wine and are found in every bar and restaurant. The variety of items presented is staggering and keeps one going until mealtime, which tends to be very late in the evening in Spain. Spaniards sometimes will skip the evening meal and feast on tapas alone.

Here in the United States, we generally define hors d'oeuvres as finger or cocktail-party food and first courses as food served on plates and preceding the meal. Salads are served as a separate course. However, with today's relaxed lifestyle, the distinction between hors d'oeuvres and first courses is becoming less clear.

Whatever the distinctions, both are intended to pique the appetite and prepare for the courses that follow. Offered in this chapter are a few of the tried-and-true dishes I serve and for which I receive many requests for recipes. Pickled Shrimp, Oysters, or Crabs are very popular for picnics and barbecues to tease the appetite while the other food is being prepared. West Indies Salad is delicious when served on top of a thick slice of ripe summer tomato as a first course or as a filling to half an avocado. The White Asparagus Pâté is a unique and delicious appetizer and can be varied by replacing the white asparagus with green asparagus or artichoke hearts. Sweet and Sour Meatballs are a wonderful relief from the ubiquitous Swedish meatballs. Bacon-Wrapped Prunes and Bacon-Wrapped Kiwis will really surprise you.

These hors d'oeuvres are easy to prepare and are appetizing in appearance and taste. I hope you will enjoy one or more of them and that they will become some of the best in your collection of recipes for good living.

ASPERGES BLANCS EN PUREE
WHITE ASPARAGUS PATE

This recipe is a variation of an appetizer I had at a friend's home that used canned, chopped artichoke hearts. It was very popular. I experimented with asparagus, one of my favorite vegetables, and was very pleased with the results.

2 cans white asparagus*   **2 dashes Tabasco**
1 cup mayonnaise
1 cup Parmesan cheese,
  grated

Drain asparagus and chop finely. Add mayonnaise, Parmesan, and Tabasco. Pour into an ovenproof bowl. Bake at 350 degrees until brown on top (about 45 minutes). Serve at room temperature with French bread slices or assorted crackers. Serves 12.

*Green asparagus can be substituted with only a slight change in flavor.

CREME D'AUBERGINES
CREAMED EGGPLANT

Eggplant, with only 30 calories per cup, should appeal to today's health-conscious cooks. Except for the small amount of olive oil, this dish is not only low in calories but also very fat-free and high in flavor. I had this appetizer on a visit to the French Riviera and fell in love with it.

3 large eggplants   **4 tbsp. olive oil**
3 cloves garlic, chopped   **Salt and pepper**
4 tbsp. lemon juice   **3 tbsp. parsley, chopped**

Prick eggplants with a fork. Cut in half lengthwise. Place on an oiled baking sheet. Bake at 375 degrees for 40 minutes. Remove and cool.

Scrape flesh from skins and place in the bowl of a food processor. Add garlic and lemon juice. Process while adding olive oil little by little. Transfer to a bowl. Incorporate salt, pepper, and parsley. Serve with thin slices of French bread or assorted crackers. Serves 12.

CAPONATA
ITALIAN EGGPLANT APPETIZER

This classic Sicilian appetizer is a common item in an Italian antipasto—and with good reason. The combination of eggplant, olive, tomato, and aromatics is always welcome. It improves in taste when made a day or two before use. It will keep 8 to 10 days in the refrigerator.

1 large eggplant, peeled and cut into 1-inch cubes
Salt and pepper
⅓ cup olive oil
2 medium onions, sliced into slivers
3 cloves garlic, chopped
3 tbsp. additional olive oil
3 stalks celery, sliced into slivers

2 cups tomatoes, peeled, seeded, and diced
1 cup green olives cut in half
¼ cup pine nuts
¼ cup capers
¼ cup red-wine vinegar

Salt and pepper eggplant cubes. Sauté in olive oil until tender. Remove and set aside.

Sauté onions and garlic in additional olive oil. Add celery, tomatoes, and olives. Simmer 10 minutes. Incorporate reserved eggplant, pine nuts, and capers. Blend in vinegar. Salt and pepper. Simmer 5 minutes. Turn into a bowl and chill. Serves 12.

CREVETTES MARINEES
PICKLED SHRIMP

A perennial favorite along the Gulf Coast, Pickled Shrimp are frequently served as an appetizer at a cocktail party or as finger food at a picnic or barbecue. Marinated in vinegar and oil, the shrimp develop a delicious flavor and improve as they age. They will keep about one week in the refrigerator.

2 lb. shrimp, boiled, shelled, and deveined
2 cups onions, sliced
8 bay leaves
1 cup olive oil
¾ cup vinegar
2 tbsp. capers
1½ tsp. salt
2 tsp. celery seeds

Layer shrimp and onion in a bowl. Place bay leaves on top. Combine olive oil, vinegar, capers, salt, and celery seed. Pour over shrimp and onions. Cover and refrigerate for 24 hours. Serves 6.

HUITRES MARINEES
PICKLED OYSTERS

Twenty years ago I tasted Pickled Oysters at a party given by my very dear friend Mrs. Sis Lipson, who shared the recipe with me. I have prepared this dish many, many times, always to raves and requests for the recipe. So here it is. I hope you enjoy them as I do.

2 qt. oysters and their liquid
½ cup black peppercorns
6 small red peppers
1 tbsp. whole allspice*
1 tbsp. salt
2 whole mace
8 whole cloves
2 cups white-wine vinegar

Poach oysters in their liquid until they begin to curl. Remove oysters and save liquid.

Scald peppercorns, red peppers, allspice, salt, mace, and cloves in wine vinegar. Pour over oysters. Add 2 cups of reserved oyster liquid. Cover and refrigerate. Serves 8.

*Allspice is the dried fruit or berry of a tropical American tree sometimes called "pimento," about a ¼-inch in size. It has the aroma and flavor of a combination of cinnamon, nutmeg, and cloves. It is used whole in pickling combinations, as in this recipe, or in ground form in baking cakes and cookies.

DOIGTS DES CRABES
EN SAUCE BORDELAISE
CRAB FINGERS BORDELAISE

Elegant and simple to prepare, Crab Fingers Bordelaise—shelled crab claws marinated in a sauce of butter, olive oil, and garlic—will be the hit of your party. This is a classic New Orleans dish, one that I have been serving since I lived there more than 35 years ago.

**1 lb. crab claws, cooked
and shelled
4 tbsp. butter
4 tbsp. olive oil**

**⅓ cup parsley, chopped
2 cloves garlic, chopped
Salt and pepper**

Heat butter and olive oil in a skillet. Add parsley, garlic, salt, and pepper. Add crab claws and toss gently in sauce until hot. Serve in a chafing dish. Serves 6.

CRABES MARINES
PICKLED CRABS

Pickled Crabs, like Pickled Shrimp, is a very popular recipe on the Gulf Coast, where the blue crab is so plentiful. In summer, when we go crabbing and are lucky, we have an abundance to boil in special seasonings, shuck, and then eat, accompanied by a good bottle of beer. The excess crabs, if there are any, are frequently pickled, thus prolonging their freshness and flavor for another meal. They are excellent at a picnic or barbecue.

1 cup olive oil	2 stalks celery, chopped
⅓ cup red-wine vinegar	1 large onion, chopped
4 cloves garlic, chopped	4 green onions, chopped
1 tsp. dry mustard*	4 tbsp. parsley, chopped
1 tbsp. horseradish	Salt and pepper
1 tbsp. Worcestershire sauce	12 crabs, boiled, cleaned,
Juice of 2 lemons	and bodies broken in half

Blend together olive oil, vinegar, garlic, mustard, horseradish, Worcestershire, and lemon juice. Add celery, onion, green onions, and parsley. Salt and pepper generously. Pour over crabs to cover. Refrigerate 24 hours. Serves 6.

*Mustard is a member of the cress family of greens. The seeds from this plant are various shades of yellow to brown, ground, and combined with vinegars, wines, and other flavoring to make the condiment we call mustard. Dry mustard, or mustard powder, is made from yellow mustard seeds and packaged in dry form. The yellow mustard we commonly use on hot dogs is a combination of dry yellow mustard seed, vinegars, and turmeric, which give it its bright color.

FROMAGE DE PIMENT DOUX A LA MAISON
HOMEMADE SWEET PIMENTO CHEESE

This cheese recipe was given to me by a very dear friend, Doe Bercaw, 30 years ago. Doe always served this flavorful cheese at parties held in the antique shop she and her husband owned and operated, and it was always a hit. Its flavor improves when refrigerated a day or two before being served.

1 lb. sharp cheddar cheese, grated
1 cup pimento, chopped
1½ cup mayonnaise
1 medium green bell pepper, seeded and chopped
1 medium red bell pepper, seeded and chopped

Blend together the cheddar cheese, pimento, and mayonnaise. Transfer to a well-oiled mold or bowl. Refrigerate for several hours. Just before serving, unmold the cheese onto a serving dish. Garnish with chopped green and red bell pepper mixed together around the edges. Serve with French bread slices or crackers. Serves 12 to 15.

PETIT CROQUE-MONSIEUR
SMALL FRENCH HAM AND CHEESE APPETIZERS

If you have ever traveled to Paris, you would certainly have had a *Croque-Monsieur*, the ubiquitous French ham and cheese sandwich. This recipe adapts this French institution to make a great appetizer. If you substitute sliced chicken for the ham, you then will have a *Croque-Madam*.

8 slices thin sandwich bread   **8 slices of Gruyère cheese**
   with a coarse texture   **8 oz. butter, melted**
4 slices boiled or baked ham

Butter one side of each slice of bread. Place a slice of Gruyère cheese on buttered side of 4 slices of bread. Arrange a slice of ham on top of cheese and a second slice of cheese on top of the ham. Cover with the remaining slices of bread, buttered side down.

Butter one side of each sandwich and place in a lightly buttered hot skillet, grilling the sandwich until golden. Brush butter on the upside of the sandwich and turn sandwich over to grill the other side.

Remove to paper towels and allow the sandwiches to cool. Trim crusts from the 4 sides of each sandwich. Cut the sandwich in half diagonally. Cut each half in half, then cut each quarter in half.

Before serving, place in a 350-degree oven for 5 minutes. Makes 32 sandwiches.

PRUNEAUX AU LARD
BACON-WRAPPED PRUNES

This French appetizer will surprise you. I always include it on my menu for a cocktail party because it is inexpensive and makes an excellent conversation piece. I have never found a guest who did not like them, even among people who do not like prunes. The counterbalance of the sweetness of the prunes and the saltiness of the bacon makes an unusual and delicious combination.

30 large prunes, pitted*   **15 slices bacon, cut in half**

Wrap each prune in a half-slice of bacon. Skewer with wooden toothpicks.** Place on a rack on a baking pan. Bake at 400 degrees for 15 to 20 minutes until bacon is cooked. Arrange on a serving plate and allow to cool 10 minutes. Serves 10.

*Variation: Substitute dried apricots for the prunes.

**Soak toothpicks in water before using to prevent them from burning.

KIWIS ROULES A LA GASCONNE
BACON-WRAPPED KIWIS

Another unique recipe from France, this hors d'oeuvre is similar to the prunes wrapped in bacon. The natural sweetness of the kiwi fruit acts as a counterpoint to the saltiness of the bacon. The colors of the fruit and bacon make it a visually appealing appetizer that also follows through with a wonderful taste.

2 tbsp. lemon juice   **6 firm kiwis, peeled***
2 tsp. honey   **24 slices center-cut bacon**
3 tbsp. olive oil

Combine the lemon juice, honey, and olive oil in a bowl. Cut the kiwis in quarters and wrap each quarter in a slice of bacon. Skewer with a wooden toothpick. Marinate the skewered kiwis in the lemon-juice/honey/olive-oil marinade 30 minutes.

Place the kiwis rolls on a baking sheet and broil 5 minutes, turning several times until the bacon is cooked. Transfer to a serving plate. Serves 8.

*Kiwi fruit, also know as Chinese gooseberry, became popular in the United States during the 1950s. It was originally imported from New Zealand, where it had been brought from China and developed as an export product. It has been a cash crop in the United States since the 1960s.

FOIES DE VOLAILLE HACHES
CHOPPED CHICKEN LIVER

This recipe was a traditional one for my mother, who prepared it for holiday meals, especially Thanksgiving. She obtained it from an Irish lady who was married to a Jewish gentleman. The secret is to chop the livers and egg coarsely so as not to purée. The elements should be identifiable but held together by the fat used to cook the livers. I like it best served with Ritz crackers.

1 lb. chicken livers, cleaned   **6 medium eggs, hard-boiled**
4 tbsp. chicken fat, rendered*   **Salt and pepper to taste**

Sauté livers in chicken fat. Drain and save the drippings. Chop the livers coarsely. Chop the eggs coarsely. Blend liver and eggs together. Salt and pepper to taste. Add the saved drippings to bind the mixture. Chill. Serve with crackers. Serves 8.

*The chicken fat can be replaced by an equal amount of butter, margarine, or peanut oil. This liver appetizer is excellent served with various crackers or with thinly sliced French bread.

CREVETTES SAUCE REMOULADE
SHRIMP REMOULADE

In French cuisine, a classic remoulade sauce is a mayonnaise-based garlic sauce used with fish dishes and certain vegetable salads. However, this Shrimp Remoulade, of New Orleans origin, is the catsup-mustard-horseradish version so common in that city. There are many variations of this sauce. This one is my simplification of others.

3 qt. water
1 large onion, sliced
1 large lemon, sliced
3 stalks celery and their
    tops, sliced
⅓ cup liquid Crab Boil*
½ cup salt

2 lb. headless shrimp
½ cup catsup
½ cup Creole brown mustard
¼ cup prepared horseradish
1 clove garlic, chopped
¼ cup olive oil
4 cups lettuce, shredded

Bring water, onion, lemon, celery, Crab Boil, and salt to a hard boil. Add shrimp and return water to a boil. Boil 7 minutes for medium shrimp. Remove from heat. Pour 1 cup cold water into pot. Allow to rest 10 minutes. Drain, cool, peel, and devein shrimp. Chill. Blend together the catsup, mustard, horseradish, garlic, and olive oil. Chill. Divide the lettuce onto individual plates. Combine ½ cup sauce with the shrimp. Arrange shrimp over lettuce. Serve remaining sauce on the side. Serves 6.

*Crab Boil, an extract made from a combination of spices and herbs, is used to season the boiling liquid for crabs, shrimp, and crawfish and is packaged and sold by a number of New Orleans firms. To produce a satisfactory substitute, try my recipe below.

CRAB BOIL

Combine 2 tsp. mustard seeds, 1 tsp. coriander seeds, ½ tsp. cayenne pepper, 3 bay leaves, 1 tsp. dill seed, 1 tsp. whole allspice, 1 tsp. whole cloves, and ¾ cup water. Bring to a boil. Simmer until liquid is reduced to about ½ cup. Strain. Use as directed by specific recipes.

SALADE DES ANTILLES
WEST INDIES CRAB SALAD

This favorite on the Alabama and northwest Florida Gulf Coast was brought from the Caribbean in the 1940s by William Bayley, who owned a restaurant in Mobile. It was featured along with deep-fried crab claws in his restaurant and at Wintzell's Oyster House in Mobile for many years. Unfortunately, both restaurants are defunct, but the West Indies Crab Salad is still available in Mobile and Pensacola.

2 cups lump crabmeat
1 large onion, finely chopped
½ cup olive oil
½ cup red-wine vinegar

1 tbsp. parsley, chopped
1 dash Tabasco
Salt and pepper to taste

Place crabmeat in a bowl. Cover with chopped onions. Blend together olive oil, vinegar, parsley, Tabasco, salt, and pepper. Pour over crabmeat and onions. Refrigerate 24 hours. Serve with avocado, tomato slices, mixed greens, or a combination of these. Serves 4.

TERRINES DE POULET VARIEES
VARIOUS CHICKEN TERRINES

Four flavors of a chicken terrine cut into generous slices and arranged on attractive plates make a very eye-appealing and tasty first course. The terrines are delicious served cold or at room temperature. You will hear many raves over this. Leftovers make wonderful sandwiches.

2 lb. chicken breasts,
deboned, skinned, and cut
into pieces
1 tsp. salt
½ tsp. white pepper
½ cup vermouth
2 egg whites, beaten
1 cup cream, lightly beaten
2 tbsp. butter
2 cloves garlic, crushed

½ lb. mushrooms, chopped
½ lb. shrimp, boiled, shelled,
and deveined
2 tsp. dill weed
½ lb. ham, chopped
2 tbsp. dill pickles, chopped
4 chicken livers
4 tbsp. peanut oil
2 tbsp. tomato paste

Process chicken, salt, and pepper in a food processor 1 minute. Add vermouth and process until incorporated. Transfer mixture to a mixing bowl. Fold in beaten egg whites and cream. Cover chicken mousse and refrigerate.

Sauté garlic and mushrooms in butter 2 minutes and set aside. Combine shrimp and dill and set aside. Combine ham and pickles and set aside. Sauté chicken livers in peanut oil 2 minutes. Drain and chop livers. Blend chopped livers with tomato paste and set aside.

Retrieve chicken mousse and divide into 4 portions. Incorporate into each portion 1 of the reserved mixtures. Oil 4 miniature bread pans or other molds. Line the bottoms with parchment paper. Fill molds with 1 of the 4 mixtures. Cover with a strip of oiled parchment. Place in a pan of water halfway up the sides. Cover pans with aluminum foil. Bring to a boil and simmer 12 minutes. Remove from heat. Allow to cool, then chill several hours.

Unmold and slice into ½-inch slices. Serve 1 slice of each terrine per person. Serves 8.

BOULES DE PERLES AU PORC
PORK PEARL BALLS

This popular appetizer recipe always brings compliments. I learned this many years ago when I took some cooking classes from a charming Chinese woman. If you do not have a Chinese steamer, you can improvise by placing four small glasses full of water in a roasting pan and placing a roasting-pan rack on top. Add water to roasting pan to just below rack. Place pearl balls on rack.

1 cup rice	½ lb. mushrooms chopped
1 lb. lean ground pork	½ cup water chestnuts,
1 egg, lightly beaten	chopped**
1 tbsp. soy sauce	2 green onions, chopped
1 tsp. salt	24 small pieces of waxed
1 tbsp. fresh ginger root,	paper cut into 1-inch
grated*	squares

Cover rice with cold water in a bowl and soak for 2 hours. Drain and spread on a towel to absorb the excess moisture.

Combine pork, egg, soy sauce, and salt. Add ginger root, mushrooms, water chestnuts, and green onions, blending well.

Shape into balls about 1-inch in diameter. Roll each ball in the rice to coat with rice. Place each ball on a piece of waxed paper and set into the top part of a steamer. Cover the steamer and steam over boiling water 30 minutes.

Remove pearl balls to a serving platter and serve with Chinese hot mustard and plum sauce. Serves 8.

*Fresh ginger is the root of a lilylike perennial plant that found its way into western European cuisines from India and southern China, through Alexandria, and then to Greece and Rome before the time of Christ. Today, the largest supplier of ginger to the U.S. market is Jamaica.

**Water chestnuts are the nutlike fruit of an aquatic plant that grows along the edges of ponds, lakes, and marshes in China. When peeled, their firm white flesh retains its crisp quality when cooked, providing a special texture and flavor to the dish. They are sometimes found fresh and whole in supermarkets. They are most commonly used canned and are available whole or sliced.

BOULETTES DE BOEUF A L'AIGRE-DOUCE
SWEET AND SOUR SMALL BEEF BALLS

Tired of Swedish meatballs? Try these bite-size, Chinese-style meatballs in a sweet and sour sauce. These tiny morsels are baked rather than fried, and most of the fat is rendered before they are sauced.

1 medium onion, chopped	**¼ cup milk**
2 tbsp. butter	**1 egg, lightly beaten**
1 lb. lean ground beef	**Salt and pepper to taste**
¼ lb. ground pork	**1 tsp. sage**
1 cup stale French bread, cut in cubes	**1 recipe Sweet and Sour Sauce (recipe follows)**

Sauté onions in butter until transparent. Combine sautéed onions, ground beef, and ground pork, blending well.

Soften bread with the milk until bread absorbs the milk. Blend in egg, salt, pepper, and sage. Combine this mixture with the meat-and-onion mixture.

Shape mixture into small balls and arrange on a rack in a baking pan. Bake at 375 degrees 15 minutes until lightly browned. Transfer to a chafing dish. Pour Sweet and Sour Sauce over meatballs. Makes about 30 meatballs.

SAUCE AIGRE-DOUCE
SWEET AND SOUR SAUCE

½ cup sugar
1 tbsp. cornstarch
2 tsp. salt
½ cup red-wine vinegar

¼ cup orange juice
½ cup pineapple juice
3 oz. tomato paste

Blend together sugar, cornstarch, and salt. Stir in vinegar, orange and pineapple juices, and tomato paste. Cook on medium heat, stirring constantly, until sauce thickens. Use as directed in whatever recipe calls for this sauce. Makes 1½ cups.

Salads and
Their Dressings

The classic salad in France is lettuce and other greens with a very straightforward vinaigrette dressing ($\frac{1}{4}$ cup vinegar, $\frac{3}{4}$ cup olive oil, salt, pepper, and optionally a dab of Dijon mustard). In France it is often (especially in homes) served with the main course or, as in times gone by, as an interlude between the main course and the dessert. The salad was sometimes served in the same plate as the main course so that small amounts of sauce or bits of food could be gathered with the lettuce and enjoyed as a palate cleanser before dessert. However, salads are not limited to greens alone. A classic vegetable salad is French Potato Salad, dressed with wine, vinegar, and olive oil while hot so the potatoes will absorb the flavors. Celery Root Salad in Mustard Sauce is another classically French creation. What would Salade Niçoise, the well-known salad from Provence, be without green bean salad, potato salad, and tuna fish? Many other kinds of salads (vegetable, seafood, poultry, and meats) are usually served as a first course or appetizer. My preference is to serve any salad with the main course. I sometimes prefer the salad as the main course.

The Creoles and Cajuns enjoy a variety of salads and usually serve them with the main course. Red Bean Salad, White Bean and Shrimp Salad, and Creole Potato Salad are but a few examples of Creole/Cajun creative styles. Cajuns particularly like a large spoon of Creole Potato Salad in their Seafood Gumbo. They also like a Creole Vinaigrette, which substitutes Creole brown mustard (1 tsp.) and horseradish (1 tsp.) for the Dijon. They sometimes make a Creamy Creole Vinaigrette by adding $\frac{1}{2}$ cup cream.

Along the Gulf Coast, one finds many salads with seafood as well as vegetables. I particularly recommend the West Indies Crab Salad (in chapter 1) and the Pensacola Gazpacho Salad for their uniqueness. Besides, they just taste good.

All over the United States, salads play a multiplicity of roles. As above, the basic greens and vinaigrette are popular, but we have created many styles: salads to be served before a meal; salads to be served with a meal; salads to be served as a meal; salads to take on picnics and barbecues, etc. In this chapter we present salads composed of a variety of vegetables, both familiar and unfamiliar, each with its own sauce or dressing.

However you like your salad—before, during, after a meal, as the meal itself, or as a complement to picnics and barbecues—here are a few I hope you will enjoy.

SALADE DE POMME DE TERRE CREOLE
CREOLE POTATO SALAD

Of all the recipes for potato salad that I have come across over the years, this one stands out above all the rest. I incorporated it into my permanent repertoire many years ago. Its rich and creamy taste, spiced with the mustard and mayonnaise, sets it apart from any other.

3 lb. potatoes, peeled and
  cut into bite-size pieces
1 tbsp. white distilled vinegar*
6 large eggs
8 large green onions, sliced
2 stalks celery, strings
  removed and chopped

Salt and pepper
1 cup mayonnaise
½ cup cream
1 tbsp. Dijon mustard
1 tbsp. red-wine vinegar

Place potatoes, vinegar, and eggs in salted water to cover. Bring to a boil and simmer 15 minutes. Drain and place the potatoes in a mixing bowl.

Peel the eggs, cut into bite-size pieces and add to the mixing bowl. Add the green onions, celery, salt, and pepper.

Blend together the mayonnaise, cream, mustard, and red-wine vinegar. Combine with the potato/egg mixture, blending gently. Chill until ready to serve. Serves 8.

*This recipe presents a cooking tip worth mentioning. When boiling peeled potatoes, add a small amount of white distilled vinegar to the water. The vinegar causes a very light crust to form on the potatoes that helps them hold their shape when blended with other foods. This can be applied to other root vegetables such as beets, Jerusalem artichokes, turnips, or rutabagas.

SALADE DE POMME DE TERRE FRANÇAISE
FRENCH POTATO SALAD

The classic French potato salad combines heated white-wine vinegar and dry white wine with hot potatoes and seasonings, allowing them to absorb the liquid flavors. A light coating of a good olive oil is all that is needed to bring out the wonderful flavor of the potatoes. This salad is best served warm or room temperature.

3 lb. potatoes, peeled and
  cut into bite-size pieces
1 tbsp. salt
1 tbsp. distilled vinegar
½ tsp. white pepper

½ tsp. celery salt
2 shallots, chopped
½ cup white-wine vinegar
½ cup dry white wine
½ cup olive oil

Place potatoes, salt, and distilled vinegar in a pot of cold water. Bring to a boil and simmer 15 minutes. Drain and transfer to a mixing bowl. Add white pepper, celery salt, and chopped shallots.

Heat white-wine vinegar and dry white wine until almost boiling. Pour over potato mixture and gently blend together. Pour off any excess vinegar and wine. Pour olive oil over and toss lightly. Serve warm or at room temperature. Serves 8.

SALADE DE POMME DE TERRE TIEDE
WARM POTATO SALAD

For a change from the traditional egg and mayonnaise-based potato salad, try this very French style, spiced with mustard, garlic, and chervil. Served warm or hot, it is an excellent accompaniment to fried fish, sautéed ham steaks, and fried chicken.

6 tbsp. red-wine vinegar
2 tsp. Dijon mustard
2 cloves garlic, chopped
Salt and pepper

2 tbsp. chervil, chopped
½ cup olive oil
3 lb. small new potatoes, peeled

Blend together vinegar, mustard, garlic, salt, pepper, and chervil. Whisk in olive oil and set aside.

Boil potatoes 15 minutes until tender. Drain and transfer to a serving bowl. Pour vinaigrette over immediately. Serve warm or hot. Serves 8.

SALADE DE POMME DE TERRE A LA MOUTARD
MUSTARD POTATO SALAD

For an interesting change of pace, try this new-potato salad with a mustard-cream dressing. Best served at room temperature, this salad goes well with fish and chicken dishes.

3 lb. small new potatoes, cut in half
1 tbsp. white distilled vinegar*
Salt to taste

White pepper to taste
3 tbsp. brown mustard (Creole or Meaux)
1 cup cream

Boil potatoes in vinegar, salt, and water 15 minutes until tender. Drain and cool. Salt and pepper potatoes to taste. Combine mustard and cream. Pour over potatoes. Turn gently. Transfer to a serving platter. Serves 8.

*Adding a small amount of vinegar to the boiling water will cause the potatoes to form a light crust. When tossing with other ingredients as above, the potatoes will hold their shape.

SALADE DE POMME DE TERRE AU RADIS
POTATO AND RADISH SALAD

Sliced radishes, garlic, chives, and mint provide a rather interesting garnish for a vinaigrette-dressed potato salad.

3 lb. small new potatoes	**1 clove garlic, chopped**
Salt	**1 tbsp. chives, chopped**
1 tbsp. white vinegar	**8 tbsp. olive oil**
6 tbsp. white-wine vinegar	**3 tbsp. mint, chopped**
Salt and pepper	**1 cup sliced radishes**

Boil potatoes in vinegar, salt, and water 15 minutes until tender. Drain and transfer to a serving bowl.

Combine wine vinegar, salt, pepper, garlic, and chives. Whisk in olive oil. Pour over hot potatoes. Allow to reach room temperature. Add mint and radishes and blend well. Serves 8.

CELERI-RAVE REMOULADE
CELERY ROOT SALAD IN MUSTARD SAUCE

Salads made with celeriac, or celery root, are to be found in bistros all over France, especially with a French remoulade dressing. I am delighted to see that this root vegetable is more readily available in our U.S. markets. Although unattractive in appearance, when stripped of its gnarled exterior, the interior flesh has a celery-and-parsley taste that is complemented by the mayonnaise-mustard dressing. Try it— you'll like it.

2 lb. celery root, peeled and cut into julienne strips*	**4 tbsp. mayonnaise**
4 tbsp. mustard (Creole, Dijon, or your choice)	**3 tbsp. cream**
	1 tbsp. lemon juice
	1 tbsp. parsley, chopped

Blanch celery-root strips in salted water 2 minutes. Drain and refresh in cold water.

Blend together mustard, mayonnaise, cream, and lemon juice. Pour over celery root and toss well. Transfer to a serving dish. Garnish with parsley. Serves 6.

Julienne is the French term to describe a method of cutting vegetables or meats into thin, uniform strips. This shape makes the cooking go faster and provides an attractive appearance. Just cut the vegetables into 2- or 3-inch lengths and ¼-inch-wide slices, stack the slices, and cut again into ¼-inch slices.

SALADE ROUGE ET JAUNE
RED AND YELLOW SALAD

Sliced red beets and yellow orange slices give this recipe its name. Round slices of these two vegetables are layered in overlapping fashion, each layer becoming smaller, thereby allowing the edges of the previous layer to show. Seasoned with a garlic vinaigrette, this dish is both a sight to behold and a taste to remember.

Zest of 4 oranges, grated	**¼ cup olive oil**
¼ cup red-wine vinegar	**2 large cans sliced beets**
Salt and pepper	**4 oranges, peeled and sliced**
2 cloves garlic, chopped	

Combine orange zest, vinegar, salt, pepper, and garlic. Whisk in olive oil. Set aside.

Place a layer of oranges on the bottom of a round serving platter. Arrange a layer of beets over oranges, allowing the oranges to show around the edges. Continue layering oranges and beets, making each layer a little smaller around than the previous.

Pour orange vinaigrette over orange and beet layers. Cover and refrigerate before serving. Serves 8.

SALADE DE CAROTTES ET NAVETS
CARROT AND TURNIP SALAD

Colorful and flavorful carrots and turnips are accompanied by sweet raisins and crunchy sesame seeds with a vinaigrette dressing for a unique combination. This salad is very refreshing and complements chicken and pork dishes.

2 lb. carrots, peeled, shredded	**4 tbsp. lemon juice**
1 lb. turnips, peeled, shredded	**2 tbsp. peanut oil**
1 cup raisins	**4 tbsp. olive oil**
2 tbsp. sesame seeds, toasted	**Salt and pepper**
2 tbsp. chives, chopped	

Combine carrots and turnips in a salad bowl. Blend in raisins, sesame seeds, and chives. Blend together lemon juice, peanut oil, olive oil, salt, and pepper. Pour over vegetables. Toss well. Serves 8.

SALADE DE TOPINAMBOURS
JERUSALEM ARTICHOKE SALAD

This truly American Indian vegetable, which they called "sunroot," was transplanted to Europe by French explorers in the 1600s and became very popular in France and Italy. The name has nothing to with Jerusalem or the globe artichoke but rather is a corruption of the Italian *Girasole Articiocco*. This root vegetable is delicious when cooked like potatoes—boiled, mashed, fried—or served in this salad.

3 lb. Jerusalem artichokes*   **2 tbsp. lemon juice**
Salt and pepper   **2 tbsp. parsley, chopped**
½ cup olive oil   **½ cup walnuts, chopped**

Cut artichokes into bite size. Blanch in salted water, covered, for 15 minutes until tender. Drain and refresh in cold water.

Blend together the salt, pepper, olive oil, lemon juice, and parsley. Pour over the artichokes and toss well. Transfer to a serving bowl. Garnish with walnuts. Serves 8.

*Scrub Jerusalem artichokes with a vegetable brush to remove all dirt. They do not have to be peeled; however, they can be peeled before cooking and dropped into water with lemon juice. To preserve their whiteness, cook in an *à blanc* liquid, that is, 2 tablespoons of flour and the juice of 1 lemon added to 1 quart of water. This method of cooking prevents the vegetable from discoloring and can also be used with artichoke bottoms and cauliflower. Caution: Do not use an aluminum pot.

SALADE DE CHOU ROUGE MARINE
MARINATED RED CABBAGE SALAD

I usually associate red cabbage with German cooking, especially Sweet and Sour Red Cabbage. Flavorful and very colorful, it can be prepared in the same manner as green cabbage, but it tends to be a little tougher, thus needing longer or slower cooking. In this French version of coleslaw, the cabbage is blanched to tenderize while preserving its crispness and color. A teaspoon or 2 of white vinegar in the blanching water will help preserve its color.

**1 large red cabbage, thickly
    shredded
4 tbsp. powdered sugar
2 cloves garlic, chopped
1 large onion, chopped
Salt to taste
1 cup red-wine vinegar
1 bay leaf**

2 tsp. cumin*
**½ tsp. pepper, coarsely
    ground
2 tbsp. Dijon mustard,
    grainy style
½ tsp. salt
½ cup sunflower oil**

Blanch cabbage in salted water 5 minutes. Drain and refresh in cold water. Drain again and press out as much water as possible. Combine cabbage, sugar, garlic, onion, and salt. Marinate 1 hour.

Combine vinegar, bay leaf, cumin, and pepper in a saucepan. Bring to a boil and reduce by half. Strain. Add mustard and salt. Whisk in sunflower oil. Marinate another 15 minutes. Serves 8.

*Cumin is an ancient spice known since biblical times and is popular in Asian, North African, Middle Eastern, and Latin American cooking. It is gaining popularity in the United States and is used in chilies, meat loaf, and barbecue sauces.

SALADE DE CHOU BLANC A L'AIGRE-DOUCE
SWEET AND SOUR CABBAGE SALAD

Try this version of a slaw, which achieves a sweet and sour taste by combining tart wine vinegar and sweet brown sugar to complement the cabbage, carrots, bell pepper, and raisins. A short marination tenderizes the cabbage, which then is garnished and enriched with parsley and cream.

1 3 lb. cabbage
1 green bell pepper, cut into thin strips 2 inches long
1 red bell pepper, cut into thin strips 2 inches long
1 lb. carrots, shredded
1 cup raisins

1 cup wine vinegar
¼ cup brown sugar
1 cup cream
4 tbsp. parsley, chopped
½ tsp. cayenne pepper
Salt to taste

Cut cabbage into quarters and remove the hard stem portions. Shred the cabbage quarters thinly into a large mixing bowl. Add the green and red bell peppers, carrots, and raisins.

Blend together vinegar and brown sugar. Pour over vegetables and mix well. Marinate 3 hours, turning 3 or 4 times. Drain vegetables and place in a serving dish.

Blend together cream, parsley, cayenne, and salt. Pour over vegetables and blend. Serves 8.

SALADE DE CHOU-FLEUR
CAULIFLOWER SALAD

Although cauliflower can be eaten raw, a short swim in boiling salted water seems to bring out the wonderful flavor of this flower vegetable. A cousin of broccoli and cabbage, cauliflower can be combined with them for variations of this salad. The vinaigrette gives the salad character, and the pumpkinseeds offer a crunchy contrast.

2 lb. cauliflower, separated
   florets
2 tsp. salt
¼ cup red-wine vinegar
Salt and pepper

½ cup olive oil
1 bunch watercress, large
   stems removed
2 tbsp. dried pumpkinseeds

Place cauliflower in salted boiling water for 2 minutes. Drain and refresh in cold water. Drain again.

Blend together vinegar, salt, and pepper. Whisk in olive oil. Combine cauliflower, watercress, dried pumpkinseeds, and vinaigrette and toss well. Serve at room temperature. Serves 8.

SALADE DE PASTEQUES
WATERMELON SALAD

Are you looking for something different? Well, here it is. A unique mixture of sweet watermelon pieces, vinaigrette, and marinated onions is combined for a counterpoint of taste and textures. This is a colorful and refreshing salad for summer outdoor suppers and barbecues.

6 cups watermelon, cut into
   bite-size pieces
1 tbsp. parsley, chopped
2 tbsp. lemon juice
Salt and pepper

1 tsp. chives, chopped
½ tsp. thyme
4 tbsp. olive oil
3 small yellow onions,
   cut into rings

Combine watermelon and parsley in a serving bowl. Blend together lemon juice, salt, pepper, chives, and thyme. Whisk in olive oil. Marinate onion rings in vinaigrette 1 hour, turning frequently. Gently combine onion, vinaigrette, and watermelon. Serves 8.

CHOU-FLEUR MIMOSA AU ROQUEFORT
CAULIFLOWER IN EGG AND ROQUEFORT SAUCE

Beautiful white heads of cauliflower are the flower buds of the plant and are kept white by tying the surrounding leaves over the bud. If left exposed, the bud would open into yellow flowers that are inedible. This recipe blanches the florets until tender-crisp, refreshes to stop the cooking, and garnishes with Roquefort cheese and hard-boiled egg-cream dressing.

1 head cauliflower, divided into florets	**1 tbsp. chives, chopped***
2 oz. Roquefort cheese, crumbled	**Salt and pepper**
⅔ cup cream	**3 eggs, hard-boiled and cut into medium size pieces**
	1 tsp. additional chives

Blanch cauliflower florets in salted water 3 minutes, until tender (do not overcook). Drain and refresh in cold water.

Gently blend together the Roquefort, cream, chives, salt, and pepper. Fold in chopped eggs. Transfer cauliflower to a serving dish. Pour Roquefort sauce over cauliflower. Garnish with additional chives. Serves 4.

*This delicate member of the onion family is prized for its long, slender stalks, which produce a mild onion flavor, and its bright green color, which makes a nice garnish. They can be used in cream soups, light butter sauces for fish and shellfish, as well as in salads and dressings. I keep a pot of chives growing all year and harvest as needed by cutting 2 inches from the root.

SALADE AU GAZPACHO
PENSACOLA GAZPACHO SALAD

In the Pensacola/Mobile area of the Gulf Coast, where the Spanish influences are 400 years old, there is a salad called Gazpacho, which is a combination of tomatoes, green onions, cucumbers, and hardtack. Hardtack is a very hard sea biscuit that is baked to last and was used by sailors on the long voyages at sea. It is believed that this salad has its origin in the Spanish custom of dipping their bread (hardtack) into Gazpacho Soup (made from the same ingredients as this salad) to soften it.

Salt and pepper
1 tsp. Dijon mustard
⅓ cup red-wine vinegar
⅔ cup olive oil
2 Hardtack, broken into bite-size pieces (recipe follows)

2 large tomatoes, cut into bite-size pieces
2 medium cucumbers, peeled, seeded, and cut into pieces
10 green onions, sliced

Blend together salt, pepper, Dijon mustard, and vinegar. Gradually whisk in olive oil. Combine vinaigrette with hardtack in a salad bowl. Allow hardtack to absorb vinaigrette 1 hour or longer.

Add tomatoes, cucumbers, and green onions, tossing together. Chill for several hours. The flavor improves overnight in the refrigerator. Serves 6.

Variations:
1. Add 2 green peppers cut into bite-size to the basic recipe.
2. Replace vinaigrette with 1½ cups mayonnaise.
3. Use white onions, sliced, instead of green onions.

BISCUIT DE MER
HARDTACK (SEA BISCUIT)

Hardtack is a necessary ingredient in the Pensacola Gazpacho Salad and is hard to find in commercial stores. The Peter Pan Bakery and the Premier Baking Company in Pensacola are the last bakeries that bake them. This recipe is very easy, and the biscuits will last indefinitely in airtight containers. I much prefer these homemade to the commercial hardtack available.

4 cups flour
½ tsp. salt
1 pkg. dry yeast
½ tsp. sugar

⅓ cup water, warmed to
115 degrees
1 cup additional warm
water

Sift flour and salt into a bowl. Dissolve yeast in sugar and warm water. Incorporate yeast and additional water into the flour. Form a dough and knead 5 minutes. Form a ball and place in a buttered bowl, turning to coat. Cover and let rise in a warm place until doubled in bulk.

Punch dough down and knead 1 minute. Roll dough until ½-inch thick. Using a large pastry cutter, cut biscuits. This should produce 6 5-inch biscuits. Prick tops with a fork. Place on baking sheet and bake at 300 degrees for 1 hour. Lower heat to 250 degrees and bake 1 hour. Lower heat to 200 degrees and bake 1 hour. Turn heat off and let biscuits remain in oven until cool. Remove and store in airtight container. The hardtack will last indefinitely.

SALADE DE POIVRONS
ET COURGETTES A LA GRECQUE
PEPPERS AND ZUCCHINI SALAD GREEK STYLE

I love vegetable salads, especially those that incorporate Mediterranean-style produce. This salad does just that, with the use of zucchini, onion, and red bell peppers giving it a Greek flavor, further highlighted with black olives and feta cheese bathed in an oregano-flavored vinaigrette.

4 small zucchini, cut into
  rounds
4 tbsp. olive oil
Salt and pepper
2 medium white onions,
  cut into rings
6 medium red bell peppers,
  seeded, peeled, and
  cut into large dice

1 cup black olives, cured
  in oil
¾ lb. feta cheese, cut into
  dice
1 tbsp. oregano
¼ cup parsley leaves
¼ cup white-wine vinegar
Salt and pepper
½ cup additional olive oil

Sauté zucchini in olive oil 5 minutes. Remove from heat. Salt and pepper. Allow to come to room temperature.

Combine in a large salad bowl onions, peppers, olives, and zucchini. Add feta cheese, oregano, and parsley. Blend together vinegar, salt, and pepper. Whisk in olive oil. Pour over vegetables and toss gently. Serves 8.

SALADE PAYSANNE
PEASANT SALAD

The word "peasant" brings to mind hearty and savory ingredients. It is an appropriate descriptor for this salad because we combine black beans, bacon, red bell pepper, and celery with a garlic vinaigrette for a melange of color and flavor with substance.

4 tbsp. red-wine vinegar
Salt and pepper
1 clove garlic, chopped
1 tbsp. parsley, chopped
4 tbsp. olive oil
6 cups black beans, cooked
and drained

6 slices bacon, cut into
small strips
1 large red bell pepper,
diced
3 stalks celery, diced

Combine vinegar, salt, pepper, garlic, and parsley in a bowl. Whisk in olive oil. Pour over black beans and marinate.

Sauté bacon strips until browned. Add bacon to beans. Fold in the bell pepper and celery. Transfer to a serving dish. Serves 8.

HARICOTS VERTS EN SALADE
GREEN BEAN SALAD

The secret to cooking green beans is to avoid overcooking them until they become soft and change color to a dull grey-green. Instead, blanch the beans in boiling water until tender-crisp and then refresh them in cold water to stop the cooking and retain the color. The flavorful vegetable thus produced is then sauced with a cream-enriched tarragon and garlic vinaigrette.

**2 lb. green beans, cut into
  2-inch lengths
⅓ cup red-wine vinegar
2 tsp. Dijon mustard
Salt and pepper**

**1 tsp. tarragon
1 clove garlic, chopped
½ cup olive oil
½ cup cream**

Blanch green beans in a large pot of salted boiling water 10 to 12 minutes until tender-crisp. Drain and refresh in cold water and drain again.

Blend together the vinegar, mustard, salt, pepper, tarragon, and garlic. Whisk in olive oil. Gradually whisk in cream. Pour over green beans and toss well. Serve at room temperature. Serves 8.

SALADE DES HARICOTS VERTS AU THON
GREEN BEAN AND TUNA SALAD

Blanched green beans can be combined with a gamut of other ingredients to produce endless varieties of tasty meals. This recipe combines tuna fish with onions, bell pepper, and lettuce. Garnished with a lemon-garlic vinaigrette, it will satisfy any taste.

2 lb. green beans, cut into
   2-inch pieces
1 head soft leaf lettuce,
   broken in pieces
1 red bell pepper, diced
2 cups canned tuna fish,
   drained

2 small white onions,
   cut into rings
1 clove garlic, minced
Juice of 2 lemons
¼ cup white-wine vinegar
Salt and pepper
½ cup olive oil

Blanch green beans in a large pot of salted boiling water 10 to 12 minutes. Drain and refresh in cold water. Combine green beans, lettuce, bell pepper, tuna, and onions in a salad bowl.

Blend together garlic, lemon juice, vinegar, salt, and pepper. Whisk in olive oil. Pour over vegetables and toss well. Serve at room temperature or chilled. Serves 8.

POIS GOURMANDES EN SALADE
SUGAR SNAP PEA SALAD

When I am lucky enough to find fresh sugar snap peas in our markets, I quickly bring them home and prepare. Not only are the peas fully developed, but the pods are tender and flavorful. Although they are wonderful as a side dish to a main course, I love them as a salad with a garlic-mustard vinaigrette.

1 lb. sugar snap peas, strings removed	4 tbsp. wine vinegar
	Salt and pepper
1 large red bell pepper, cut into julienne strips	1 clove garlic, chopped
	1 tsp. Dijon mustard
1 tbsp. sesame seeds, toasted	⅓ cup olive oil

Blanch sugar snap peas and bell pepper strips in salted water 2 minutes. Drain and refresh in cold water.

Blend together sesame seeds, vinegar, salt, pepper, garlic, mustard, and olive oil. Toss vinaigrette and vegetables together. Transfer to a serving dish. Serves 4.

SALADE AUX HARICOTS ROUGES
RED BEAN SALAD

Red beans in any form are one of my favorite foods. I particularly like Creole Red Beans and Rice, but when served in a salad with tomatoes, onions, leeks, corn, vinaigrette, and feta cheese, they take on a different dimension.

3 cups canned red beans, drained and rinsed
4 medium tomatoes, peeled, seeded, and diced
2 medium onions, diced
2 medium leeks, sliced into rounds
1½ cups canned corn, drained and rinsed

⅓ cup red-wine vinegar
Salt and pepper
10 leaves basil, chopped
½ cup olive oil
½ lb. feta cheese, sliced into strips

Combine the beans, tomatoes, onions, leeks, and corn. Blend together vinegar, salt, pepper, and basil. Whisk in the olive oil until blended. Pour over vegetables.

Garnish with strips of feta cheese. Serve at room temperature. Serves 8.

HARICOTS ROUGE ET BLANC EN SALADE
RED AND WHITE BEAN SALAD

The colorful combination of red and white beans, artichoke hearts, green onions, and celery, garnished with hard-boiled eggs, is bound together with seasoned mayonnaise for a memorable taste experience.

2 cups canned red beans, drained and rinsed in cold water
2 cups canned white beans, drained and rinsed in cold water
2 cans artichoke hearts, quartered
6 green onions, chopped
3 stalks celery, chopped
1 green pepper, chopped
4 eggs, hard-boiled, peeled, and quartered
2 cloves garlic, chopped
1 cup mayonnaise
1 tbsp. parsley, chopped
1 tbsp. basil, chopped
1 tbsp. thyme, chopped
Juice of 1 lemon
Salt and pepper
2 tbsp. capers
½ lb. bacon, fried, drained, and crumbled

Combine beans, artichokes, green onions, celery, and green pepper. Gently add hard-boiled egg quarters.

Combine garlic, mayonnaise, parsley, basil, thyme, lemon juice, salt, pepper, and capers. Fold mayonnaise mixture into vegetables and egg and toss gently. Transfer to a serving platter and garnish with crumbled bacon. Serves 8.

HARICOTS BLANCS AUX CREVETTES EN SALADE
WHITE BEAN AND SHRIMP SALAD

After red beans, white beans are my next favorite. I love white beans with a leg or rack of lamb; with Italian sausage; or with boiled rice and hot dogs. But as a delightful, cold summer salad like this one with boiled shrimp, white beans are hard to beat.

2 tbsp. parsley, chopped
2 tbsp. chives, chopped
2 tbsp. chervil, chopped
⅓ cup basil, chopped
½ cup olive oil
⅓ cup vodka
Juice of 2 limes

2 cloves garlic, chopped
2 shallots, chopped
Salt and pepper to taste
2 1-lb. cans white beans,
  drained
1½ lb. shrimp, boiled and
  cleaned

Blend together parsley, chives, chervil, basil, olive oil, vodka, lime juice, garlic, shallots, salt, and pepper. Gently combine the beans and shrimp. Pour the herbal dressing over the mixture. Toss gently. Serves 8.

SALADE TOSCANE
A SALAD FROM TUSCANY

From one of the most beautiful areas of Italy comes this combination of white and butter beans, black olives, and tuna fish garnished with an oregano-flavored olive oil. Placed on a bed of radicchio or red leaf lettuce, it is as Italian as you can get.

3 cups canned white beans, drained
3 cups canned small butter beans, drained
1 medium onion, chopped
½ cup olive oil
⅓ cup black olives, pitted

1 tbsp. parsley, chopped
1 tbsp. oregano
1 cup canned white tuna fish
Salt and pepper to taste
1 head radicchio* or red leaf lettuce

Combine beans and onion in a bowl. Add olive oil, olives, parsley, and oregano. Incorporate tuna, salt, and pepper.

Place radicchio leaves on a serving platter. Arrange the bean mixture over radicchio. Cover and refrigerate until serving time. Serves 8.

*Radicchio is the Italian name for chicory and has a beautiful burgundy red color that lends itself to garnishing both salads and cooked vegetables. It has a firm leaf and a distinctly bittersweet flavor like that of endive and escarole. Italians often add lightly sautéed radicchio to spaghetti with anchovies and garlic for a colorful and flavorful pasta dish.

SALADE AUX POIS CHICHES
CHICKPEA SALAD

The chickpea, a legume, originated in the Mediterranean and was a staple food before the Romans. It figures heavily in Spanish and North African cuisines. Because of the Spanish influence, they are also common in Mexican dishes. They are used in a limited way in French cuisine, and this salad is one I experienced in the south of France many years ago.

4 tbsp. olive oil
4 tbsp. peanut oil
¾ lb. thick bacon, cut into
   thin strips
1 large red bell pepper, diced
2 medium onions, diced
2 medium carrots, cubed

2 medium zucchini, cubed
4 medium tomatoes, peeled,
   seeded, and cubed
Salt and pepper to taste
3 cups chickpeas, cooked*
Juice of 1 lemon

Sauté bacon strips in olive and peanut oil 5 minutes. Add bell pepper, onions, and carrots. Sauté 5 minutes, turning frequently. Add zucchini, tomatoes, salt, and pepper. Cover and simmer 10 minutes. Add chickpeas and simmer an additional 5 minutes, uncovered.

Allow to cool to room temperature. Sprinkle with lemon juice. Serve at room temperature or cold. Serves 8.

*I have never seen fresh chickpeas. I have soaked dried chickpeas and cooked them in salted water until tender. Usually I just open a can. Chickpeas are also known as garbanzo beans.

SALADE DE CHAMPIGNONS SAUCE A L'AIL
MUSHROOMS IN GARLIC SAUCE

Because mushrooms are so porous, they should not be washed in a large volume of water. Instead, wipe them with water and lemon juice. If you are careful and quick, you can place them in a colander, spray them with hot water, and quickly place them on clean kitchen towels to remove excess moisture. Because of their porous quality, they are marinated in an herbal vinaigrette to absorb flavors. Combined with bacon, they take on a unique flavor.

2 tbsp. herbs, chopped
  (tarragon, parsley, chives,
  thyme)
Salt and pepper to taste
1 clove garlic, chopped

¼ cup red-wine vinegar
½ cup olive oil
2 lb. button mushrooms
¼ lb. bacon, cut into strips
1 tbsp. parsley, chopped

Blend together herbs, salt, pepper, garlic, and vinegar. Whisk in olive oil. Combine mushrooms with vinaigrette. Let rest for several hours, turning from time to time.

Sauté bacon until browned. Add mushrooms, vinaigrette, and parsley. Toss well. Transfer to a serving dish. Serve warm. Serves 8.

SALADE DE CHAMPIGNONS ET CREVETTES
MUSHROOM AND SHRIMP SALAD

Boiled shrimp and mushrooms are combined with a marinade of lemon vinaigrette and garlic to develop an unusual blend of flavors. This salad can be served as either a first course or a salad course. It can also be garnished with a few strips of sliced pimento for color.

¾ cup olive oil
4 tbsp. lemon juice
Pepper to taste
2 cloves garlic
1½ lb. mushrooms

1 lb. small shrimp,
  boiled and shelled
1 tsp. salt
2 tbsp. parsley, chopped

Blend together olive oil, lemon juice, and pepper. Add garlic cloves. Gently fold in mushrooms and shrimp. Cover and refrigerate 1 hour.

At serving time, remove garlic cloves. Add salt and parsley. Transfer to a serving dish. Serves 8.

Soups, Gumbos, and Chowders

In years gone by, when eight-course meals were common, soups were served between a first course and the main course. It can still be an elegant first course or a lunch course. However, with today's lighter eating styles, soup often is the principal dish of the meal. This is certainly true of hearty soups, gumbos, and chowders.

On my many food excursions to France, Italy, and Spain, I have gathered some wonderful recipes for soups that exemplify the character of each country's cuisine. In France I experienced wonderful combinations of vegetables and seafoods, such as in Cream of Vegetable Soup (a variation of Vichyssoise), Tomato and Rice Curry Soup, and the classic Bouillabaisse (Mediterranean Fish Stew). In Italy I had a Tomato and White Bean Soup that I can still taste in my memory, and luckily I have it in my files. From Spain I was able to taste the flavor of the country with Gazpacho Andaluz (Cold Tomato Soup) and White Gazpacho Soup with Grapes.

When I was much younger and living at home in New Orleans, my mother prepared Creole Seafood Gumbo, Crawfish Bisque, Shrimp and Crab Gumbo, Turkey Oyster Gumbo, and Turtle Soup—always as the main courses. Her vegetable soup was to die for; unfortunately, I have never been able to duplicate it. These soups, gumbos, and chowders were too good to be relegated to second place as in-between courses; they were the main course. A good green salad, some French bread, and a light dessert were all that was needed to complement our main course of soup.

When I moved to Pensacola, Florida, I was introduced to a popular local soup, Red Snapper Chowder, and made it part of my repertoire. This rich chowder of potatoes, tomatoes, and fish never fails to please my guests.

From trips to California comes the well-known San Francisco Fish Stew called *Cioppino*. A fabulous combination of fish, crustaceans, and shellfish in a savory tomato broth, the dish was created by Italian and Portuguese immigrant fishermen, who simmered their leftover catch in tomato broth in the style of their countries of origin.

Some of the recipes that follow were collected on various trips to France, Spain, Italy, and assorted places within the United States.

Others are old family recipes, some of which go back to my great-grandmother. From cooking schools and seminars in Europe I have been able to build a file of some particularly wonderful soups. However, true to my roots, I am particularly fond of those of Creole and Cajun origin. I especially recommend the Oyster Soup and some of its variations. It is still my favorite and is easy to prepare.

VICHYSSOISE DE LEGUMES
CREAM OF VEGETABLE SOUP

Vichyssoise is a classic soup created by a French chef named Louis Diat. He modified a humble dish of his childhood, leek and potato soup, by puréeing the vegetables after cooking in chicken stock and adding cream. He served it chilled with chopped chives. This recipe reverses that process by substituting other root vegetables for the potatoes and serving it hot. This dish is a real winner.

2 large onions, chopped
4 large leeks, chopped and washed
3 tbsp. butter
1 lb. carrots, peeled and diced
1 lb. turnips, peeled and diced
8 stalks celery, peeled and diced
8 sprigs parsley, chopped
Salt and pepper to taste
8 cups chicken stock
1 cup cream

Sauté onions and leeks in butter until transparent. Add carrots, turnips, celery, and parsley. Salt and pepper to taste. Add chicken stock. Bring to a boil. Reduce heat and simmer 30 minutes. Add cream, blending well. Remove from heat and serve very hot. Serves 8.

SOUPE AU PISTOU
VEGETABLE SOUP WITH BASIL

Another classic French soup is this combination of vegetables, white beans, and tubular pasta cooked in chicken stock and flavored with a *pistou* (garlic/basil/olive-oil blend). A final garnish with Parmesan cheese gives this soup a hearty character.

4 medium zucchinis, diced
3 medium leeks, cut into
  rings
4 medium tomatoes, peeled
  and diced
3 medium carrots, peeled
  and diced
2 medium onions, chopped
1 lb. green beans, diced
1 cup white beans, cooked

4 cups chicken broth
Salt and pepper to taste
½ cup small tubular pasta
5 cloves garlic
½ cup fresh basil leaves,
  chopped*
6 tbsp. olive oil
4 tbsp. Parmesan cheese,
  grated

Place zucchini, leeks, tomatoes, carrots, onions, and green and white beans in a large stockpot. Add chicken broth and blend well. Salt and pepper to taste. Bring to a boil, cover, and simmer 15 minutes. Add the pasta and continue simmering 12 minutes.

Crush the garlic in a small bowl. Blend the basil leaves until they form a paste. Incorporate olive oil little by little.

When the soup is done, remove from heat. Slowly blend in the pistou (garlic/basil/olive-oil mixture). Serve as soon as possible. Garnish each serving with Parmesan. Serves 8.

*Basil: Each spring and summer I have an abundance of fresh herbs that I grow in my kitchen garden. Although I harvest many of these and dry them for use later in the year, I also preserve some, especially basil, sage, and mint. I spread a thin layer of kosher salt into a rectangular plastic container with a tight-fitting lid. Over this layer I place a layer of basil, sage, or mint. I add another light layer of salt and another layer of herbs and so on until I have covered all the herbs or filled the container. This container is covered and placed on the shelf in my pantry until needed. When a recipe calls for fresh basil, sage, or mint, I gently remove the salt until the herb is exposed. The herb will be slightly darkened in color but is soft, pliable, and full of fragrance—not to mention flavor. I use the stored herbs for fresh ones and find them much better than dried herbs.

CREME AU CAROTTES
CREAM OF CARROT SOUP

Carrots are one of the most colorful and flavorful of the aromatic vegetables and lend themselves to many different preparations. If you are lucky enough to find fresh carrots with the green tops (indicating their freshness), make this soup. The young, fresh carrots are sweet and packed with flavor. When combined with onions and milk, thickened with breadcrumbs, and puréed, they become a gourmet delight.

4 cups carrots,	**6 tbsp. butter**
peeled and sliced	**½ cup breadcrumbs**
2 cups water	**2½ cups milk**
Salt to taste	**Salt and pepper to taste**
3 medium onions, chopped	**2 tbsp. parsley, chopped**

Boil carrots in salted water until tender. Add onions, butter, breadcrumbs, and milk. Salt and pepper to taste. Bring to a boil, cover, and simmer 5 minutes. Remove from heat and cool slightly.

Blend in a food processor until puréed. Return purée to stockpot and reheat. Transfer to a soup bowl. Garnish with parsley. Serves 8.

POTAGE VERT
GREEN SOUP

Green Soup. The name does not turn on the mental taste buds. But after sampling the mild peppery taste of watercress, the mild onion flavor of chives, and the slightly acidic taste of spinach with cream, the combination proves to be an epicurean's delight.

2 bunches watercress
½ cup chives, chopped
1 lb. spinach, cleaned
   and stemmed
1 tsp. thyme
½ cup parsley, chopped

1 qt. chicken stock
Salt and pepper to taste
3 tbsp. cornstarch
1 cup cream
Juice of ½ lemon
1 lemon, cut in rounds

Combine watercress, chives, spinach, thyme, and parsley in a large stockpot. Add chicken stock, salt, and pepper. Bring to a boil, cover, and simmer 20 minutes. Remove and cool slightly.

Process in a food processor until puréed. Return purée to stockpot and reheat. Dissolve cornstarch in cream. Add to soup. Simmer while stirring until soup thickens. Add lemon juice. Transfer to a soup bowl. Garnish with lemon rounds. Serves 6.

SOUP DES TOMATES
AUX HARICOTS BLANCS
TOMATO AND WHITE BEAN SOUP

One of my favorite combinations is the slow simmering of tomatoes and onions in chicken stock garnished with cooked white beans. The resulting soup is a happy blend of tastes. Serve with crispy croutons.

3 tbsp. butter	**1 bouquet garni***
2 medium onions, chopped	**2 qt. chicken stock**
3 lb. tomatoes, peeled,	**3 cups cooked white beans**
** seeded, and crushed**	**Salt and pepper to taste**
2 cloves garlic, crushed	

Sauté onions in butter 3 minutes. Add tomatoes, garlic, and bouquet garni. Add chicken stock. Bring to a boil. Add beans and reduce heat to simmer. Salt and pepper to taste. Cover partially and simmer 40 minutes. Remove bouquet garni and discard. Serve soup with croutons. Serves 8.

*A bouquet garni is made by tying parsley, thyme, and bay leaves together with kitchen string or tied together inside several leek leaves. Dried thyme can be used instead of fresh, but the ingredients must be wrapped in cheesecloth and tied together or placed in small bags made for that purpose. Other herbs can be added, such as tarragon, basil, sage, peppercorns, etc. The other ingredients in the dish will dictate the use of additional herbs. I like to tie the bouquet garni to the handle of the pot so I can find it later and remove it. The purpose of the bouquet garni is to allow the herbs to flavor the food and to permit easy removal if you do not want to leave them in the dish.

POTAGE DE TOMATES ET RIZ AU CURRY
TOMATO AND RICE CURRY SOUP

This soup is particularly good when made with fresh summer tomatoes. The combination of aromatic vegetables and tomatoes is complemented with the flavor of curry powder. When cooked with rice and chicken stock, the soup takes on a creamy texture. Sour cream is the perfect garnish.

4 medium onions, sliced
6 tbsp. butter
4 stalks celery, sliced
4 tsp. curry powder
3 cups crushed tomatoes
   and their juice

1 cup rice
2 cups chicken stock
Salt and pepper to taste
3 cups water
½ cup sour cream

Sauté onions in butter until browned. Add celery and curry and sauté 3 minutes while stirring. Blend in tomatoes and their juice, rice, chicken stock, salt, and pepper. Add water, bring to a boil, reduce heat, and cover. Simmer 25 minutes, stirring from time to time. Serve soup garnished with 1 tablespoon of sour cream. Serves 8.

SOUPE DE MAIS
CORN SOUP

My Corn Soup is a smooth purée of simmered onions, potatoes, milk, bay leaf, and corn thickened by a roux, enriched with cream and whole kernels of corn, and garnished with crumbled bacon. This is a soup with character.

1 large onion, chopped
4 tbsp. butter
2 medium potatoes, cut into
   dice
⅓ cup flour
1½ cups milk

2 bay leaves
Salt and pepper to taste
4 cups canned corn, drained
¼ cup cream
4 slices bacon, fried
   and crumbled

Sauté onion in butter 5 minutes. Add potatoes and sauté 2 minutes. Add flour and blend well. Incorporate milk little by little. Bring to a boil and add bay leaves, salt, and pepper. Add half the corn. Cover and simmer 20 minutes.

Remove bay leaves. Allow to cool slightly. Blend in a food processor until puréed. Return to stockpot and reheat. Add remaining cream and corn. Transfer to a serving bowl. Garnish with bacon. Serves 8.

SOUPE DE NOUVELLE-ANGLETERRE
NEW ENGLAND SOUP

This French version of New England Clam Chowder is a combination of potatoes, onions, and corn with clams and shrimp enriched with cream. Fast and easy to prepare, it is a hearty seafood soup with great taste.

6 green onions, chopped	1 lb. shrimp, shelled/ deveined
4 tbsp. butter	
½ cup flour	2 cups canned corn, drained
1 pinch cayenne	
Salt and pepper to taste	3 large potatoes, peeled and diced
4 cups fish stock or clam juice	
2 cups shucked clams	1 cup cream
	2 tbsp. parsley, chopped

Sauté green onions in butter 3 minutes. Add flour, cayenne, salt, and pepper. Sauté 1 minute. Add fish stock little by little. Bring to a boil. Add clams, shrimp, corn, and potatoes. Simmer 15 minutes. Blend in cream. Transfer to a soup bowl. Garnish with parsley. Serves 8.

SOUPE DE CONCOMBER ET CREVETTES GLACEE
CHILLED CUCUMBER AND SHRIMP SOUP

For a real summer refresher, try this cold cucumber and shrimp combination. The tangy taste of puréed cucumbers, flavored with garlic and bay leaves simmered in milk, is garnished with shrimp, mint, and cream. Refrigerated to allow the flavors to blend, it is served ice cold.

2 medium cucumbers,
   unpeeled and cut into
   small dice
4 shallots, chopped
4 tbsp. butter
2½ cups milk
4 cloves garlic, crushed

2 bay leaves
Salt and pepper to taste
2 tbsp. mint, chopped
2 tbsp. chives, chopped
1 lb. shrimp, boiled and
   shelled
2 cups cream

Sauté cucumbers and shallots in butter, covered, 5 minutes. Add milk, garlic, bay leaves, salt, and pepper. Simmer 10 minutes.

Remove bay leaves. Process mixture in a food processor. Pour into a soup bowl. Add mint, chives, shrimp, and cream. Blend well. Refrigerate 2 hours. Serves 8.

POTAGE DE MAIS ET CREVETTES CREOLE
CREOLE CORN AND SHRIMP SOUP

The "holy trinity" of Creole cooking—onions, celery, and bell pepper—is sautéed with garlic and fresh Gulf shrimp until the shrimp turn pink. Corn and tomato sauce are added. The mélange is given a Creole character by the addition of spicy Crab Boil, thickened by filé powder and mellowed by bay leaves.

1 large onion, chopped	3 cups corn kernels
3 cloves garlic, chopped	3 cups tomato sauce
2 tbsp. butter	½ tsp. liquid Crab Boil*
2 stalks celery, chopped	½ tsp. filé powder*
1 small bell pepper	2 bay leaves
1½ lb. shrimp, shelled	Salt and pepper to taste
and deveined	

Sauté onion and garlic in butter for 3 minutes. Add celery, bell pepper, and shrimp. Sauté 5 minutes. Add corn and tomato sauce, blending well. Stir in liquid Crab Boil, filé powder, bay leaves, salt, and pepper. Simmer 15 minutes. Remove bay leaves. Serves 8.

*See recipe for Shrimp Remoulade in the first chapter for description of liquid Crab Boil and the recipe Creole Gumbo Peyroux later in this chapter for an explanation of filé powder.

BOUILLABAISSE
MEDITERRANEAN FISH STEW

There are as many variations of this classic French fish stew as there are variations of Louisiana gumbo. I was very fortunate in 1982 on a visit to San Raphael, France, to have been invited to a local businessman's home where *vrai Bouillabaisse* was prepared. This recipe comes close to that experience. The varieties of Mediterranean fish, such as rascasse, are not available here in the United States, but our local fish do just fine.

2 lb. fish back bones
2 qt. water
4 tbsp. olive oil
2 large onions, chopped
3 cloves garlic, chopped
3 lb. tomatoes, peeled, seeded, and chopped
3 cups dry white wine
3 strips of orange zest 1½-inches long
2 tbsp. parsley, chopped
1 stalk of fennel

2 bay leaves
1 stem thyme
1 tsp. saffron
Salt and pepper to taste
3 lb. various fish, cut into pieces
½ cup olive oil
8 slices French bread, toasted lightly
2 additional cloves garlic
1 serving Rouille (recipe follows)

Place fish bones and water in a stockpot. Bring to a boil, then reduce heat. Simmer 35 minutes. Strain and save 1 quart of stock.

Sauté onions in olive oil 3 minutes. Add garlic, tomatoes, wine, orange zest, parsley, fennel, bay leaves, thyme, saffron, salt, pepper, and reserved fish stock. Bring to a boil, then reduce heat. Simmer 15 minutes.

Add the various pieces of fish and simmer 10 minutes. Incorporate the additional olive oil and simmer 5 minutes. Remove from heat, cover, and keep warm.

Rub the slices of toasted French bread with the garlic cloves and set aside.

Remove the fish to a serving platter and moisten with a little of the liquid. Transfer the broth to a soup bowl.

To serve, place some of the fish pieces on individual plates for each person and serve the broth in individual soup plates. Place a slice of French bread on top of the broth and serve the Rouille on the side. Serves 8.

ROUILLE
RED GARLIC SAUCE

This classic garlic sauce is a must with Bouillabaisse.

4 large cloves garlic, puréed*
½ cup pimentos, puréed*
¾ cup plain breadcrumbs

½ cup olive oil
Salt and pepper to taste

Blend together the puréed garlic, pimentos, and breadcrumbs. Slowly incorporate the olive oil, a little at a time, until blended. The result should be a thick sauce like mayonnaise. Add more or less olive oil to achieve the desired consistency. Season with salt and pepper to taste. Serves 8.

*To purée, pass garlic and pimentos through a strainer pressing with a wooden spoon.

CIOPPINO
SAN FRANCISCO FISH STEW

Some years ago I had this wonderful soup in a Los Angeles hotel restaurant, and it was one of the best dishes I have ever eaten in this country. This savory soup has its origin in the latter part of the nineteenth century among the Italian and Portuguese fishermen in the San Francisco Bay area. Various combinations of seafood, left over from the day's catch, were simmered in a tomato broth in the Old World tradition to take on a unique character. This soup has become an American classic.

2 lb. fish bones
1 large onion, cut into pieces
6 stalks celery, cut into pieces
Salt and pepper to taste
1 tbsp. dried leaf thyme
4 cups water (to cover bones)
½ cup olive oil
2 medium onions, chopped
1 large green bell pepper,
    chopped
2 cloves garlic, chopped
2 cups crushed tomatoes
2 tbsp. tomato paste
2 bay leaves
1 tsp. thyme
1 tsp. basil
3 tbsp. parsley, chopped

2 cups red wine
Salt and pepper to taste
5 or more of the following
    seafoods:
3 lb. sea bass, snapper,
    amberjack, etc., cut into
    bite size
1 qt. mussels, clams
    (steamed), and/or oysters
1 lb. Alaskan king or snow
    crab, cut into pieces
1 lb. headless shrimp,
    shelled and deveined
1 lb. scallops
1 lobster tail, cooked and
    cut into pieces
Sourdough bread, sliced

Place fish bones, onion, and celery in a large stockpot. Add salt, pepper, and thyme. Add water to cover ingredients. Bring to a boil, reduce heat, and simmer half-hour. Strain and reserve stock.

Sauté onions in olive oil until transparent. Add bell pepper and garlic and sauté 3 minutes. Add tomatoes, tomato paste, bay leaves, thyme, basil, parsley, seafood stock, red wine, salt, and pepper. Bring to a boil, reduce heat, and simmer 20 minutes.

Add chosen fish, crab, shrimp, and lobster. Continue cooking 10 minutes. Add mussels, clams, oysters, and scallops. Simmer 5 minutes. Serve seafood and broth in soup bowls with slices of sourdough bread. Serves 8.

SOUPE AUX POISSON ROUGE
RED SNAPPER CHOWDER

At the turn of the century Pensacola was the snapper capital of the world, and red snapper was the fish of choice. The dish is still very popular in homes and restaurants, and while recipes vary somewhat, all seem to adhere to a basic set of ingredients: aromatic vegetables, a light roux, tomatoes, seasonings, potatoes, and fish.

2 lb. fish bones
1 large onion, cut into pieces
6 stalks celery, cut into pieces
Salt and pepper to taste
1 tbsp. dried leaf thyme
4 cups water (to cover bones)
2 large additional onions, chopped
1 large green bell pepper, diced

2 cloves garlic, chopped
3 tbsp. butter
3 tbsp. flour
4 cups tomatoes, diced
3 cups potatoes, diced
2 bay leaves
Salt and pepper to taste
3 lb. red snapper fillets, cut into 1-inch cubes

Place fish bones, onion, and celery in a large stockpot. Add salt, pepper, and thyme. Add water to cover ingredients. Bring to a boil, reduce heat, and simmer half-hour. Strain and reserve stock.

Sauté additional onions, bell pepper, and garlic in butter 3 minutes. Add flour and stir 2 minutes. Blend in the tomatoes and cook 5 minutes. Add 3 cups of reserved stock and the potatoes. Bring to a boil and simmer 15 minutes.

Blend in bay leaves, salt, and pepper. Simmer uncovered 15 minutes. Add snapper fillets and simmer 15 minutes. Be careful not to overcook fish. Serves 8.

Note: This recipe was handed down through Pensacola's Baars family for at least three generations. It was given to me by Mrs. Lelia Baars, who was a very capable cook.

SOUPE DES HUITRES
OYSTER SOUP

This soup is a family treasure that it has been passed through four generations of the Peyroux family. This was a must soup for Thanksgiving when my mother was alive. I have taught this soup to many students in cooking classes. It always gets raves.

1 qt. oysters and liqueur
2 tbsp. butter
2 tbsp. flour
2 cups white onions, chopped
1½ cups green onions, chopped

½ cup parsley, chopped
1 cup water
4 tbsp. butter (optional)
Salt and pepper to taste

Drain oysters and save oyster liquid. Melt butter in a 3-qt. stockpot. Blend in flour, stirring until well blended, 1 minute. Add onions and sauté until soft. Incorporate green onions and parsley. Add water and reserved oyster liquid. Chop half the oysters finely. Add to soup. Simmer 30 minutes. Add remaining oysters, butter, salt, and pepper. Simmer 15 minutes longer. Serves 8.

Variations:
1. For Oyster Rockefeller Soup, add 2 cups shredded fresh spinach when remaining oysters and butter are added and 1 oz. of Pernod liquor the last 1 minute of cooking.
2. For Oyster Artichoke Soup, add 2 cups of quartered artichoke hearts at the same time as the chopped oysters.

VELOUTE AUX HUITRES
CREAMED OYSTER SOUP

This version of oyster soup, which is a fish-stock and cream-based soup, is probably the best-known type of oyster soup. Its rich, creamy texture complements the salty taste of oysters and is an excellent first course or supper on cold winter nights.

1 qt. oysters and their liquid
2 leeks, white part only, chopped
8 shallots, chopped
4 stalks celery, peeled and cut into 2-inch pieces
4 tbsp. butter

Salt and pepper to taste
1½ cups white wine
3 cups fish stock or clam juice*
1 cup cream
Coarse ground black pepper
2 tbsp. chopped chervil, parsley, or cilantro

Drain oysters in a colander and save liquid. Set both aside.

Sauté leeks, shallots, and celery in butter until tender. Add salt, pepper, and wine and bring to a boil. Blend in fish stock or clam juice and saved oyster liquid. Simmer 45 minutes.

Strain mixture into another soup pot. Bring to a boil and immediately poach oysters in this broth for 2 minutes. Remove from heat and blend in cream. Garnish with coarse ground pepper and chopped chervil, parsley, or cilantro leaves. Serves 8.

*Lacking fresh fish stock, fish bouillon cubes can be used to make required fish stock or bottled clam juice can be substituted. See recipe for Fish Stock in "Fish, Crustaceans, and Shellfish" chapter for instructions for making fresh fish stock.

BISQUE DE CREVETTES
SHRIMP BISQUE

Don't let the list of ingredients frighten you. This is relatively simple to prepare and well worth the effort. I serve this as the main course along with a salad such as Warm Potato Salad, Celery Root

Salad, or Peppers and Zucchini Salad Greek Style (all in the salads chapter). Some hot, crispy French bread will complete the meal.

3 lb. shrimp, shelled and deveined, saving shells
1 medium onion, coarsely chopped
3 stalks celery, sliced
1 tsp. thyme
Salt and pepper to taste
4 cups water
1 cup additional onions, chopped
1 small bell pepper, chopped
1 cup celery, chopped
2 cloves garlic, chopped
4 tbsp. parsley, chopped
Salt and pepper to taste
1 egg, slightly beaten
½ cup flour
½ cup peanut oil
1 large additional onion, chopped
2 tbsp. butter
1 tbsp. additional peanut oil
1 cup additional celery, chopped
3 tbsp. browned roux*
1 tbsp. tomato paste
4 cups chicken stock
6 green onions, chopped

Place shrimp shells, onion, celery, thyme, salt, pepper, and water in a stockpot. Bring to a boil and simmer 30 minutes. Strain and reserve 4 cups of shrimp stock.

Process shrimp in a food processor with onion, bell pepper, celery, garlic, parsley, salt, pepper, and egg until smooth. Save 1 cup of the mixture and put aside. Roll remaining mixture into 1-inch balls. Dust with flour. Fry shrimp balls in peanut oil until brown. Remove and reserve.

Sauté additional onion in butter and oil until brown. Add celery, roux, tomato paste, and reserved shrimp mixture. Blend in chicken stock. Bring to a boil, then simmer 15 minutes.

Add reserved shrimp balls. Simmer 5 minutes. Garnish with green onions. Serve with boiled rice. Serves 8.

*Browned roux is prepared by cooking flour in a skillet without any liquid until it turns the color of pecans. Allowed to cool, it can be stored in a jar until needed. By using prebrowned flour in a recipe that calls for a roux, you can save a good deal of time. I keep a cup or two of browned roux on my shelf all the time.

GUMBO FRUITS DE MER PEYROUX
CREOLE GUMBO PEYROUX

This is another of my family recipes that has been passed on through four or five generations. It is somewhat unique in that it uses ham along with seafood. I have never seen another recipe (and there are hundreds of variations) for gumbo that does. It gives the dish a unique taste. This recipe will serve 8 to 10 people as a main course, depending upon the appetites.

⅓ cup olive oil
4 cups white onions, chopped
3 cloves garlic, chopped
2 cups celery, chopped
2 cups ham, diced
1 cup bell pepper, chopped
4 cups okra, cut into pieces
⅓ cup brown roux*
6 tbsp. tomato paste
4 cups shrimp stock

1 cup oyster liquid
6 bay leaves
½ cup parsley, chopped
Salt and pepper to taste
2 lb. shrimp, shelled and
    deveined
1 qt. oysters
1 lb. dark crabmeat
2 tbsp. filé powder**

Sauté onions and garlic in olive oil until soft. Halfway through cooking, add celery, ham, bell pepper, and okra. Add browned roux and blend with the olive oil. Blend in tomato paste. Add shrimp stock and oyster liquid, blending well. Add bay leaves, parsley, salt, and pepper. Incorporate shrimp, oysters, and crab. Simmer 15 minutes. Add filé powder and blend well. Simmer 5 minutes (do not allow to boil). Serve with boiled rice. Serves 8.

*See previous recipe for Shrimp Bisque for an explanation of browned roux.

**Filé powder (pronounced "fee-lay") is an herb inherited from the Louisiana Choctaw Indians that is prepared by grinding dried sassafras leaves into a fine powder. It imparts a unique flavor to gumbos and acts as a thickening agent. It originally was used in winter because okra, which is also a thickening agent, was not available. I use both for their special flavors and for thickening. Boiling filé causes it to become stringy and unpalatable, so it should be added at the end of cooking and never be brought to the boil.

POTAGE SENEGLAISE
COLD CHICKEN CURRY SOUP

This soup of disputed origin combines the assertive flavors of curry and ginger with the sweetness of apples in a purée of chicken and stock for a memorable taste experience. The enrichment of cream and the garnishment of chicken slivers complete this cold cream of chicken soup.

1 large onion, chopped
1 cup celery, strings
   removed and chopped
1½ tbsp. butter
1½ tbsp. flour
1 tbsp. curry powder
1 tbsp. fresh ginger,
   grated

1 large apple, peeled and
   diced
2 cups cooked chicken
   breast meat, slivered
4 cups chicken stock
Salt and pepper to taste
1 bay leaf
2 cups cream

Sauté onions and celery in butter until soft. Add flour, curry, and ginger and cook on low heat 2 minutes. Remove from the heat and add the apple, half the chicken, 1 cup of stock, salt, and pepper. Purée the mixture in a food processor and return to saucepan. Add remaining chicken broth and bay leaf. Bring to a boil and simmer 5 minutes. Transfer to a bowl and refrigerate until very cold.

At serving time, add the cream and remaining chicken slivers. Serves 8.

SOUPE DE BROCOLI AUX AMANDE
BROCCOLI SOUP AMANDINE

Another cold soup for summer is this purée of broccoli and almond. But for the garnish of broccoli florets and almonds, you would be hard-pressed to guess the ingredients. A student in my cooking classes introduced me to this soup many years ago, but only after I had failed to guess the primary ingredients.

4 cups broccoli florets, separated	4 tbsp. butter
2 cups broccoli stems, peeled and cut into pieces	2 tbsp. flour
½ cup blanched almonds	2 tbsp. lemon juice
1 medium onion, chopped	1 cup sour cream
2 cups chicken stock	½ cup toasted slivered almonds

Blanch broccoli florets and stems in salted water 3 minutes. Drain and reserve 1 cup of florets for garnish. Combine the remaining broccoli, almonds, and onions in the bowl of a food processor. Process until smooth. Add ½ cup of chicken broth and process 30 seconds. Set aside.

Sauté flour in butter to make a light roux. Blend in remaining chicken stock, lemon juice, and puréed vegetables. Bring to a boil and simmer 2 minutes. Remove from heat and transfer to a bowl. Refrigerate for 3 hours.

At serving time, blend in sour cream. Garnish soup with reserved broccoli florets and toasted almonds. Serves 8.

GAZPACHO ANDALUZ
ANDALUSIAN COLD TOMATO SOUP

This cold tomato soup comes from the area of Andalusia, Spain, and has become a standard the world over. When garnished with the additional vegetables and bread croutons, it is like eating a liquid salad*. Cool and refreshing, it is to be enjoyed during the hot days of summer, when the ingredients are fresh and flavorful.

8 large ripe tomatoes, peeled, seeded, and quartered
2 medium onions, peeled and quartered
2 small green peppers, seeded
1 large cucumber, peeled and seeded
2 cloves garlic
1 tsp. salt
½ tsp. pepper
2 tsp. paprika
½ cup breadcrumbs, plain
½ cup olive oil

⅓ cup red-wine vinegar
3 drops Tabasco (optional)
1 cup red onion, chopped
1 cup additional tomatoes, peeled, seeded and chopped
1 cup additional cucumber, peeled, seeded and chopped
1 cup additional green pepper, seeded and chopped
1 cup croutons

Blend the tomatoes, onions, green peppers, cucumber, garlic, salt, and pepper in a food processor until smooth. Add paprika, breadcrumbs, olive oil, vinegar, and optional Tabasco. Process until well blended. Transfer to a bowl and refrigerate.

Place the red onion, additional tomatoes, cucumbers, green peppers, and croutons in separate bowls or arrange on a large platter.

At serving, each person garnishes his or her soup with the chopped vegetables as desired. Serves 8.

*See salads chapter for the Pensacola Gazpacho Salad.

AJO BLANCO CON UVAS
WHITE GAZPACHO SOUP WITH GRAPES

On a trip to Madrid, Spain, some years ago, I visited a Spanish cooking school called Alambique, run by a very elegant lady, Clara Maria Amezua de Llamas. Among the recipes she gave me was one for White Gazpacho, which produces a milky soup complemented with green grapes. This is a refreshing and unique soup for a summer menu.

½ cup breadcrumbs, plain
¼ cup milk
2 cups almonds, blanched
1 clove garlic
¾ cup olive oil
Salt and white pepper to
    taste

4 cups ice water
3 tbsp. red-wine vinegar
2 cups seedless green
    grapes, chilled

Blend together the breadcrumbs and milk. Place moistened breadcrumbs, almonds, and garlic in the bowl of a food processor. With the motor running, gradually add the olive oil and process for 3 minutes. Add salt and white pepper to taste. Gradually add ice water and vinegar. If this is not to be served immediately, refrigerate. At serving, garnish with cold green grapes. Serves 8.

Fish, Crustaceans, and Shellfish

FISH

I am very fortunate. Living on the Gulf of Mexico with its supply so many varieties of fish and other seafood, I have available this wonderful resource to cook and enjoy. The seafood markets of Pensacola (once the red snapper capital of the world) abound with red snapper, black snapper, pink snapper, mingo snapper, as well as trout, amberjack, grouper, scamp, flounder, bass, mullet, shrimp (grey, white, royal reds), blue crabs, crawfish, scallops (bay and sea), squid, octopus, etc., etc., etc. This supply allows me to prepare such dishes as Trout Amandine, Poached Fish with Green Grapes, Pecan-Fried Triggerfish, and Red Snapper with Mustard Sauce.

Having lived my early life in New Orleans, I learned as second nature the Creole, Cajun, and the French methods for preparing the seafood available from the Gulf as well as the bayous and lakes of Louisiana. The Creoles and Cajuns also incorporated the skills of the Spanish, Africans, Indians, and Italians who have brought their cooking skills and cuisines to Louisiana over the course of hundreds of years. This potpourri of cuisines has emerged as Creole and Cajun—or Louisiana—cooking.

CRUSTACEANS

This wonderful category of seafood—comprised of shrimp, crawfish, lobster, and crab—includes any aquatic arthropods having a segmented body, a semitransparent exoskeleton, and paired, joined limbs. Although it doesn't sound very appetizing, this category of seafood is probably America's most popular, especially shrimp.

The shrimp recipes in this volume are samples of Oriental, Creole, and Italian styles of cooking. Probably the most popular of my shrimp recipes is Dilled Shrimp Margaret. This recipe is great for a large group when doubled or tripled and serves well as a buffet dish; a little goes a long way.

Crawfish, a very popular food in south Louisiana and the New

Orleans area, has become more famous in the past fifteen years because of the efforts of the Cajun chef Paul Prudhomme. Here I present two classics in the Cajun/Creole genre, Crawfish Pie and Crawfish Étouffée.

For the crab category I present the most popular crab recipe I have taught in cooking classes, Crab Pie. It, too, is a crowd pleaser.

MOLLUSKS

This class of seafood is another of America's favorites, especially oysters, which are found all over the world. The Creole classic is Creamed Oysters, which was once popular in New Orleans restaurants and is one of my favorites.

Marinated Mussels remind me of many happy meals on the French Riviera, and I am so happy to have them available here in the Deep South thanks to modern shipping methods.

A scallop is a bivalve with two fluted shells. A large adductor muscle joins the two shells together and controls the hinge that opens and closes them. The scallop propels itself by forcing water in and out around the hinge. Inside the shell, besides the adductor muscle, there are digestive organs, the crescent-shaped sex organ (white in the male and orange-red in the female), and the frill of sensory organs around the inner circumference of each shell. The marshmallow-shaped adductor muscle is what Americans know as a "scallop." The rest of the scallop is usually discarded.

There are more than 360 species of scallops worldwide, but only a few make it to market. Most commonly available are sea scallops (gathered from deep water, they are the largest at 25 to 30 per pound); bay scallops (smaller than sea scallops, live inshore, are medium size, 50 to 60 per pound); and calico scallops (very small, 80 to 200 per pound), coming from deep water from the Carolinas all the way to Brazil.

The English name for this bivalve comes from its scalloped shape, while the Italian name (*pellegrini de San Giacomo*, or "pilgrims of

Saint James") and the French name (*coquilles Saint Jacques*, or "shells of Saint James") derive their names from the fact that pilgrims in the Middle Ages going to the holy site of Santiago di Compostella in northern Spain carried the shells as their drinking vessels. Our scallop recipes are samples of various cuisines, and I highly recommend the Grilled Skewered Scallops and Shrimp.

CURRY DE FRUITS DE MER
SEAFOOD CURRY

The fun of curry dishes is the unique flavors provided by garnishes. Each person adds one or more garnishes. The garnishes are sometimes called "boys" because at large banquets each was presented to the diner by a young boy. Some suggested boys are diced avocado, shredded coconut, chutney, chopped peanuts, sliced banana, kumquats, bacon, diced bell pepper, hard-cooked egg, or crushed almonds.

3 tbsp. olive oil
1 large onion, chopped
1 red bell pepper, chopped
3 stalks celery, chopped
½ lb. mushrooms, sliced
3 tbsp. curry powder*
2 apples, peeled, seeded, and diced
1 lb. firm white fish filets, cut into bite-size pieces

1 lb. shrimp, shelled and deveined
½ cup raisins
2 tsp. Worcestershire sauce
4 tbsp. tomato paste
1 cup white wine
½ cup water
Salt and pepper to taste
4 tbsp. plain yogurt
Juice of 1 lemon

Sauté onion, bell pepper, celery, and mushrooms in olive oil 5 minutes. Add curry powder and sauté 2 minutes while stirring. Incorporate apples, fish, shrimp, raisins, Worcestershire, and tomato paste, blending well. Add wine, water, salt, and pepper. Cover and simmer 10 minutes.

Blend in yogurt and lemon juice. Serve with boiled rice. Serves 8.

*There are many recipes for curry powder, which is a blend of many spices (turmeric, chilies, salt, cumin seeds, fennel seeds, black pepper, garlic, ginger, fenugreek, cinnamon, cloves, anise, and mustard). In India, powders are rarely used; each cook compounds them as needed. The British East India Company developed spice powders to allow the sailors who became fond of spicy dishes take them home. From England, curry powder spread throughout the world. Be sure to buy a quality brand such as Madras to ensure a successful curry.

POISSON BOULANGER
BAKERS' FISH CASSEROLE

Layers of potatoes, fish, and onions baked with butter, garlic, and vinegar provide a simple prepare-ahead casserole for a family supper or a luncheon. Serve this with Carrot and Turnip Salad or Mushrooms and Garlic Salad in the salad chapter.

**2 lb. potatoes, peeled and
  cut into rounds
1 tbsp. white vinegar
Salt to taste
4 tbsp. butter, softened
2 cloves garlic, chopped**

**3 lb. fish filets, skinned and
  cut into 2-inch pieces
Salt and pepper to taste
2 large onions, cut into
  rounds
4 tbsp. additional butter**

Boil the potatoes in salted water and vinegar 8 minutes. Drain and reserve. Combine butter and garlic. Spread over the bottom of a baking dish. Arrange the fish pieces over butter. Salt and pepper to taste. Place a layer of onions over fish. Arrange potatoes over fish and onions in overlapping fashion. Dot with additional butter. Bake at 350 degrees for 40 minutes until potatoes are brown. Serves 8.

RAGOUT MEDITERRANEEN
MEDITERRANEAN FISH STEW

Fish stews abound in most European cuisines, and this one from the Mediterranean classically combines fish, mussels, and shrimp in a tomato-flavored broth for a dish that reminds one of the Côte d'Azur.

4 tbsp. olive oil
2 large onions, cut into rings
3 cloves garlic, crushed
6 medium tomatoes, diced
¼ cup water
¾ cup white wine
2 bay leaves
Salt and pepper to taste
2 tbsp. parsley, chopped

2 lb. fish filets (cod, bass, amberjack, etc.), cut into 1½-inch pieces
½ lb. mussels, washed and tightly closed
½ cup additional water
½ lb. shrimp, shelled and deveined

Sauté onions and garlic in olive oil 3 minutes. Add tomatoes, water, wine, bay leaves, salt, and pepper. Simmer 15 minutes.

Add the fish pieces and simmer an additional 10 minutes.

Place mussels and additional water in a saucepan. Cover and bring to a boil 5 minutes. Remove mussels and separate the shells, discarding the top portion. Place mussels in the bottom shells and their cooking liquid into the tomato/fish preparation. Add shrimp, blending well. Simmer 5 minutes. Transfer to a serving bowl. Garnish with chopped parsley. Serves 8.

FILET DE POISSON VERONIQUE
POACHED FISH FILETS IN
GREEN-GRAPE VELOUTE SAUCE

This recipe introduces a unique technique in the use of plastic wrap. By enclosing the filets in plastic wrap, you hold the flesh together so it doesn't fall apart when handled and keeps the fish moist while resting. This method also can be used when poaching chicken breasts to help them hold an attractive shape.

½ cup green onions, chopped
1 cup clam juice or Fish Stock
  (recipe follows)
1 cup white wine
8 4-oz. filets of fish (trout,
  snapper, sea bass, etc.)
Salt and pepper to taste
8 pieces saran wrap
  (12 x 12 inches)

1 piece of waxed paper
3 tbsp. butter
3 tbsp. flour
½ tsp. salt
⅛ tsp. cayenne pepper
2 egg yolks
3 tbsp. cream
1 cup green seedless
  grapes

Place green onions, clam juice or stock, and white wine in a deep skillet. Bring to a boil, reduce heat, and simmer.

Salt and pepper fish filets. Wrap each in saran wrap. Place wrapped filets in poaching liquid. Cover with a piece of waxed paper. Poach 8 minutes. Remove filets and keep warm. Strain poaching liquid and reserve.

Melt butter in a saucepan. Add flour and blend well. Gradually add reserved poaching liquid. Whisk until sauce thickens. Add salt and cayenne. Blend in egg yolks and cream. Add grapes and heat thoroughly.

Unwrap fish filets and arrange on a serving plate. Pour grape sauce over and serve. Serves 8.

Note: The classic dish that uses grapes is Trout Veronique, which covers poached filets of trout with a hollandaise sauce with green grapes. This recipe is a variation on that theme.

FUMET DE POISSON
FISH STOCK

1 lb. fish parts (backbones, heads, pieces)*
1 large onion, chopped
1 cup celery, chopped
Salt and pepper to taste
1 tsp. thyme
4 cups water

Combine fish parts, onion, celery, salt, pepper, and thyme in a large stockpot. Add water to cover ingredients. Bring to a boil. Simmer 30 minutes.

Strain liquid and discard solids.

*I usually have fish parts because I either am able to buy the whole fresh fish and clean it myself or buy backbones at my fishmonger. However, if I don't, I use bottled clam juice as a reasonable substitute.

TRIGGERFISH FRIT AU PACANE
PECAN-FRIED TRIGGERFISH

This very interesting dish is a favorite at Madison's Cafe in Pensacola, Florida. Chef Jim Shirley has sealed small, firm, sweet, flat filets from the triggerfish in a pecan-flavored coating. Sautéed in olive oil for flavor, it is delicious served with Roasted-Corn Tartar Sauce. It's a very popular item on the menu.

½ cup pecans, finely chopped
¼ cup pecan meal*
½ cup flour
1 tsp. garlic powder
1 tsp. onion powder
Salt and pepper to taste
1 tsp. sugar
1 egg
½ cup milk
2 lb. triggerfish filets**
½ cup breadcrumbs, plain
Peanut oil for frying
1 recipe Roasted-Corn
  Tartar Sauce
  (recipe follows)

Blend together pecan pieces, meal, flour, garlic and onion powders, salt, pepper, and sugar. Blend together egg and milk. Dip triggerfish filets in egg/milk mixture. Pass filets in seasoned flour mixture. Pass filets a second time in egg wash. Coat filets in breadcrumbs. Sauté in ¼-inch peanut oil in a sauté pan, 3 minutes on each side until golden. Transfer to a serving plate. Serve with a tablespoon of Roasted-Corn Tartar Sauce. Serves 8.

*Pecan meal is a by-product of shelling pecans and is available from Renfroe Pecan Company in Pensacola. It can be made at home by toasting the pecans in a 300-degree oven about 10 minutes. Cool the pecans and grate them. Because they have a high oil content, the meal may be a little coarse, but it still works.

**Triggerfish is a flat-sided fish with a pointed nose and powerful teeth used to crush shellfish, which is its preferred food. With a leathery and rough skin, it does not look very appetizing, but don't let that fool you. Its flesh is firm and sweet when cooked, and it holds up well when sautéed, grilled, poached, or broiled.

SAUCE TARTAR AU MAIS ROTI
ROASTED CORN TARTAR SAUCE

This variation of tartar sauce is an excellent accompaniment to many fish dishes as well as shrimp, scallop, and crab recipes.

1 cup mayonnaise
1 tsp. Worcestershire sauce
¼ tsp. lemon juice
2 tbsp. sweet relish
¼ tsp. garlic powder

¼ tsp. onion powder
1 ear corn, chucked, baked at 350 degrees 15 minutes, and cut off the cob

Combine mayonnaise, Worcestershire, lemon juice, relish, and garlic and onion powders. Add roasted corn kernels. Blend well. Serve as a garnish with fish.

TRUITE AUX AMANDES
TROUT AMANDINE

This recipe is a classic in the French and Creole repertoire. The French use filets of sole, which is a common fish in colder waters. The Creoles adapted this recipe to use fish available in the Gulf of Mexico and the lakes and bayous of Louisiana: trout. Other fish, such as redfish and red snapper, can be substituted.

8 6-oz trout filets, skin on (other fish can be used)
1 cup milk
Salt and pepper to taste
6 tbsp. flour
½ cup clarified butter*

¼ cup additional clarified butter
¾ cup sliced almonds
Juice of 1 lemon
2 tbsp. parsley, chopped

Soak filets in milk 1 hour. Drain filets. Salt, pepper, and flour filets. Sauté filets in butter skin-side-up 3 minutes. Turn and sauté skin-side-down 3 minutes. Transfer to a serving dish and keep warm. Add additional clarified butter to the skillet. Sauté almonds until browned. Add lemon juice and bring to a boil. Pour over filets. Garnish with parsley. Serves 8.

*Because butter burns at a high temperature, it is desirable to clarify by melting, which causes the milky liquid to separate from the butter and settle to the bottom of the container. This protein is what scorches when heated. Skimming off the clear golden liquid from the top and using it to cook will yield better results.

POISSON ROUGE MILANESE
RED SNAPPER MILANESE

À La Milanese usually implies a food product (fish, veal, chicken) with a coating of flour/egg/breadcrumbs sautéed in butter. What better fish than red snapper to prepare this classic?

½ cup olive oil
2 tbsp. lemon juice
2 tbsp. onion, grated
Salt and pepper to taste
8 4-oz. red snapper filets
1 cup flour
2 eggs, well beaten
2 tbsp. water

1 cup breadcrumbs
4 tbsp. butter
2 tbsp. additional olive oil
2 tbsp. additional butter
1 tbsp. capers
1 tbsp. parsley, chopped
2 lemons, quartered

Blend together the olive oil, lemon juice, onion, salt, and pepper. Marinate the fish in this mixture. Dredge fish filets in flour. Pass filets in egg mixed with water. Coat with breadcrumbs.

Melt butter with additional olive oil over medium heat. Sauté snapper filets in butter 3 minutes each side, until coating is golden. Place on a serving plate.

Add additional butter to skillet and cook until it turns light brown. Add capers and parsley. Pour over snapper filets. Garnish with lemon slices. Serves 8.

FLET A LA KIEV
FLOUNDER KIEV

I learned this variation on Chicken Kiev fifteen years ago from a fellow cooking-school teacher, Julie Josephs, and have adapted it as my own ever since. This recipe substitutes filets of flounder for pounded chicken breasts. Surrounded in garlic- and parsley-flavored butter, the filets are breaded and deep-fried. The burst of aroma and flavor when cut is a culinary delight.

8 tbsp. butter, softened
1/4 cup parsley, chopped
1 tsp. Worcestershire sauce
2 cloves garlic, chopped
1 tbsp. lemon juice
1 dash Tabasco
8 flounder filets
1 cup flour

2 tbsp. water (to combine with eggs)
4 eggs, lightly beaten
1 cup breadcrumbs
Peanut oil for deep-frying
2 lemons, quartered
1 recipe Lemon Caper Sauce (recipe follows)

Blend together softened butter, parsley, Worcestershire sauce, garlic, lemon juice, and Tabasco. Mold into a cylinder 1/2-inch thick, wrap in plastic wrap, and freeze.

Flatten flounder filets between pieces of plastic wrap. Cut frozen butter cylinder into 1 1/4-inch lengths. Place a piece of butter on each flounder filet. Fold sides of filet over edges of butter. Roll filet to enclose butter. Dust well with flour. Pass in egg/water mixture. Coat well with breadcrumbs.

Deep-fry 3 minutes in peanut oil at 375 degrees. Drain. Garnish with lemon slices and Lemon Caper Sauce on the side. Serves 8.

SAUCE CITRON AU CAPRES
LEMON CAPER SAUCE

4 tbsp. butter
4 tbsp. flour
1⅓ cups milk

⅓ cup lemon juice
⅓ cups capers*
Salt and pepper to taste

Melt butter in a saucepan. Add flour and blend 2 minutes. Whisk in milk gradually until thickened. Add lemon juice, capers, salt, and pepper. Serve as a garnish to fish dishes. Makes about 2 cups.

*Capers are the unopened flower buds of a Mediterranean trailing shrub called a caper bush, which grows wild. They are picked before flowering, pickled, and bottled. They have been used as a condiment for thousands of years. They have a salty and lemony taste and complement fish dishes extremely well.

POISSON ROUGE AU SAUCE PACANE
REDFISH WITH PECAN SAUCE

This recipe is a good example of the Creoles' adaptation to the food products available in early colonial times. Not having their familiar almonds readily available for garnishing fish, the Creoles substituted pecans, which grow in abundance in south Louisiana. A Creole classic was thus created. While redfish, a type of drum fish, is most popular in Louisiana, other firm-flesh fish—such as sea bass, amberjack, triggerfish, and snapper—can be cooked in this manner.

2 tbsp. butter
½ cup pecan pieces
½ cup pecan halves
2 eggs, beaten
2 tbsp. milk
Salt and pepper to taste
3 drops Tabasco

8 6-oz. fish filets (redfish,
   snapper, flounder,
   amberjack)
1 cup flour
6 oz. clarified butter*
2 tbsp. lemon juice

Sauté pecan pieces and halves in butter until "toasted," then set aside.

Blend together eggs, milk, salt, pepper, and Tabasco. Pass fish filets in flour and shake off excess. Place in egg mixture and drain excess egg. Pass again in flour and set aside.

Heat clarified butter in a skillet over medium heat. Sauté fish filets in butter 3 minutes until browned. Turn filets over and brown second sides. Transfer to a serving dish.

Add reserved toasted pecans and lemon juice to skillet and heat 1 minute. Pour over the fish filets. Serves 8.

*For clarified butter, see recipe for Trout Amandine.

FILET DE POISSON
A LA SAUCE CITRON AU FOUR
BAKED FISH FILETS WITH LEMON SAUCE

These individual packages of firm, white filets of fish and a slice of smoked salmon rest on a bed of spinach in a lemon béchamel sauce. They are a delight to both the taste and the eye.

2 lb. spinach, blanched and drained
16 3-oz. fish filets (flounder, trout, snapper, etc.)
8 slices smoked salmon
4 tbsp. butter
4 tbsp. flour
2 cups milk
½ cup lemon juice
Salt and pepper to taste
2 lemons, cut in quarters

Divide the spinach into 8 equal portions in individual baking dishes. Place 1 filet of fish on top of spinach. Cover each filet with a slice of salmon. Top each with a second filet.

Dissolve flour in butter in a saucepan. Gradually add milk while whisking. When sauce thickens, add lemon juice, salt, and pepper. Mask each fish package with sauce. Bake at 350 degrees 15 minutes. Garnish with lemon slices. Serves 8.

POISSON ROUGE VAL DE LOIRE
RED SNAPPER WITH MUSTARD SAUCE

In 1979 I had the privilege of escorting a group of food enthusiasts on a trip to Angers, France, where we took classes with a young French chef, Phillipe Bezout. Phillipe introduced us to the unique foods of the Loire valley and taught us some interesting techniques. One of these "tricks" was the wrapping of fish filets in lettuce leaves, which keeps the fish firm and moist during the cooking process and provides an attractive presentation. The mustard-cream sauce is a perfect complement to the snapper.

8 6-oz. filets of red snapper
  (or other firm fish)
8 large lettuce leaves*
4 tbsp. butter
½ cup shallots, chopped
1 cup Fish Stock or bottled
  clam juice

2 cups cream
6 tbsp. additional butter
4 tbsp. brown Creole or
  Meaux mustard
⅓ cup parsley leaves or
  watercress

Blanch lettuce leaves in boiling water 30 seconds. Drain and refresh in cold water. Place a fish filet on each lettuce leaf, folding lettuce over to enclose the fish. Sprinkle chopped shallots in a large buttered skillet and place the fish packages on top. Add Fish Stock or clam juice to barely cover fish. Cover loosely with a piece of waxed paper. Bring to a simmer and cook 15 minutes. Remove filets to an ovenproof plate, cover loosely with foil, and keep warm in a 275-degree oven.

Strain the poaching liquid into another pan. Reduce over high heat until about 2 tablespoons of liquid remain. Add cream and reduce again by one-third. Incorporate additional butter and mustard.

Pour sauce into a serving platter. Arrange the fish packages over sauce. Garnish with parsley or watercress. Serves 8.

*To separate the large outer leaves from the lettuce, remove the core with a sharp knife. Holding the lettuce upside down, allow running water to flow through the lettuce. The leaves will separate easily without damage.

CREVETTES FOO YUNG
SHRIMP FOO YUNG

Although much of Oriental cooking requires a lot of pre-preparation of many ingredients, this recipe is the exception. The ingredients are few and quickly prepared. I serve this for a simple but flavorful light supper because it is quick and needs only a simple salad, such as marinated cucumbers in vinaigrette, to complete the meal.

1 cup chicken stock	1 cup green onions, chopped
2 tbsp. soy sauce	2 cups shrimp, boiled and
2 tbsp. sherry wine	cleaned
2 tbsp. cornstarch	Salt and pepper to taste
8 medium eggs, well beaten	3 tbsp. peanut oil
1 cup fresh bean sprouts*	1 cup green peas, cooked

Blend stock, soy, sherry, and cornstarch. Heat over medium heat until thickened. Set aside.

Combine eggs, sprouts, green onions, shrimp, salt, and pepper. Heat oil in a large pan or grill. Pour ¼ cup of egg mixture to make small pancakes. Sauté until egg sets. Turn and sauté second side. Remove to a serving platter. Keep warm.

Reheat soy/sherry sauce. Pour over pancakes. Garnish with green peas. Serves 8.

*Bean sprouts, the small white shoots of the pealike mung bean plant, have a mild and crunchy taste and are used in many Oriental dishes. They are available fresh or canned. Canned sprouts should be washed before using to remove a metallic taste. Unused fresh or canned sprouts should be covered with water in the refrigerator.

CREVETTES ET FROMAGE DE SOYA FRIT-RAPIDE
STIR-FRY OF SHRIMP AND TOFU WITH OYSTER SAUCE

Bean curd (Chinese) or tofu (Japanese) is a low-fat protein product of soybean milk (soybeans soaked, ground, and strained) turned into a curd. Smooth and creamy in texture and bland in taste, it has the ability to absorb the flavors of other foods. Stir-fried with shrimp, it is garnished with oyster sauce for a unique flavor.

½ cup chicken stock
2 tbsp. cornstarch
¼ cup oyster sauce*
¼ cup sherry wine
¼ cup soy sauce
1 tbsp. peanut oil
½ lb. bean curd (tofu),
  cut into ½-inch slices
1 tbsp. additional peanut oil
2 cloves garlic, sliced

2 tbsp. ginger root, shredded
1½ lb. shrimp, shelled and
  deveined
½ cup green onions, sliced
1 medium red bell pepper,
  large dice
½ cup snow peas
1 recipe Pan-Fried Noodles
  (recipe follows)

Blend together stock, cornstarch, oyster sauce, sherry, and soy sauce and set aside.

Add peanut oil to a very hot wok. Add bean curd and toss gently 3 minutes until browned. Remove and set aside.

Add additional peanut oil to wok. Stir-fry garlic and ginger 1 minute. Add shrimp and stir-fry 3 minutes. Add onions, bell pepper, and snow peas. Stir-fry an additional 2 minutes. Add reserved bean curd and sauce mixture. Cook until sauce thickens. Serve with Pan-Fried Noodles. Serves 8.

*Oyster sauce is made from oysters, salt, soy sauce, and seasonings. It is a thick, brown, bottled sauce with a rich, subtle oyster flavor that enhances sauces. It will keep indefinitely in a covered container in the refrigerator.

NOUILLES A POELE
PAN-FRIED NOODLES

½ lb. Chinese noodles*   1 tbsp. soy sauce
2 tbsp. peanut oil

Boil noodles in salted water until al dente, about 3 to 5 minutes. Drain and dry with towels. Add peanut oil to a hot wok. Add noodles and soy sauce. Stir-fry until light brown, about 2 minutes. Place on a serving dish.

*Chinese noodles come in a variety of shapes, thin and round, flat, or wide and square. They usually are made from flour, water, and translucent noodles, which are extremely thin and are made from dried mung beans, rice, potatoes, or taro root. The noodles required for this recipe are the thin, round variety that, after boiling and drying, are stir-fried to become *chow mein (chow* meaning "stir-fried" and *mein* meaning "noodles"). Thin spaghetti can be substituted if necessary. There also is a type of precooked noodle called "instant noodles" or "ramen," which comes packaged in blocks with a seasoning pouch to make quick soups. These can be used in this recipe without the seasonings (boil as directed on package).

CREVETTE A LA NOUVELLE ORLEANS
CREAMED SHRIMP NEW ORLEANS STYLE

Sauced seafood mixtures filling puff-pastry patty shells (or *bouchées*) are very popular menu items in Creole homes and restaurants in New Orleans. This recipe combines shrimp and mushrooms in a Veloute sauce as the filling for puff-pastry shells.

1 cup green onions, sliced
4 oz. butter
2 lb. shrimp, shelled and deveined
¾ cup mushrooms, sliced
4 oz. additional butter
½ cup flour
1 cup milk
1 cup Shrimp Stock (recipe follows) or clam juice

½ cup sherry wine
⅓ cup lemon juice
2 egg yolks
2 tbsp. parsley, chopped
Salt and cayenne pepper
8 puff-pastry patty shells, baked*

Sauté green onions in butter 2 minutes. Add shrimp and mushrooms and sauté 5 minutes. Remove shrimp and mushrooms and set aside.

Add additional butter to the skillet. Dissolve flour in butter, stirring 2 minutes. Whisk in milk, shrimp stock or clam juice, sherry, and lemon juice. Return shrimp and mushrooms to the skillet. Blend in egg yolks, parsley, salt, and cayenne. Fill patty shells with shrimp mixture. Serves 8.

*Puff-paste pastry is known in French cuisine as *pate feuilletée*, or "flaky dough," which is made by enclosing butter in pastry dough, rolling and folding into thirds, re-rolling and folding six times, thus creating more than one thousand layers of dough, butter, dough. When baked, the butter keeps the dough separated and causes the dough to puff up to five or more times its original thickness. This is sometimes referred to as *millefeuille* or "a thousand leaves" or sheets.

When cut into 2-inch rounds, baked, and the central uncooked portion removed, it forms a pastry container referred to as *bouchées,* or "patty shells." These patty shells are available frozen from Pepperidge Farms and can be found in your supermarket freezer.

FONDS DES CREVETTES
SHRIMP STOCK

Heads and shells of shrimp	**Salt and pepper to taste**
1 large onion, chopped	**1 tsp. thyme**
1 cup celery, chopped	**4 cups water**

Combine heads, shells, onion, celery, salt, pepper, and thyme in a large stockpot. Add water to cover ingredients. Bring to a boil. Simmer 30 minutes.

Strain liquid and discard solids.

Note: I usually have shrimp shells because I am able to buy the shrimp fresh or have them frozen in my freezer. However, if I don't, I use bottled clam juice as a reasonable substitute.

AUBERGINES FARCIES AUX CREVETTES
SHRIMP-STUFFED EGGPLANTS

Louisiana Creoles are fond of stuffing eggplants with a variety of flavorings, such as beef, lamb, sausage, crab, crawfish, shrimp, or simply aromatic vegetables and seasonings. Probably the most popular stuffing is shrimp. This dish truly represents *la bouche Creole,* "the Creole taste."

4 medium eggplants, cut in
  half lengthwise
2 tbsp. olive oil
2 large onions, chopped
2 cloves garlic, chopped
2 tsp. thyme
1 tsp. Quatre-Epices
  (recipe follows)
⅛ tsp. cayenne pepper

1½ lb. shrimp, boiled
  and shelled
½ cup parsley, chopped
Salt and pepper to taste
1 cup breadcrumbs
3 medium eggs, beaten
½ cup additional bread
  crumbs

Place eggplants, cut-side down, on an oiled baking pan. Bake at 350 degrees for 20 minutes. Remove from the oven. Allow eggplants to cool. Scoop out flesh and chop, reserving shells.

Sauté onions* and garlic in olive oil until browned. Add reserved chopped eggplant flesh. Add thyme, Quatre-Epices, and cayenne. Blend in shrimp, parsley, salt, and pepper. Add breadcrumbs, mixing well. Incorporate beaten eggs, stirring well. Fill reserved eggplant shells with mixture. Sprinkle with additional breadcrumbs. Bake at 350 degrees for 20 minutes. Serves 8.

*Sautéeing the onions slowly in olive oil until they turn a light brown color causes the sugars in the onions to caramelize, which imparts a delightful sweet taste to the onions and thus the entire dish when added.

QUATRE-EPICES
FRENCH FOUR-SPICE BLEND

Quatre-Epices, a blend of four spices available in bottled form in France, is used to flavor vegetables, grilled or braised pork, beef, and meat mixtures such as meat loaf, pâtés, and terrines. I usually combine a tablespoon of each and keep in a jar on my spice shelf.

1 part ground cloves*   **1 part ground ginger*****
1 part ground nutmeg**   **1 part ground white pepper******

Blend together. Store in a bottle on shelf. Use as directed in recipes.

*Cloves, the pink flower buds of a Southeast Asian plant, are picked before they open and are dried in the sun, where they turn a reddish brown.

**The fruit of the nutmeg tree produces a seed that is harvested as nutmeg, while the seed's outer covering becomes mace. Nutmeg is native to Indonesia and the West Indies.

***Ginger: The root of a tropical Asian plant is dried and ground into a power. Although used mainly in baking in this country, it is often used in savory dishes as well.

****White pepper: White pepper starts out as black peppercorns. The black peppercorns are soaked in water until the black shell is loosened and removed. The inner white peppercorn is then ground or is used whole.

CREVETTES AUX ANETH MARGARET
DILLED SHRIMP MARGARET

This recipe was given to me almost 40 years ago by the late Mrs. Margaret Cheer Allen, whose family owned La Louisiane restaurant in New Orleans in the early part of this century. Margaret was an avid gourmand and cook extraordinaire who encouraged my interest in cooking. It never fails to please my guests.

4 tbsp. butter
½ cup green onions, chopped
½ cup French vermouth
3 lb. shrimp, shelled
  and deveined
Salt and pepper to taste
4 tbsp. additional butter
4 tbsp. flour
1½ cups milk, heated

½ cup fresh dill weed,
  chopped (or 2 tbsp. dill
  seed, ground)*
Salt to taste
⅛ tsp. cayenne pepper
1 recipe Golden Rice
  (recipe in "Rice and
  Pasta" chapter)

Sauté green onions in butter 1 minute. Add vermouth, shrimp, salt, and pepper. Simmer 5 minutes.

In another saucepan, dissolve flour in additional butter. Whisk in heated milk until sauce thickens. Add chopped dill, salt, and cayenne. Add dill sauce to shrimp mixture. Simmer 2 minutes. Serve with Golden Rice. Serves 8.

*Dill weed, the feathery leaves of the dill plant, has a lighter and sweeter flavor than dill seed, and its bright green color adds to the appearance of this dish. Dill seeds can be used in this dish; however, they need to be processed in a blender. I use both: the weed for flavor and color, and the ground seeds to reinforce the flavor.

PENNE CON GAMBERI E CREMA
TUBULAR PASTA WITH SHRIMP IN CREAM SAUCE

This recipe offers a change from pasta with the usual tomato and meat sauces by combining fresh shrimp with wine, tomato sauce, and cream with Italian seasonings and cheese as a garnish to penne, a tubular pasta whose shape readily absorbs the sauce within its tube.

1 lb. penne pasta
2 cloves garlic, chopped
4 tbsp. butter
2 lb. shrimp, shelled
   and deveined
Salt and pepper to taste
½ cup white vermouth

½ cup tomato sauce
1 cup cream
½ tsp. basil
½ tsp. oregano
2 egg yolks
2 tbsp. Parmesan cheese
3 tbsp. parsley, chopped

Boil penne pasta until al dente. Sauté garlic in butter until soft. Add shrimp and toss until pink, 3 to 5 minutes. Salt and pepper to taste. Add vermouth, tomato sauce, cream, basil, and oregano. Bring to a simmer. Add 3 tablespoons tomato mixture to egg yolks and blend. Add to shrimp and sauce. Blend in Parmesan. Simmer until thickened. Drain pasta into a serving bowl. Pour shrimp and sauce over pasta. Garnish with chopped parsley. Serves 8.

CREVETTES SAUCE PIQUANTE ALMA
SHRIMP CREOLE ALMA

This is a classic Creole recipe that has come down through several generations of my family. My mother, Alma, learned this from my father's grandmother. This makes the recipe at least 150 years old. It is a light combination of shrimp in a broth of aromatic vegetables, seasonings, and tomatoes served on a bed of steamed Creole Rice.

3 lb. shrimp, shelled and deveined, shells reserved
1 medium onion, cut into eighths
3 stalks celery, cut into large pieces
6 stems parsley
1 tsp. thyme
2 bay leaves
Salt and pepper to taste
4 tbsp. peanut oil
2 cups additional onions, chopped
2 cloves garlic, chopped

2 tbsp. flour
2 cups additional celery, chopped
1 cup green bell pepper, chopped
6 cups tomatoes, chopped
1 tbsp. tomato paste
1 dash cayenne pepper
2 tsp. salt
3 bay leaves
2 tsp. thyme
1 recipe boiled Creole Rice (recipe in "Rice and Pasta" chapter)

Place shrimp shells, onion, celery, parsley, thyme, bay leaves, salt, and pepper in a stockpot. Cover with water. Bring to a boil and simmer 30 minutes. Strain and reserve liquid.

Sauté onions and garlic in peanut oil until they turn light brown. Incorporate flour, blending well for 2 minutes. Add celery and bell pepper, mixing well. Blend in tomatoes, tomato paste, cayenne, salt, bay leaves, and thyme. Add 2 cups reserved shrimp stock. Bring to a boil. Reduce heat and simmer 20 minutes. Add shrimp and simmer 10 minutes. Serve over boiled Creole Rice. Serves 8.

TARTE D'ECREVISSE
CRAWFISH PIE

Crawfish have been largely unknown in the United States except in south Louisiana. For centuries they have been a Creole/Cajun favorite and a major food item. Louisiana is a large producer of rice, which is grown in flooded fields, a natural habitat for these crustaceans. Thanks to chef Paul Prudhomme, who has made Louisiana cooking a household word, the popularity of this local seafood has traveled throughout the land, giving rise to a multimillion-dollar industry in crawfish farming.

2 tbsp. butter
2 cups onions, chopped
3 cloves garlic, chopped
2 tbsp. Dry Roux
   (recipe follows)
1 large bell pepper, chopped
1 cup celery, chopped
½ cup parsley, chopped

1 cup green onions, chopped
Salt and pepper to taste
⅛ tsp. cayenne pepper
2 tbsp. tomato paste
1 lb. crawfish tails
1 recipe Basic Pie Dough,
   rolled into 2 circles
   (see "Desserts" chapter)

Sauté onions and garlic in butter 3 minutes. Blend in Dry Roux. Add bell pepper, celery, parsley, and green onions. Salt and pepper to taste. Add cayenne pepper. Add tomato paste and crawfish tails. Blend until mixture thickens.

Line a pie dish with dough. Fill with crawfish mixture. Cover with second pie-dough circle. Trim excess dough. Cut several slits in top crust. Bake at 350 degrees for 40 to 45 minutes until top is golden. Serves 8.

ROUX SEC
DRY ROUX

A *roux* is a quantity of flour that has been cooked in a fat over low heat. The process prepares the particles of flour to absorb the liquid used in the recipe, eliminates the raw, pasty taste of uncooked flour, imparts a unique flavor to the dish it serves, and acts as a thickening agent. Because it saves time, many cooks, myself included, prefer a dry roux when cooking Creole and Cajun food. The dark brown dry roux is added to the fat already in the recipe, and cooking continues. If uncooked flour is used, it will take 10 minutes or longer to turn the desired color. I always keep one or more cups of browned flour on my shelf.

1 cup flour

Place flour in a heavy, dry skillet and heat slowly while stirring. Stir as flour turns light tan, tan, and then brown (about 15 minutes). Remove from heat, cool, and store in an airtight container.

ETOUFFEE D'ECREVESSE
CRAWFISH ETOUFFEE

Étouffée is the French word for "smothered." In Creole/Cajun cooking terminology, it means a method of cooking something well in a combination of the Creole/Cajun holy trinity of vegetables—onions, celery, and bell pepper—with a dark roux and a small amount of liquid. The most popular étouffée dishes in Louisiana cooking are Shrimp Étouffée and this recipe, Crawfish Étouffée. This dish is traditionally served with boiled and steamed rice, a salad, French bread, and ice-cold beer, preferably New Orleans' own Dixie beer.

½ cup Dry Roux (see previous recipe)
3 tbsp. peanut oil
3 tbsp. butter
½ cup onions, chopped
½ cup green onions, chopped
½ cup celery, chopped
½ cup green bell pepper, chopped
2 cloves garlic, chopped
½ tsp. thyme
½ tsp. basil
3 tbsp. tomato paste
Salt and cayenne pepper
1 tbsp. Worcestershire sauce
2 cups seafood stock or clam juice, heated
2 lb. crawfish tails, cooked
3 tbsp. parsley, chopped
½ cup additional green onions, sliced

Dissolve Dry Roux in oil and butter. Add onions, green onions, celery, bell pepper, garlic, thyme, basil, tomato paste, cayenne pepper, salt, and Worcestershire. Cook vegetables and seasonings 3 minutes. Add heated stock and blend well. Simmer until thick. Add crawfish tails. Heat thoroughly. Remove from heat. Add parsley. Serve over boiled rice. Garnish with green onions. Serves 8.

ETOUFFEE D'ECREVISSE AUX HARICOTS
SMOTHERED CRAWFISH WITH BEANS

At first glance, one would think this recipe was from southwest Louisiana Cajun land. Sorry, I found this one in the south of France. While crawfish are not as common in France as in south Louisiana, they show up in many recipes. This one combines seasoned red and white beans, port wine, and crawfish tails for a unique ensemble. It is delicious when served with boiled rice.

1 medium onion, chopped	Salt and pepper to taste
2 cloves garlic, chopped	1 bouquet garni including
1 large carrot, chopped	2 whole cloves
1 stalk celery, chopped	3 hot peppers, seeded and
2 tbsp. butter	chopped
½ lb. red beans	¾ cup port wine
½ lb. white beans	1 lb. crawfish tail meat

Sauté onion, garlic, carrot, and celery in butter until soft. Add the red and white beans and blend well. Salt and pepper to taste. Add water to cover. Add bouquet garni with cloves and hot peppers. Cover and simmer for 1 to 1½ hours. Add port wine. Cover and simmer an additional 30 minutes. Add crawfish tail meat. Simmer 10 more minutes until hot. Serve over boiled rice. Serves 8.

TARTE AU CRABE
CRAB PIE

I found this recipe forty-five years ago in the cooking section of the New Orleans *Times-Picayune.* I was intrigued by the use of potato chips to form a crust. I tried it, served it at a dinner party, and had to make copies of the recipe for everyone there. I have taught this recipe in cooking classes over the years, presented it on my television program, and prepared it more times than I can imagine at home. A wonderful casserole for a buffet dinner party, it can be prepared ahead and even frozen. It is the most popular recipe I have ever prepared.

2 cups potato chips, crushed
4 tbsp. butter, melted
1 tsp. paprika
1 tbsp. green onions, chopped
4 tbsp. additional butter
1 cup additional green onions, chopped
⅓ cup pimento, chopped
⅓ cup black olives, seeded and chopped
⅓ cup green bell pepper, chopped
1 lb. crabmeat
3 tbsp. flour
Salt and pepper to taste
½ cup milk
½ cup sour cream

Combine chips, butter, paprika, and green onions. Press ¾ of mixture into a 9-inch pie pan. Bake at 375 degrees 10 minutes. Remove from the oven and allow to cool.

Sauté additional green onions in additional butter. Add pimento, olives, and bell pepper. Gently fold in crabmeat. Blend in flour, salt, and pepper. Gradually incorporate milk and cook until thickened. Remove from heat. Fold in sour cream. Pour mixture into baked pie shell. Sprinkle remaining potato chips over crabmeat. Bake 20 minutes at 350 degrees. Serves 8.

CROQUETTES DES CRABS
CRAB CROQUETTES

Living in Pensacola and having grown up in New Orleans, I have been fortunate to have readily available many fresh seafood products. Probably my most favorite seafood is the blue crab from the lakes and bayous of Louisiana and the Gulf Coast. Because of my Creole heritage, I have learned many ways of preparing this delicate meat. This recipe is one of my favorites.

1 onion, chopped
3 cloves garlic, chopped
3 tbsp. butter
3 tbsp. flour
6 green onions, chopped
⅓ cup parsley, chopped
1½ lb. crabmeat
Salt and pepper to taste

⅛ tsp. cayenne pepper
1 large egg, lightly beaten
2 cups breadcrumbs
1 cup peanut oil for frying
2 lemons, sliced for garnish
1 recipe Horseradish Sauce
    (recipe follows)

Sauté onion and garlic in butter until soft. Add flour and blend well. Incorporate green onions and parsley. Fold in crabmeat. Add salt, pepper, and cayenne. Blend in beaten egg until mixture binds. Remove from heat and cool.

Form mixture into croquettes. Coat well with breadcrumbs. Fry in hot peanut oil until golden brown. Transfer to paper towels to drain. Place on a serving platter. Garnish with lemon slices. Serve with Horseradish Sauce. Serves 8.

Note: For an interesting variation, add 1 cup of cooked corn kernels along with the crabmeat. The sweet taste and the crunchiness of the corn add a new dimension to the dish.

SAUCE RAIFORT
HORSERADISH SAUCE

1 cup sour cream
1 tbsp. prepared horseradish*
1 tbsp. Dijon mustard

1 tsp. salt
2 tbsp. capers

Combine sour cream, horseradish, and mustard. Add salt to taste. Blend in capers. Transfer to a serving bowl. Chill.

*Horseradish, a plant native to Eurasia, has a thick, whitish, and very pungent root that is grated and combined with vinegar and salt to make a condiment. Prepared horseradish is sometimes combined with dry mustard in a basic béchamel sauce for a Horseradish Sauce.

FRUITS DE MER EN BATEAU DE PAIN
FRUITS OF THE SEA IN BREAD BOATS

Containerizing foods in edible receptacles is popular in French cooking. Seafood, meats, fruits, and vegetables are often served in puff-pastry cases, crêpes, scooped-out vegetables, and pie dough. In this recipe we form containers out of small French rolls or brown-and-serve rolls by cutting a slice off the tops and scooping out most of the crumbs.

3 tbsp. butter	1 cup small mushrooms
3 tbsp. flour	½ cup white wine
1 cup milk	1 tbsp. shrimp, shelled
Salt and a dash cayenne	and deveined
pepper	12 oz. bay or calico
½ tsp. nutmeg	scallops
8 small French rolls or brown-	1 lb. crab claw meat
and-serve rolls, baked	Salt and pepper to taste
⅓ cup butter, melted	2 tbsp. Parmesan cheese,
1 cup green onions, chopped	grated
4 tbsp. additional butter	1 tsp. paprika

Melt butter in a saucepan. Add flour and blend well. Whisk in milk until sauce thickens. Add salt, cayenne, and nutmeg. Set this béchamel sauce aside.

Cut a thin slice off the top of each roll. Scoop out the center to form a container. Brush insides of rolls with butter. Bake at 350 degrees for 3 minutes. Remove from the oven and reserve.

Sauté green onions in additional butter. Add mushrooms and sauté 1 minute. Add white wine. Add shrimp, scallops, and crabmeat. Simmer 5 minutes. Salt and pepper to taste. Add béchamel sauce, blending well. Fill reserved bread cases with seafood mixture. Sprinkle with Parmesan cheese. Garnish with paprika. Serves 8.

Note: The filling for the bread containers is a classic Fruits de Mer, or Fruits of the Sea recipe of creamed shellfish and mushrooms. Other ingredients, such as cubes of firm-flesh fish, crawfish, oysters, mussels, clams, etc., can be added or substituted. Small to medium shrimp are best in this recipe, and small bay scallops are ideal. I prefer the dark crab claw meat because it is sweeter in taste and holds its shape better than the white. However, white lump crabmeat is delicious in this dish.

COQUILLE SAINT JACQUES PROVENÇALE
SAUTEED SCALLOPS WITH TOMATO AND GARLIC

Provence, one of the most colorful and beautiful parts of France, is situated on the Mediterranean coast. Full of sunlight, the area is known for the production of wonderful vegetables such as tomatoes, garlic, eggplant, and all sorts of herbs, such as basil, thyme, rosemary, and other fragrant plants. Dishes named Provençale generally contain tomatoes, garlic, thyme, shallots, and/or basil and are usually cooked in olive oil.

2 lb. sea scallops, cut horizontally into thirds
Salt and pepper to taste
¼ cup flour
¼ cup olive oil
2 cloves garlic
¼ cup shallots, chopped
2 cups tomatoes, peeled, seeded, and diced

¼ cup French vermouth
2 tbsp. fresh basil, chopped
2 tbsp. parsley, chopped
8 scallop shells
1 recipe Sautéed Bread crumbs (recipe follows)

Salt and pepper scallops and dust lightly with flour. Heat oil in a large skillet until very hot. Add scallops. Sauté for 1 minute until browned. Blend in garlic, shallots, and tomatoes. Add French vermouth. Toss over high heat until juices thicken, about 1 minute. Fold in basil and parsley. Put scallop mixture into 8 scallop shells. Sprinkle with Sautéed Breadcrumbs. Serves 8.

SAUTE DE CHAPLURE
Sauteed Breadcrumbs

1½ tbsp. butter   **½ cup breadcrumbs**

Melt butter in a small skillet. Stir in breadcrumbs. Cook until butter is absorbed and breadcrumbs are golden.

Note: Sautéed Breadcrumbs are a wonderful garnish for vegetable dishes such as cauliflower and broccoli.

PORC ET COQUILLES SAINT-JACQUES FRIT-RAPIDE
STIR-FRIED PORK TENDERLOIN AND SCALLOPS

Pork tenderloin slices and scallops are a unique combination for this Chinese stir-fry. Each ingredient contributes its own special texture and flavor when marinated in ginger, soy, and sherry. Rice is the natural accompaniment.

**1½ lb. pork tenderloin,
  thinly sliced
2 tsp. sugar
½ tsp. salt
1 tsp. ginger, grated
4 tbsp. soy sauce
2 tbsp. sherry wine**

**3 green onions, sliced
2 tsp. cornstarch*
2 tsp. chicken stock
2 tbsp. peanut oil
1 lb. sea scallops, sliced
  horizontally**

Marinate pork in a blend of sugar, salt, ginger, soy, sherry, and onions 15 minutes. Blend together cornstarch and stock. Drain pork, reserving marinade.

Add peanut oil to a hot wok. Add pork and stir-fry 2 minutes. Add scallops and stir-fry 1½ minutes. Add reserved marinade and dissolved cornstarch. Toss for 30 seconds until sauce thickens. Transfer to a serving dish. Serves 8.

*Cornstarch, a purified starch made from corn, is used in cooking as a thickening agent for sauces. It has twice the thickening power of flour. It must be dissolved in a cold liquid before adding to hot foods; otherwise it will lump. It also imparts a silky, shiny appearance to a sauce. It is the preferred thickening agent in Chinese cookery.

SPIEDINI DE CANESTRILLE E GAMBERI ALLA GRIGLIA
GRILLED SKEWERED SCALLOPS AND SHRIMP

Of the more than 360 species of scallops, the most commonly available are sea scallops (gathered from deep water, 25 to 30 per pound), bay scallops (live inshore, 50 to 60 per pound), and calico scallops (very small, 80 to 200 per pound). In this recipe the large sea scallops and large shrimp are marinated in garlic-, rosemary-, and thyme-flavored olive oil. Each scallop is surrounded by a large shrimp and skewered, then broiled or grilled, for a unique dish.

½ cup seasoned breadcrumbs	3 tbsp. olive oil
3 tbsp. parsley, chopped	24 large sea scallops
2 cloves garlic, chopped	24 large shrimp, shelled
1 tsp. rosemary leaves, crushed	and deveined
1 tsp. thyme	8 bamboo skewers (8-inch), soaked in water*
½ tsp. salt	4 cups cooked rice

Blend together breadcrumbs, parsley, garlic, rosemary, thyme, and salt. Stir in olive oil. Combine scallops, shrimp, and breadcrumb mixture and coat seafood well. Skewer a shrimp through the tail end. Add a scallop, skewering through the side. Pass skewer through the head end of the shrimp. The scallop should be almost surrounded by the shrimp. Repeat 2 more times. Skewer 3 shrimp and 3 scallops on the remaining skewers. Grill or broil 3 minutes. Turn skewers over and grill 3 minutes. Serve on a bed of boiled rice. Serves 8.

*Soaking bamboo skewers in water helps prevent them from burning under the broiler or on the grill.

BOUCHEES DES HUITRES CREME
A LA NOUVELLE ORLEANS
CREAMED OYSTERS IN PATTY SHELLS
NEW ORLEANS STYLE

This recipe was one of my mother's specialties and is typical of the Creole style of cooking. Oysters are combined with onions, both white and green, and parsley in a cream-enriched velouté sauce and served in crisp puff-pastry shells.

2 cups large oysters
2 large onions, chopped
2 tbsp. butter
8 green onions, chopped
½ cup parsley, chopped
8 tbsp. additional butter
1 cup flour
1 egg yolk

1 cup cream
2 cups additional oysters, drained (reserve liquid) and chopped
8 puff-pastry patty shells, baked*
2 tbsp. additional parsley, chopped

Poach oysters in their liquid until edges curl. Drain, set aside, and reserve liquid, adding to the liquid drained from the additional 2 cups of chopped oysters.

Sauté onions in butter until well done. Add green onions and parsley. Add additional butter and flour, blending well. Add 1½ cups of the reserved oyster liquid. Stir until thickened. Blend in egg yolk and cream. Add additional chopped oysters. Add reserved poached oysters. Simmer 5 minutes. Spoon into baked patty shells. Garnish with additional chopped parsley. Serves 8.

*Puff-pastry shells are called "patty shells" in New Orleans and *bouchees* in France. They are available in the frozen-food section of your supermarket from Pepperidge Farms. These frozen puff-pasty shells will rise into a light, flaky pastry shell five times their original thickness. When baked, it is necessary to remove the small scored top, setting it aside, and to scoop out the uncooked portion in the center. The result is a flaky container for this recipe or other creamed dishes.

TARTE AUX HUITRE
OYSTER PIE

This Cajun delight is a hearty dish of aromatic vegetables, mushrooms, and oysters bound together by an oyster-flavored roux as a filling for a double-crust pie. Worcestershire sauce, Tabasco, and cayenne pepper give the dish a distinct Cajun characteristic.

2 tbsp. butter
1 cup white onions, chopped
1 cup green onions, chopped
1 cup mushrooms,
    stems and pieces
½ cup celery, chopped
1 tsp. thyme
3 tbsp. Dry Roux (see recipe
    for Crawfish Pie earlier
    in this chapter)
2 cups oysters and
    their liquid

½ cup parsley, chopped
1 tbsp. lemon juice
2 tsp. Worcestershire sauce
2 dashes Tabasco
Salt and pepper to taste
⅛ tsp. cayenne pepper
1 recipe Basic Pie Dough
    (recipe in "Desserts"
    chapter)
1 egg, lightly beaten

Sauté green and white onions in butter until soft. Add mushrooms, celery, and thyme. Sauté 3 minutes. Add Dry Roux and blend well. Add oysters and their liquid. Stir until thickened. Add parsley and lemon juice. Blend in Worcestershire sauce, Tabasco, salt, pepper, and cayenne.

Line a pie dish with pie dough. Pour oyster mixture into pie shell. Cover filling with second piece of pie dough. Seal edges well. Brush with beaten egg. Cut several slits in top to vent steam. Bake at 350 degrees for 45 minutes. Serves 8.

MOULES MARINIERES
MARINATED MUSSELS

One of the fondest memories I have of my many visits to France is the opportunity I had to experience this classic French dish, especially in Nice. Fortunately, thanks to today's fast transportation, I am able to buy fresh mussels here in the Deep South, so I can enjoy the delicious broth of wine and mussel juices blended with butter, shallots, and French seasonings. French bread dipped into the broth and consumed with the mussels is a gourmet delight.

6 oz. butter	Salt and pepper
8 shallots, chopped	4 qt. live mussels, cleaned
1 bouquet garni (parsley,	well
thyme, and bay leaf)	3 tbsp. parsley, chopped
4 cups white wine	French bread, sliced

Sauté shallots in butter. Add bouquet garni, wine, salt, and pepper. Bring to a boil. Discard any mussels that are open and will not close when tapped. Add mussels to poaching liquid. Cover and simmer 5 minutes. Remove mussels with a skimmer to a bowl. Discard any mussels that have not opened.

Add parsley to poaching liquids. Raise heat and reduce liquid by half. Remove bouquet garni and discard. Pour sauce over mussels. Dip French bread into sauce and consume mussels. Serves 8.

Beef, Veal,
Pork, and Lamb

BEEF

Beef has become the meat of choice for most Americans in the twentieth century, especially those naturally tender cuts of meat that become steaks and roasts. The less tender parts, which must be braised (cooked slowly in liquid), and the tougher pieces, which are usually ground and chopped, can be used in a host of special recipes. The steaks and roast I leave to other books. Here I present recipes for various kinds of stews, braised dishes, and ground-beef mixtures.

Beef braised in wine, beer, or plain water makes memorable meals, and ground beef in cabbage leaves, with sauces, pasta, croquettes, or pies, are hearty ways to use this most popular meat.

VEAL

Veal, the meat of a young cow, is much more readily available in France and Italy, where it seems to be the meat of choice. When I was young, we had veal more often than beef at home because it was less expensive, but today it is much more expensive. However, veal is becoming more and more popular and is more easily found in the markets today. It was the meat of choice for New Orleans Grillades and Grits, which was a popular breakfast dish at the turn of the century. We frequently had it for supper.

I present in this chapter some of my favorite veal recipes. I especially enjoy Breaded Veal Parmesan Cheese Turci and Venetian-Style Liver.

PORK

The pork industry, conscious of the public's concern for fat, has made great efforts to breed pigs that provide considerably leaner flesh, so much that they call it "the other white meat" and go to great lengths to compare its calorie and fat content to that of veal and chicken. If one removes most of the visible fat from the flesh, the meat still retains good flavor and can be eaten without guilt.

I present in this chapter a few recipes that take advantage of this lower-fat meat. The Sautéed Pork Chops Dijon Style—with all visible fat removed, bathed in Dijon mustard, and coated with seasoned breadcrumbs—is my favorite. The tang of the mustard and the counterpoint flavor of the sweet pickles provide a taste experience, and the Pork Rolls Stuffed with Sauerkraut is a wonderful combination of pork, sauerkraut, potatoes, and spices that will surprise you.

LAMB

Lamb, the meat of choice for many centuries in several Mediterranean countries and in northern France, has become more and more popular in the United States in the past twenty or so years. The flesh of a young sheep less than a year old has found its way into menus and cookbooks around the country, especially where Americans of Greek, Turkish, and North African descent are living.

This assertively flavored meat is often served as a rack of lamb (part of the rib cage) or as chops (the individual ribs). Both cuts are rather expensive but are well worth the price on special occasions. Another choice part of the animal is the hind leg, which is usually roasted with cloves of garlic inserted into the flesh and sprigs of rosemary, an herb that marries extremely well with lamb.

The French prepare a classic stew called Navarin d'Agneau, which is a blend of cubes of lamb with carrots, turnips, onions, leeks, and potatoes, while the Greeks and Turks prepare different recipes of ground lamb and eggplant called Moussaka.

RAGOUT DE BOEUF
BEEF STEW

Beef Stew, one of those dishes I call comfort food, is a favorite from my childhood that brings back wonderful memories of the aromas and tastes of my Creole roots. Tasty beef—braised in red wine, beef stock, and aromatic vegetables and garnished with additional vegetables—was and still is a classic. Since I rarely find it in restaurants anymore, I frequently prepare it at home.

3 lb. beef, cut into 1-inch pieces
Salt and pepper to taste
3 tbsp. flour
3 tbsp. peanut oil
2 cups onions, sliced
1 cup carrots, sliced
3 cloves garlic, chopped
2 cups red wine
4 cups beef stock
2 cups tomatoes, crushed
1 bay leaf

1 tsp. thyme
Salt and pepper to taste
3 cups potatoes, peeled, cut into 1-inch pieces and parboiled*
3 cups additional carrots, peeled, cut into 1-inch cylinders, and parboiled*
2 cups pearl onions, peeled and parboiled*

Salt and pepper beef cubes. Dust with flour. Brown beef in peanut oil in 2 batches, placing beef in an ovenproof casserole dish.

Pour out all but 1 tablespoon of the cooking oil. Add remaining flour from the dusting of the beef. Add onions, carrots, and garlic and sauté until lightly brown. Place the cooked vegetables over the beef. Deglaze the sauté pan with red wine. Add beef stock, tomatoes, bay leaf, thyme, salt, and pepper. Pour over beef in casserole dish to cover beef (add additional stock if necessary). Bring to a boil. Cover and place in a 325-degree oven for 2½ hours.

Add additional potatoes, carrots, and pearl onions. Cook another 30 to 40 minutes until meat and vegetables are tender. Serve with rice or egg noodles. Serves 8.

*To parboil the root vegetables, cover with cold salted water. Bring to a boil. Drain immediately and refresh in cold water to stop the cooking. Add to the recipe as requested.

NOISETTES DE BOEUF
BEEF NUGGETS IN WINE SAUCE

Noisettes de Boeuf was a very popular item on the menu of Masson's Beach House, a now-defunct restaurant in New Orleans. I have tried to duplicate the recipe and often serve it when I have guests. It also makes a wonderful item for a large buffet party because it can be prepared ahead of time and served from a chafing dish along with very thin boiled noodles or rice.

2 lb. beef (filet or sirloin), cut into ½-inch cubes
1 tsp. garlic, minced very finely
Salt and pepper to taste
2 tbsp. butter
2 tbsp. peanut oil
6 large green onions, chopped
1 cup white onions, sliced
3 tbsp. Dry Roux (see recipe for Crawfish Pie, chapter 4)
1 cup beef stock
¾ cup red wine
3 tbsp. tomato paste
1 tsp. Kitchen Bouquet (sold in stores)
2 cups mushrooms, quartered
½ cup parsley, chopped

Season beef cubes with garlic, salt, and pepper. Heat butter and oil in a large pot until very hot. Sauté beef nuggets in small batches in butter and oil until brown. Remove beef and set aside.

Add green and white onions to drippings and sauté until lightly brown. Add browned roux, blending well. Gradually add beef stock and red wine while stirring. Blend in tomato paste and Kitchen Bouquet. Simmer 5 minutes, then add mushrooms and parsley. Return reserved beef to sauce. Simmer partially covered 30 minutes. Serve with rice or egg noodles. Serves 8.

FILET DE BOEUF STROGANOFF
BEEF STROGANOFF

This universally popular recipe was created by a Russian chef whose name has long been forgotten. He named it for his patron, Count Paul Stroganoff, a member of the court of Czar Alexander III. I like it best when served with very thin boiled egg noodles.

2 lb. beef filet, cut into
   1-inch cubes
Salt and pepper to taste
2 tbsp. butter
1 tbsp. peanut oil
3 tbsp. Cognac or brandy
2 tbsp. additional butter
2 lbs. mushrooms,
   sliced or quartered

1 tsp. garlic, chopped
1 tsp. tomato paste
1 tsp. beef extract*
3 tbsp. flour
⅓ cup chicken stock
1 cup sour cream
1 tbsp. dill weed

Salt and pepper beef filet cubes. Heat butter and oil until hot. Sauté beef cubes in batches, until browned. Return browned beef to skillet. Add Cognac and ignite. When flames subside, remove beef to a serving dish.

Add additional butter to skillet. Sauté mushrooms and garlic 2 minutes. Add tomato paste, beef extract, flour, and chicken stock, blending well. Lower heat and gradually blend in sour cream. Incorporate dill weed. Return beef to skillet and warm 2 minutes. Transfer to serving bowl. Serve with egg noodles. Serves 8.

*Beef extract is the commercial name for the classic French *Glace de Viande*, a greatly reduced beef stock that is very thick and concentrated in flavor. One brand name I use is Bovril. Substitution: Boil ½ cup beef broth until reduced to 1 tablespoon.

CARBONADE DE BOEUF
BEER-BRAISED BEEF

The word *carbonade* in French cooking terms means "to braise in beer." Although beef and chicken stocks and red and white wines are more often used, beer is sometimes used as the preferred liquid for braising (slow cooking in a liquid) because it adds a special flavor to the dish. Here it is used to braise beef chuck (which is flavorful but not tender) with onions, garlic, and mushrooms to produce a tender and flavorable carbonade.

3 large onions, cut into rounds
3 tbsp. peanut oil
1 lb. mushrooms, cut in half
3 lb. beef chuck, cut into
   8 6-oz. pieces
Salt and pepper to taste

4 tbsp. flour
2½ cups beer
2 cloves garlic, crushed
1 tbsp. brown sugar
Salt and pepper to taste

Sauté onions in peanut oil until soft. Add mushrooms and sauté another 1 minute. Transfer onions and mushrooms to a Dutch oven, leaving as much of the cooking oil as possible in the skillet.

Salt and pepper beef chuck pieces. Dust with flour. Brown beef on all sides in same skillet. Transfer to Dutch oven.

Add the remaining flour to skillet and stir until it begins to turn color. Add beer a little at the time. Add garlic, sugar, salt, and pepper. Bring to a boil. Transfer to the Dutch oven. Cover and bake 2½ hours at 325 degrees. Serves 8.

POITRINE DE BOEUF
BOUILLI SAUCE RAIFORT
BOILED BRISKET OF BEEF
WITH HORSERADISH SAUCE

Boiled brisket is an old New Orleans favorite that can still be found in homes and restaurants. The recipe for boiled beef brisket is a dish that has been featured on the menu at a long time landmark in New Orleans, Tujaque's Restaurant. This very old restaurant with a fixed menu has become famous for serving boiled brisket with horseradish sauce as a first course along with vegetable soup. I sometimes prepare this dish and serve it along with braised cabbage as a main course.

5 lb. beef brisket*	2 large carrots, sliced
2 qt. boiling water	2 stalks celery, sliced
1 bouquet garni**	1 recipe Horseradish Sauce
1 large onion, sliced	(recipe follows)

Place brisket of beef in a heavy stockpot and cover with boiling water. Return to a boil and reduce heat to simmer. Skim off any film that develops. Add bouquet garni, onion, carrots, and celery. Simmer 3 hours until fork-tender, adding water as needed to keep beef covered.

Remove brisket to a serving platter and allow to rest 10 minutes. Slice across the grain. Serve with horseradish sauce as a first course or larger portions as a main course. Leftovers make wonderful sandwiches. Serves 8 to 10.

*Beef brisket is the cut of beef from the breast of the cow between the front legs. The boneless, flat muscle with a layer of fat is excellent for braising or boiling and makes beautiful slices. It is the preferred piece of beef for making corned beef.

**Recipe for bouquet garni accompanies Tomato and White Bean Soup dish in soups chapter)

SAUCE RAIFORT
HORSERADISH SAUCE

1 cup catsup or mayonnaise
½ cup prepared horseradish
½ cup brown Creole mustard

Blend together the catsup or mayonnaise, horseradish, and mustard. Chill. Serve with boiled meat. Keeps for several months under refrigeration.

Note: This sauce is excellent with boiled shrimp, crabmeat, or poached, baked, or fried fish. Some people prefer the red-catsup version, the one most common in New Orleans. However, the mayonnaise style is excellent, and I prefer it for Boiled Brisket of Beef.

PAIN DE BOEUF
MEAT LOAF

A good flavorful meat loaf is hard to come by. After eating many mediocre loafs, I came across this excellent recipe while having a family supper with friends. My friend gave me her recipe, which I now call mine. I now pass it on to you.

1 cup onions, chopped	2 tsp. paprika
2 tbsp. peanut oil	1 tsp. allspice
3 cloves, garlic crushed	1 tbsp. oregano
2 lb. lean ground beef	2 medium eggs, lightly
1 lb. ground pork	beaten
1 cup seasoned breadcrumbs	4 bay leaves
2 tsp. salt	1 recipe Tomato Sauce
½ tsp. pepper	(recipe follows)
2 tsp. thyme	

Sauté onions in peanut oil 3 minutes. Add garlic and sauté another 3 minutes. Set aside.

Blend together beef and pork. Incorporate breadcrumbs, salt, pepper, thyme, paprika, allspice, and oregano. Add beaten eggs and reserved onions and garlic, blending all well. Press mixture into a 2-qt. meatloaf pan. Arrange bay leaves on top. Bake at 350 degrees 1½ hours until a meat thermometer reaches 155 degrees.

Remove from the oven and let rest 30 minutes. Pour off fat and juices. Transfer to a platter and slice into ½-inch slices. Serve with Tomato Sauce and mashed potatoes or rice. Serves 8.

SAUCE TOMATE
TOMATO SAUCE

1 cup onions, chopped
2 cloves garlic, chopped
2 tbsp. olive oil
1 32-oz. can crushed tomatoes

1 14-oz. can tomato sauce
Salt and pepper to taste
1 tsp. Italian seasoning*

Sauté onions and garlic in olive oil until lightly brown. Add crushed tomatoes and tomato sauce, blending well. Add salt, pepper, and Italian seasonings. Simmer 1 hour.

*Italian seasoning is sold in the spice section of your supermarket. It is a blend of seven herbs; oregano, rosemary, savory, thyme, marjoram, sage, and basil. These herbs, individually and in combination, are common in many Italian recipes.

LAHANODOLADES
STUFFED CABBAGE LEAVES GREEK STYLE

This recipe is a variation of the classic Greek dish called *Dolamthes,* grape leaves stuffed with lamb and rice. Cabbage leaves are filled with a savory beef stuffing, rolled to enclose the filling, and braised in chicken stock. They are garnished with an egg-and-lemon sauce.

1 large cabbage, leaves separated*	**Salt and pepper to taste**
2½ lb. ground beef	**1 cup chicken stock, boiling**
¾ cup raw rice	**2 egg whites**
3 tbsp. parsley	**2 egg yolks**
1 tbsp. dill weed	**Juice of 2 lemons**
2 onions, chopped	**1 tbsp. cornstarch**

Blanch the cabbage leaves in boiling water until soft and pliable. Drain and refresh in cold water. Drain again and set aside.

Combine ground beef, rice, parsley, dill, onions, salt, and pepper. Place 3 or 4 tablespoons of meat mixture on each cabbage leaf. Fold the stem end over the stuffing and both sides inward. Roll the stuffed leaf to form a bundle. Line the bottom of a baking dish with extra cabbage leaves. Place rolls over leaves. Add boiling chicken stock. Cover with foil and place another baking dish on top to weigh the rolls down. Bake at 350 degrees 1½ hours.

Remove from the oven and pour off the cooking liquid into a 1-cup measure. Beat egg whites until stiff. While beating, gradually add the egg yolks, lemon juice, cornstarch, and reserved broth. Pour over cabbage bundles. Serves 8.

*To separate cabbage leaves, remove core of cabbage and hold cabbage stem side up under running cold water. As the water finds its way in between the leaves, they will begin to fall away from the head. Continue until all the larger leaves separate.

PASTITSIO
MACARONI AND MEAT PIE

The Greek answer to Baked Italian Lasagna is Pastitsio. Layers of boiled large macaroni are separated by a layer of sautéed lamb (or beef) with aromatic vegetables, seasonings, tomatoes, and Parmesan cheese. A final layer of Greek-style white sauce prepares the dish for a 20-minute stay in the oven. This is really delicious.

2 medium onions, chopped
3 tbsp. olive oil
1¼ lb. ground lamb or beef
3 medium tomatoes, peeled,
    seeded, and chopped
Salt and pepper to taste
1 bay leaf
¼ tsp. basil
⅓ cup water
1½ lb. macaroni
    (No. 3 thick)
⅔ cup Parmesan cheese
1 recipe Béchamel Sauce
    (recipe follows)

Sauté onions in olive oil until brown. Add ground meat and sauté until medium-cooked, about 8 minutes. Add tomatoes, salt, pepper, bay leaf, basil, and water. Simmer 30 minutes.

Boil macaroni until al dente in salted water. Drain and refresh in cold water. Make a layer with half the macaroni in a baking dish. Distribute half the cheese over the pasta. Spread meat mixture over macaroni and cheese. Cover with remaining pasta and half the remaining cheese. Pour Béchamel Sauce over the top. Sprinkle with remaining cheese. Bake at 375 degrees 20 minutes. Remove from oven and allow to cool 10 minutes.

Cut into 3-inch squares and serve. Serves 8.

SALTA KREMA BESSAMEL
BECHAMEL SAUCE

½ cup butter
½ cup flour
2 cups milk, heated
3 eggs, beaten lightly

Salt and pepper to taste
¼ tsp. nutmeg
½ cup Parmesan cheese

Heat butter in a saucepan. Add flour and blend well. Whisk in milk gradually until well blended and sauce thickens. Remove from heat and add eggs, salt, pepper, nutmeg, and cheese. Stir until well blended and smooth. Makes 3 cups.

BOULETTES DE BOEUF EN SAUCE AU CITRON
MEATBALLS IN LEMON SAUCE

The term *gourmet* is often misconstrued to mean "elegant, unusual, and expensive." This, of course, is not true. Gourmet simply means "fresh food of good quality that is prepared to taste good," and this recipe illustrates this premise. Beef meatballs sautéed and garnished with a lemon velouté sauce are "gourmet" by my standards.

4 slices bread, cubed
4 tbsp. milk
2 lb. ground beef
2 tbsp. Dijon mustard
Salt and pepper to taste
2 eggs, beaten
Flour for coating

4 tbsp. butter
2 tbsp. additional butter
4 tbsp. additional flour
2 cups chicken stock
2 tbsp. lemon juice
Salt and pepper to taste
2 tbsp. parsley, chopped

Moisten bread with milk. Combine bread, ground beef, mustard, salt, pepper, and beaten eggs. Flouring your hands, form balls of the beef mixture about the size of golf balls. Sauté the meatballs in butter 8 minutes, turning frequently. Remove and set aside.

Add the additional butter to the skillet. Blend in the additional flour and cook 1 minute. Whisk in the chicken stock and bring to a boil. Add lemon juice, salt, and pepper. Whisk until sauce thickens. Return meatballs to the skillet. Cover and simmer 2 minutes. Transfer to a serving dish. Garnish with parsley. Serves 8.

CHAUSSON DE BOEUF DE CONSERVE
CORNED-BEEF TURNOVER

This is an old Southern dish that was passed on to me by the late Mrs. Geraldine Gillmore of Pensacola. I make these in small Pyrex bowls and freeze them. They are welcome when I need something in a hurry and don't want to do any heavy cooking.

1½ cups onions, chopped
6 tbsp. butter
6 tbsp. flour
3 cups canned corned
  beef, diced

3 cups diced tomatoes
Salt and pepper to taste
8 squares pie dough
  (8 x 8 inches)
1 egg, beaten lightly

Sauté onions in butter until well done. Add flour and blend well. Blend in corned beef. Add tomatoes and their liquid. Salt and pepper to taste. Bring to a boil. Reduce heat and simmer 10 minutes until thickened. Remove from heat and cool.

Line individual 4-inch ovenproof bowls with pastry squares, allowing dough to hang over. Fill pastry with cooled corned-beef mixture. Fold overhanging dough over filling, pinching together to enclose. Brush with beaten egg. Bake at 425 degrees for 20 minutes. Serves 8.

GRILLADES A LA NOUVELLE ORLEANS
BRAISED VEAL ROUNDS NEW ORLEANS STYLE

This classic dish is traditionally served at a New Orleans brunch or breakfast, especially at open house on Mardi Gras day. It is served with old-fashioned boiled grits. I often serve it as a supper menu with Fried Grits*.

2 lb. veal rounds, ½-inch thick, cut into pieces (2" x 3")
Salt and pepper to taste
¼ cup flour for dusting
3 tbsp. peanut oil
4 tbsp. butter
4 tbsp. Dry Roux (see seafood chapter, Crawfish Pie)
2 onions, chopped

2 cloves garlic, chopped
2 cups tomatoes, chopped
2 cups chicken stock
2 tbsp. parsley, chopped
1 cup green bell pepper, sliced
1 bay leaf
Salt and pepper to taste
6 green onions, chopped

Pound veal between pieces of plastic wrap until ¼-inch thick. Salt, pepper, and dust with flour. Sauté veal in peanut oil until brown. Set aside.

Add butter to the skillet. Blend in Dry Roux. Add onions, garlic, tomatoes, stock, parsley, bell peppers, and bay leaf. Salt and pepper to taste. Bring to a boil. Return veal to the pan. Reduce heat to simmer. Cover and cook slowly until meat is tender (45 minutes to 1 hour). Serve with grits or rice. Garnish with chopped green onions. Serves 8.

*Fried Grits: Leftover grits are poured into a loaf pan and become firm when chilled, allowing them to be cut into ¾-inch-thick slices. The slices are sautéed in very hot butter until lightly browned. These slices are excellent when covered with the gravy from this recipe. They also can be served as a simple family dessert with syrup or sprinkled sugar.

OSSOBUCCO PIEMONTAISE
BRAISED VEAL SHANKS WITH RICE

I learned this classic Italian dish at Le Cordon Bleu in Paris. Whenever I see meaty veal shanks, I buy them and make this recipe. What we don't eat for supper I freeze. It is excellent with Italian Risotto (whose recipe is presented in the "Rice and Pasta" chapter).

8 veal shanks, ½-lb. each,
   2-inches thick
Salt and pepper to taste
Flour for dusting
3 tbsp. butter
2 tbsp. peanut oil
1 cup onions, chopped
1 cup carrots, chopped
1 cup celery, chopped
2 cloves garlic, chopped
1 tbsp. flour

1½ lb. tomatoes, peeled,
   seeded, and chopped
1 cup white wine
1 tbsp. lemon zest
1 bouquet garni
4 cups beef or chicken stock
3 tbsp. parsley
1 recipe Risotto (see "Rice
   and Pasta" chapter)

Salt and pepper veal shanks and dust with flour. Sauté shanks in butter and oil until browned. Remove shanks to a baking pan.

Sauté onions in pan juices until soft. Add carrots, celery, and garlic. Blend in flour and cook 1 minute. Add tomatoes, wine, lemon zest, bouquet garni, and stock. Bring to a boil. Pour over veal shanks and return to a boil. Place in a 350-degree oven 1 hour. Turn shanks halfway through cooking and add parsley. Remove shanks to a serving dish.

Strain pan liquids. Skim grease from sauce. Moisten veal with some of the sauce. Serve rest on the side. Serve with Risotto. Serves 8.

QUENELLES DE VEAU A L'ESTRAGON
VEAL DUMPLINGS WITH TARRAGON SAUCE

This unique French dumpling dish is best known when made with pike, but it is sometimes made with other fish, such as salmon, or with other products, such as chicken, liver, or with veal, as in this recipe. This blend of tarragon-flavored veal mousse poached in chicken stock creates light and gossamer dumplings that are garnished with a mushroom and tarragon cream sauce. This is one recipe you will long remember.

$\frac{2}{3}$ cup water
$\frac{1}{2}$ tsp. salt
2 tbsp. butter
1 cup flour
2 lb. ground veal
1 tbsp. fresh tarragon (or
   1$\frac{1}{2}$ tsp. dried tarragon)

Salt and pepper to taste
$\frac{1}{2}$ cup cream
3 cups chicken stock
1 recipe Tarragon Sauce
   (recipe follows)

Bring water, salt, and butter to a boil. Remove from heat. Add flour all at once and blend well. Return to heat and stir with a wooden spoon until dry and mixture forms a ball. Blend flour mixture, ground veal, tarragon, salt, and pepper together. Slowly incorporate cream. Refrigerate 1 hour.

Butter an ovenproof pan generously. Shape veal mixture into oval dumplings using 2 tablespoons dipped in water. Place each quenelle onto baking pan. Delicately add stock to just cover. Cover with foil loosely. Bring to simmering on top of stove and then place in a 350-degree oven. Poach 12 minutes.

Remove from the oven. Gently extract quenelles from liquid and arrange on a serving platter. Pour Tarragon Sauce over quenelles. Garnish each with a tarragon leaf or parsley. Serves 8.

SAUCE ESTRAGON
TARRAGON SAUCE

This sauce can be used to complement many fish and chicken dishes as well as the above quenelles.

1 lb. mushrooms, sliced	4 tbsp. additional butter
2 tbsp. butter	2 cups chicken stock
1 tbsp. fresh tarragon (or	Salt and pepper to taste
1½ tsp. dried tarragon)*	1 cup cream
4 tbsp. flour	2 egg yolks

Sauté mushrooms in butter 5 minutes. Add tarragon. Set aside. Sauté flour in butter to make a light roux. Gradually add stock, stirring until mixture thickens (coats the back of a spoon). Salt and pepper to taste. Blend in cream and egg yolks. Add reserved mushrooms. Keep warm.

*Tarragon is probably the most popular of the French herbs. It is especially well paired with veal, chicken, or as in this cream sauce.

COTELETTES POJARSKI
VEAL POJARSKI

While this recipe is part of that body of French cuisine called *haute cuisine* (high-class cookery), it is Russian in origin, having been created by an innkeeper in the days of the czars. His name? What else but Pojarski? The French, typically, embellished a good thing. They took his original concoction of ground wild game, bread, cream, and seasonings, substituted the more delicate veal, and shaped it to look like a chop. Sautéed in butter and oil, its coating of breadcrumbs becomes golden, and the mousse mixture is light and delicate.

4 slices French bread	**2 eggs, beaten with**
⅓ cup milk	**1 tbsp. water**
1½ lb. veal, ground, very cold	**1 cup breadcrumbs,**
6 oz. butter, very cold	**unseasoned**
2 egg yolks	**4 tbsp. butter**
Salt and pepper to taste	**2 tbsp. peanut oil**
¼ tsp. nutmeg	**3 tbsp. additional butter,**
1 cup cream, very cold	**melted**
½ cup flour	**8 lemon slices**

Soak bread in milk and then drain. Place veal in the bowl of a food processor and process for 1 minute. Add bread, cold butter, egg yolks, salt, pepper, and nutmeg. With processor running, add the cream gradually (mixture should be firm). Remove mixture from processor bowl and chill.

Divide veal mixture into 8 equal balls. Coat lightly with flour. Flatten into rounds about ½-inch thick (like a hamburger). Gently shape the mixture to resemble a pork chop. Pass into beaten eggs and then into breadcrumbs. Chill for 1 hour.

Sauté "chops" in butter and oil until golden brown, 4 minutes on 1 side and 3 minutes on the other. Place on a serving platter. Drizzle with melted butter and garnish with lemon slices. Serves 8.

Note: I often use a variation of the recipe. I substitute deboned and skinned chicken breasts and thighs for the veal and seasoned breadcrumbs for the plain. I also increase the quantity of nutmeg to at least a ½-teaspoon. The Tarragon Sauce from the preceding recipe without the mushrooms is an excellent accompaniment.

CROQUETTES DE VEAU
AUX CHAMPIGNONS
VEAL CROQUETTES WITH MUSHROOMS

A quick check with the bible of cookbooks—*Le Guide Culinaire* by Auguste Escoffier, the famed chef of the Ritz in Paris and the Carlton in London during "*la Belle Epoque*" (1880-1900)—reveals thirty-four recipes for *croquettes*. Croquettes are made from poultry, game, fish, and veal, as well as rice and vegetable mixtures. In all cases the principal ingredient is shaped, breaded, and fried. This recipe for veal croquettes is garnished with a mushroom sauce that is very traditional.

2 lb. ground veal
½ lb. bulk pork sausage
2 medium onions, chopped
2 eggs
2 dashes Tabasco
Salt and pepper to taste
2 additional eggs, beaten
   with 1 tbsp. water
6 tbsp. breadcrumbs
1 large additional onion,
   chopped

4 tbsp. butter
½ lb. mushrooms, sliced
4 tsp. cornstarch, dissolved
   in 1 cup cream
¼ tsp. additional Tabasco
Salt and pepper to taste
¼ tsp. nutmeg
6 tbsp. peanut oil

Blend together veal, sausage, onions, eggs, Tabasco, salt, and pepper. Divide mixture into 8 equal portions and form into patty shape (like an oval-shaped hamburger). Pass croquettes in beaten egg and then into breadcrumbs to coat. Refrigerate 1 hour.

Sauté additional onions in butter until soft. Add mushrooms and sauté 5 minutes. Add cream/cornstarch mixture, Tabasco, salt, pepper, and nutmeg. Keep warm.

Heat peanut oil in a skillet. Sauté croquettes 6 minutes on each side. Remove to paper towel. Transfer to a serving platter. Coat lightly with sauce and serve remaining sauce on the side. Serves 8.

SCALOPPINE DE VITELLA
ALLA PARMIGIANA TURCI
BREADED VEAL WITH PARMESAN CHEESE TURCI

This was specialty of Senora Theresa Turci, who with her husband, Ettore, owned and operated Turci's Italian Restaurant in New Orleans for many years. Senora would very delicately pound a ½-inch-thick piece of the eye of a veal round until it was about ¼-inch thick. After coating it with flour, she dipped it in egg and then breadcrumbs twice. She sautéed it quickly (1 to 2 minutes) in butter until golden, sprinkled it with Parmesan cheese, and poured hot browned butter over it, melting the cheese.

8 veal (eye of the round) cutlets, ½-inch thick	**4 cups breadcrumbs**
Salt and pepper to taste	**Oil for frying**
2 cups flour	**1 cup Parmesan cheese**
4 eggs, beaten	**2 sticks butter**
	8 lemon wedges

Pound veal gently until ¼-inch thick and double in size. Salt and pepper the cutlets. Dust with flour. Dip in beaten eggs. Coat with breadcrumbs. Dip in egg a second time and coat with breadcrumbs a second time.

Heat oil (1 inch deep) in a skillet. Fry cutlets 1 to 2 minutes until golden brown on both sides. Remove to paper towel. Arrange on a serving platter. Generously sprinkle with Parmesan cheese.

Melt butter in a small skillet until it turns light brown. Pour over cheese and cutlets to melt cheese. Garnish with lemon wedges. Serves 8.

CHAUSSONS DE VEAU EN PAPILLOTE
VEAL TURNOVERS IN PARCHMENT PAPER

Enclosing food in parchment (or aluminum foil) tends to keep the item moist while cooking and allows the flavors to blend together. This recipe is a variation of a classic Cordon Bleu, where ham and cheese are stuffed into a pocket of the veal, breaded, and deep-fried. The variation comes in the enclosing in parchment and baking. Wonderful to prepare ahead and bake at the last minute.

8 veal scallops, ½-inch thick
4 slices boiled ham, cut in half
4 slices Gruyère cheese,
  cut in half
Salt and pepper to taste
8 pieces parchment paper*
  or aluminum foil, cut into
  6 x 8-inch rectangles

2 tbsp. butter
8 lettuce leaves
1 cup mayonnaise
2 tsp. tomato paste
⅛ tsp. cayenne pepper

With a sharp knife, form a pocket in each veal scallop. Slide a piece of ham and a piece of cheese into the pocket. Press the veal with the palm of the hand to flatten and seal the open side. Salt and pepper the scallops. Place each scallop on a piece of parchment paper. Dot with a small piece of butter. Cover with a lettuce leaf. Fold the parchment to enclose the scallop. Place scallops on a baking sheet. Bake at 400 degrees for 25 minutes.

Blend together mayonnaise, tomato paste, and cayenne pepper. Serve the veal packages, cutting open the paper to expose the scallop. Serve mayonnaise sauce on the side. Serves 8.

*Parchment paper, sometimes called "baking paper" and known in France as *sulfurise,* is paper treated to prevent foods from sticking and to withstand high temperatures during baking. It is the desired product when making any foods *en papillote,* a method of cooking by enclosing the food in paper so that the food steams in its own juices. Aluminum foil can be used instead but will not present as well. Parchment paper is available in specialty kitchen-supply stores. Its nonstick quality lends itself extremely well to baking pastry products.

ESCALOPES DE VEAU A LA CREME
SAUTEED VEAL SCALLOPS IN CREAM

Quick, easy, and elegant, this recipe enrobes tender veal scallops in a mushroom cream sauce flavored with Madeira wine. This traditional French treatment of veal can be found in restaurants all over Paris.

1 lb. mushrooms, sliced	1 cup Madeira wine
2 cloves garlic, crushed	1 cup cream
3 tbsp. butter	Salt and pepper to taste
8 5-oz. veal scallops	2 tbsp. parsley, chopped
2 tbsp. additional butter	

Sauté mushrooms and garlic in butter 5 minutes. Set aside. Add additional butter to skillet. Sauté veal scallops 3 minutes on each side. Add Madeira wine and continue cooking 3 minutes. Add cream and reserved mushrooms. Simmer until sauce thickens. Add salt and pepper to taste. Transfer to a serving platter and garnish with parsley. Serves 8.

FOIS DE VEAU AU POMMES
SAUTEED CALF'S LIVER WITH APPLES

On my first visit to Le Cordon Bleu in 1976, we were taught to prepare calf's liver with green grapes. On another visit some years later, I saw a demonstration for this recipe, which combines the unique taste of liver with salty bacon and sweet apples. It is a happy marriage of flavors I know you will enjoy.

3 tbsp. butter
4 apples, peeled, cored, and
   sliced into ½-inch rounds
8 slices thick bacon

3 tbsp. additional butter
2 lb. calf's liver slices
   ¼-inch thick

Sauté apple slices in butter until they brown slightly. Remove and keep warm. Fry bacon slices in the same skillet until crisp. Remove and set aside.

Add additional butter to skillet. Sauté liver slices 5 minutes on each side on low heat. Arrange overlapping liver slices in center of a serving platter. Place an apple slice in between each slice of liver. Place bacon slices alongside liver and apples. Serve as soon as possible. Serves 8.

FEGATO ALLA VENEZIANA
VENETIAN-STYLE LIVER

After a week of classes with Giuliano Bugialli in Florence, Italy, in 1985, I traveled to Venice to experience both the food and the charm of this unique city. There I had liver in the Venetian style, a classic Italian preparation that is a simple combination of onions and liver cut in strips, sautéed in butter, and deglazed in white wine. Try this and you will know why it is a classic.

2 onions, cut into slivers	2 lb. calf's liver, cut into
4 tbsp. butter	¼-inch strips
4 tbsp. olive oil	½ cup white wine

Sauté onions in butter and olive oil until limp but not browned over medium heat. Turn heat to high. Add liver strips and toss to coat with oil. Cook 5 minutes, stirring often. Transfer liver and onions to a serving plate.

Deglaze the pan with white wine. Reduce sauce 1 minute on very high heat. Pour over liver and onions. Serves 8.

ROTI DE PORC EN COURONNE
AUX RIZ D'ORANGE
CROWN ROAST OF PORK WITH ORANGE RICE

Probably the most glamorous preparation for a pork roast is to form a crown from two loins, fill the center with an orange-flavored rice, and present it with paper frills on each rib. The preparation is elegant, tastes wonderful, and is well worth any effort.

2 pork loins, center cuts,
8 ribs each, backbone
removed
6 cloves garlic, peeled
Salt and pepper to taste
1 large onion, chopped
4 tbsp. butter
2 cups raw rice
Salt to taste

2 tsp. leaf thyme
1 cup white raisins
½ cup orange juice
¼ cup dry sherry wine
4 cups chicken broth
2 tbsp. orange zest
2 oranges, peeled and
segmented

Cut a 1-inch slit between each rib where the backbone was removed. Make 3 slits in each loin in the meaty parts. Place a clove of garlic in each slit. Tie the 2 loins together (bone side in) with kitchen string to form a circle. Trim between and around each rib about 1-inch down the bone.* Season the roast with salt and pepper. Place in a roasting pan. Bake in a preheated oven at 350 degrees for 20 minutes per pound (meat thermometer to 160 degrees) or about 2½ to 3 hours.

Sauté onion in butter until soft. Add rice and sauté 1 minute. Add salt, thyme, raisins, orange juice, sherry, and chicken broth. Bring to a boil, reduce heat, cover, and cook 20 minutes. Add orange zest and orange segments, blending well.

About 15 minutes before roast is done, remove from the oven. Pour off the accumulated pan juices. Fill the center of crown with orange rice and place remaining rice around the base of roast. Cover loosely with foil and return to the oven until roast reaches 165 degrees on a meat thermometer.

To serve cut in between ribs and serve 2 ribs per person with some of the orange rice. Serves 8.

*If you can persuade your butcher to do the forming of the roast (omitting the garlic), you can eliminate this chore. Then just insert the garlic as described and proceed with the recipe at this point.

COTE DE PORC DIJONNAISE
SAUTEED PORK CHOPS DIJON STYLE

This recipe was presented at Le Cordon Bleu on my first visit in 1976 and has become one of the most popular with students in my classes. The tangy taste of the mustard and the crispiness of the sautéed breadcrumbs keep the chops juicy and spicy. The sweet pickle is a great counterpoint in taste.

8 boneless pork chops,
  ½-inch thick
3 tbsp. Dijon mustard
1 cup seasoned breadcrumbs
3 tbsp. butter
2 tbsp. peanut oil
3 tbsp. red-wine vinegar
1 cup chicken stock

1 cup cream
3 tbsp. additional Dijon
  mustard
2 tbsp. green peppercorns*
Salt and pepper to taste
8 small sweet pickles, sliced
  lengthwise but attached
  at 1 end

Brush all sides of chops with Dijon mustard. Pass in breadcrumbs and coat generously. Sauté in butter and oil until brown on both sides. Remove and keep warm. Deglaze sauté pan with vinegar. Add chicken stock and bring to a boil. Blend in cream and mustard and simmer until sauce thickens. Add green peppercorns. Salt and pepper to taste. Pour sauce into a serving platter. Place reserved pork chops over sauce. Spread the sliced pickles into a fan shape. Place 1 pickle on each chop for garnish. Serves 8.

*Green peppercorns are the unripe berries of the pepper vines and are harvested while still green. They are preserved in brine, white vinegar, or water and are bottled or canned. They also are air-dried. The berries are milder than black or white pepper and impart a wonderful flavor without excessive heat.

FILETS DE PROC AUX PRUNES
BRAISED PORK FILETS WITH PLUMS

Pork and fruit of all kinds have an affinity to each other. There are pork recipes with grapes, peaches, pineapples, apples, prunes, and apricots. This recipe, however, combines plums, cinnamon, and red wine to form a braising sauce for sautéed pork chops. Although the recipe calls for canned plums, fresh can be used when available.

2 lb. pork filet, cut into
  8 4-oz. pieces
Salt and pepper to taste
4 tbsp. flour
3 oz. butter

1 1-lb. canned red plums,
  drained and pitted
¼ tsp. cinnamon
1 cup red wine
1 tbsp. parsley, chopped

Salt and pepper pork filets to taste. Pass in flour to coat. Sauté filets in butter until brown on all sides. Place filets in a baking dish.

Crush plums well. Add cinnamon and red wine. Pour over filets. Cover and bake at 350 degrees for 30 minutes. Garnish with parsley. Serves 8.

GRILLADES DE PORC AUX POMMES
GRILLED PORK FILET WITH APPLES

This recipe continues the concept of fruit and pork affinity. Apples are probably paired with pork chops more than any other fruit. Here the chops are marinated, and the apples are sautéed with caraway and coriander seeds to provide a unique flavor.

1 tsp. caraway seeds*
1 tsp. coriander seeds*
1 tsp. leaf thyme
4 tbsp. olive oil
1 tbsp. Worcestershire sauce
Salt and pepper to taste
3 lb. pork filet, cut into
   ½-inch slices

1 large onion, chopped
4 tbsp. butter
3 apples, peeled, cored,
   and sliced in rounds
1 lemon, juiced

Blend together the caraway and coriander seeds with the thyme and divide into 2 batches. Combine 1 batch of spices, olive oil, Worcestershire sauce, salt, and pepper. Marinate the pork slices in the mixture 1 hour.

Sauté onion in butter 2 minutes. Add apples, lemon juice, and the remaining batch of spices and continue sautéeing 3 minutes.

Broil or grill the pork slices, brushing with the marinade 3 to 5 minutes on each side. Transfer to a serving platter along with the apples. Serves 8.

*Originally from Asia Minor, caraway seeds were carried throughout the known world by the Romans. Best known for its use in rye bread, caraway seeds are popular in many Dutch and German dishes of pork, sauerkraut, or boiled cabbage. Caraway with cumin and anise gives the German liquor Kummel its distinctive flavor. Coriander, a Mediterranean native, also has a proud history, having been grown in the Hanging Gardens of Babylon and placed in Egyptian tombs 3,000 years ago. Coriander has a pleasing taste that suggests a combination of lemon peel, sage, and cumin.

COTES DE PORC GRATINEE
BAKED PORK CHOP

A good dish to prepare ahead and bake at the last minute is this recipe for layering thick pork chops with layers of apples, onions, sage, and mushrooms with apple cider. Topped with breadcrumbs and Gruyère cheese, a real pork treat emerges after a 45-minute stay in the oven.

4 tbsp. butter
4 apples, peeled, seeded,
  and cut into slices
2 medium red onions, sliced
2 tsp. sage
8 boneless pork chops,
  ¾-inch thick

Salt and pepper to taste
½ lb. mushrooms, sliced
1¼ cups apple cider, dry*
1 cup breadcrumbs
¾ cup Gruyère cheese,
  grated

Brush a baking dish with some of the butter. Arrange half the apple slices over the bottom. Sprinkle half the onions and sage over apples. Place the pork chops over the onions. Salt and pepper to taste. Cover the chops with the mushrooms. Repeat layers with remaining apples, onions, and sage. Pour apple cider over the layers. Mix together breadcrumbs and cheese. Sprinkle mixture over ingredients. Dot with remaining butter. Bake at 400 degrees for 45 minutes. Serves 8.

*The juice of apples produces several different products called cider. Fresh apple juice is often referred to as "sweet" cider and has no alcoholic content. The juice is sometimes fermented and referred to as "hard" cider. In its distilled form it is called "applejack," and in Normandy, France, it becomes Calvados. This dish can be made with any of the three according to your preference.

COTE DE PORC SAUCE MOUTARDE
PORK CHOPS WITH MUSTARD SAUCE

I like to prepare this recipe with thick boneless pork chops. I cut off all visible fat and coat lightly with flour, salt, and pepper. After sautée-ing, they are combined with sautéed onions, white wine, and stock for a 25-minute simmer. The burst of flavor is created by a sauce that combines Dijon mustard with the juices in the pan.

2 medium onions, sliced	**2 tbsp. additional butter**
2 tbsp. butter	**1 cup Madeira wine**
Salt and pepper to taste	**1½ cups chicken stock**
8 pork chops, ½-inch thick	**2 tbsp. Dijon mustard**
2 tbsp. flour	**Salt and pepper to taste**

Sauté onions in butter until they are soft and transparent. Remove from skillet and reserve. Salt and pepper pork chops. Pass in flour to coat. Add additional butter to skillet. Brown chops on both sides. Return onions to skillet. Add wine and stock. Cover and simmer 25 minutes. Transfer chops to a serving platter and keep warm. Add mustard to the sauce in the skillet. Blend well and add salt and pepper as needed. Pour over chops and serve as soon as possible. Serves 8.

COTE DE PORC A LA VALENCIENNE
PORK CHOPS WITH ORANGE SAUCE

Citrus fruit marries very well with pork, as in this dish, which combines orange juice and orange-flavored Cointreau liquor as a braising medium for lightly browned pork chops. The sauce that develops is fantastic and is enhanced by sautéed orange slices. This is a wonderful combination.

**8 pork chops, deboned,
¾-inch thick
1 tbsp. butter
1 tsp. peanut oil
Salt and pepper to taste**

**3 oz. Cointreau liquor
Juice of 1 orange
5 oranges, sliced in rounds
2 tbsp. additional butter
1 tbsp. parsley, chopped**

Brown pork chops in butter and peanut oil 4 minutes on each side. Salt and pepper to taste. Add Cointreau and ignite. Add orange juice. Cover and simmer 10 minutes.

Sauté the orange slices in the additional butter 2 minutes on each side.

Transfer pork chops to a serving dish. Strain orange sauce over the chops. Garnish with orange slices and sprinkle with parsley. Serves 8.

PAUPIETTES DE PORC A L'ALSACIENNE
PORK ROLLS STUFFED WITH SAUERKRAUT

The term *paupiettes* in French cooking refers to bundles of meat or poultry that are stuffed and rolled. This recipe is a play on the classic Alsacienne dish Choucroute Garni. Butterflied pork chops are stuffed with sausage and sauerkraut, then sautéed, and braised in wine with potatoes. The pan drippings are enriched with cream to create a flavorful sauce.

4 tbsp. Dijon mustard
¼ tsp. paprika
¼ tsp. cumin
8 breakfast sausages
1 medium onion, sliced
   into thin slivers
2 cups sauerkraut, drained
4 juniper berries*

8 boneless pork chops,
   ½-inch thick
3 tbsp. butter
16 small parboiled potatoes**
Salt and pepper to taste
½ cup white wine
½ cup chicken stock
⅓ cup cream

Blend together mustard, paprika, and cumin and set aside. Cook the breakfast sausages until brown and set aside.

Pour out all but 2 tablespoons of sausage drippings. Sauté onion in sausage drippings until soft. Add sauerkraut and juniper berries and sauté 3 minutes. Set aside and cool. Butterfly the pork chops by cutting horizontally almost all the way through. Open the cut pork chops and pound between plastic wrap until its size is increased by half. Spread each chop with ½-teaspoon of the mustard mixture. Distribute ¼-cup sauerkraut over each chop. Place a sausage in the center of each chop. Fold the sides of the chop towards the center, partially covering the sausage. Fold the side nearest you over the sausage and roll the chop to enclose sausage and filling. Secure with a toothpick. Brown the pork rolls in butter until brown on all sides. Add the parboiled potatoes and toss in the pan drippings. Salt and pepper the potatoes. Add white wine and chicken stock, cover, and simmer 25 minutes.

Transfer pork rolls and potatoes to a serving platter. Add cream to braising liquids and reduce 1 minute. Pour over pork and potatoes. Serves 8.

*This bluish-grey berrylike fruit of evergreen trees and shrubs is called a juniper berry and is used in recipes for sauerkraut, pa%Atés, and gin. It imparts a mildly sweet aroma of pine. If you do not have access to juniper berries, substitute a dash of gin.

**Place potatoes in a pot of salted cold water. Bring to a boil. Drain immediately and refresh in cold water.

GHIOUVESTI
ROAST LEG OF LAMB

Lamb, so popular in Mediterranean countries, has been a neglected meat source in the United States for many years but seems to be finding more and more popularity. The leg and rack (ribs) of lamb are the cuts most often seen in supermarkets and restaurants. The leg, seasoned with rosemary and garlic and providing delicious slices of medium-rare lamb in a flavorful sauce, is one of my favorite foods. It also provides leftover meat to produce one of the recipes that follow.

1 leg of lamb, 6½ to 7 lb.
2 tbsp. rosemary leaves, chopped*
Salt and pepper to taste
2 tbsp. olive oil
4 cloves garlic, cut in half lengthwise

1 lb. orzo pasta, cooked al dente**
1 cup water
2 medium onions, chopped

Blend together rosemary, salt, pepper, olive oil, and garlic-clove halves. Make 8 slits in lamb about 2-inches deep in the meatiest parts. Insert a piece of seasoned garlic into each slit. Rub remaining oil/rosemary mixture over leg. Bake at 325 degrees, 11 minutes per pound, 140 degrees for medium-rare, 150 degrees for medium. Remove and let rest 15 minutes.

Skim fat from roasting pan and deglaze with water. Add onions and cook for 10 minutes. Pour into a blender and puree. Combine puree with orzo. Serve leg of lamb on a platter surrounded by orzo. Serves 8, with leftovers.

*Rosemary is an aromatic evergreen shrub of the mint family, with wonderfully fragrant slender grayish-green leaves that are used to season seafood, chicken, and meats, especially lamb. Combined with garlic, it complements lamb extremely well. I keep a large pot of rosemary growing in my garden so that I can snip a sprig or two when needed. I also dry some and keep it bottled on my shelf. Rosemary is also used in the manufacture of perfumes.

**Orzo pasta, an egg pasta shaped like oversized grains of rice, is boiled in salted water until al dente and drained. Do not wash. If the pasta is to be held for more than 5 minutes, toss with 2 tablespoons of olive oil to prevent sticking together.

MOUSSAKAS ME MELITZANES
EGGPLANT MOUSSAKA GREEK STYLE

This style of eggplant and lamb casserole is in the Greek style of layering fried eggplant with lamb and tomato sauce and topping with a white sauce and Parmesan cheese. It is a wonderful baked casserole for a buffet or a large gathering.

3 medium onions, chopped	**6 medium eggplants, cut**
⅓ cup olive oil	**into ¼-inch slices**
2 lb. ground lamb*	**Flour for dusting**
4 tomatoes, peeled, seeded,	**Oil for frying**
and chopped	**Salt and pepper to taste**
2 cloves garlic, chopped	**1 recipe Béchamel Sauce****
2 bay leaves	**⅓ cup Parmesan cheese,**
Salt and pepper to taste	**grated**

Sauté onions in oil until soft. Add ground lamb and cook 10 minutes. Blend in tomatoes, garlic, bay leaves, salt, and pepper, and simmer 1 hour.

Coat eggplant slices with flour. Fry in hot oil and drain on paper towels. Make a layer of eggplant slices in a baking dish. Salt and pepper to taste. Spread a layer of meat sauce over eggplant. Continue layering ending with meat sauce. Top with Béchamel Sauce over the ingredients. Sprinkle with Parmesan cheese. Bake at 375 degrees for 20 to 25 minutes. Remove from the oven and let rest

10 minutes. Cut into 4-inch squares and serve. Serves 8.

*Leftover cooked lamb from the preceding recipe for Roast Leg of Lamb can be substituted for the uncooked ground lamb. Eliminate the sautéeing of the lamb for 10 minutes in the recipe and proceed to add the rest of the ingredients.

**See Béchamel Sauce recipe presented earlier in this chapter.

MOUSSAKA A LA TURQUIE
MOUSSAKA TURKISH STYLE

This spectacular dish is excellent and beautiful in its presentation. A savory mixture of lamb, eggplant, aromatic vegetables, and mushrooms fills a mold lined with the skins of the eggplant and baked. When unmolded, the colorful purple eggplant skins enclose the savory filling and are surrounded by a flavorful herbal tomato sauce. I like to make a tomato rose from the skin of a fresh tomato and place on top for the final presentation. This dish can be served both hot or cold.

4 medium eggplants,
  quartered lengthwise
1 large onion, chopped
2 cloves garlic, chopped
⅓ cup olive oil
2 additional eggplants,
  peeled and diced
2 lb. ground lamb
½ lb. mushrooms, chopped

1 cup tomatoes, peeled,
  seeded, and diced
½ tsp. thyme
½ tsp. rosemary
Salt and pepper to taste
3 eggs, lightly beaten
1 recipe Tomato Coulis
  (recipe follows)

Place quartered eggplants in a baking dish, adding water ½-inch deep. Bake at 350 degrees 30 minutes. Remove from the oven. Scrape flesh from skins, saving skins and flesh.

Sauté onion and garlic in olive oil 3 minutes. Add diced eggplant and sauté 3 minutes. Add ground lamb and sauté until browned. Incorporate baked reserved eggplant flesh, mushrooms, tomatoes, thyme, rosemary, salt, and pepper. Blend in beaten eggs.

Line a charlotte mold with eggplant skins, with the narrow end in the center and the wide end hanging over the edge. Fill with eggplant/lamb mixture. Fold overhanging eggplant skin over mixture. Place mold in a pan of water halfway up the side of the mold. Bake at 375 degrees 1½ hours. Remove from oven and allow to cool 5 minutes.

Unmold on a serving platter. Surround with Tomato Coulis. Serves 8.

COULIS DES TOMATES
TOMATO COULIS

2 medium onions, chopped
⅓ cup olive oil
3 cups tomatoes, peeled,
   seeded, and chopped

2 cloves garlic, chopped
1 tbsp. fresh basil, chopped
   (or 1½ tsp. dried basil)
1 tsp. tomato paste

Sauté onions in olive oil 10 minutes. Add tomatoes, garlic, and basil. Cover and simmer 10 minutes. Uncover, add tomato paste, and simmer 20 minutes. Makes 4 cups.

AUBERGINES FARCIES A L'AGNEAU
LAMB-STUFFED EGGPLANT

This recipe is a less elegant but no less delicious variation of the Turkish Moussaka recipe above. The basic ingredients of lamb, onions, tomatoes, and seasonings are blended together to create a filling for the hollowed-out shells of the eggplant, allowing individual servings. The ground lamb can be substituted with leftover lamb roast, finely chopped. The stuffed eggplants freeze very well and should be frozen before baking.

4 medium eggplants
3 tbsp. olive oil
1½ lb. ground lamb
1 tbsp. additional olive oil
2 medium onions, chopped
2 cloves garlic, chopped
1 tbsp. additional olive oil
1 large green pepper, diced
4 tbsp. parsley, chopped

2 large tomatoes, peeled,
**   seeded, and diced**
Salt and pepper to taste
¼ tsp. cumin
¼ tsp. paprika
¼ tsp. nutmeg
⅛ tsp. cayenne pepper
4 tbsp. Parmesan cheese,
**   grated**

Cut eggplants in half lengthwise. Place in a baking dish (cut side up) and brush with olive oil. Bake at 350 degrees 20 minutes.

Remove from the oven and scoop out the eggplant flesh, leaving ¼-inch flesh attached to skin, reserving both.

Sauté lamb in additional olive oil until browned. Remove lamb and reserve. Add the additional olive oil and sauté onions and garlic until soft. Return reserved lamb to skillet. Add reserved eggplant flesh, bell pepper, tomatoes, parsley, salt, and pepper. Add cumin, paprika, nutmeg, and cayenne. Fill reserved eggplant shells with the mixture. Sprinkle with Parmesan cheese. Bake at 350 degrees 40 minutes. Serves 8.

Chicken, Turkey, and Duck

CHICKEN

Chicken is the most popular of the poultry products available today, with millions of birds bred annually for consumption. The proliferation of fast-food chicken establishments is probably the best evidence of its popularity. Chicken also is one of the most versatile meats. It can be braised, boiled, broiled, fried, roasted, stewed, or grilled. Chicken can be prepared simply (as fried chicken, chicken and dumplings, in stews), elegantly (such as dressed with French sauces), or family style (as baked chicken).

Chicken is the prime ingredient in many ethnic recipes, such as the Chinese Almond Chicken, or the French Dijon Mustard Chicken, or the Italian Chicken Cacciatore, to mention a few. Typical American recipes include Chicken Potpie and Chicken and Dumplings.

The types of chicken we find in our supermarkets fall into several types, based on the age of the bird. The most common chicken, referred to as a "broiler" or "fryer," is about 1½ to 3½ pounds and about 9 to 12 weeks old. These are best used for boiling whole or cutting into parts for frying, broiling, or barbecuing. "Roasting" chickens weigh from 5 to 7 pounds, have firmer, more flavorful flesh, and are best for roasting, poaching, or stewing. Older birds (about 12 months old) are ideal for stewing, will have a richer flavor, but are harder to find. Capon (9 to 10 months old), a castrated rooster bred for improved quality of its flesh and tenderness, is generally used for roasting and is a must for such recipes as *Coq au Vin*.

TURKEY

Turkey, once reserved for Thanksgiving and Christmas holiday meals, is becoming more and more popular, appearing in recipes resembling those for chicken, and the bird is now found in our markets divided into its parts as well as sold whole. Turkey flesh is often sold ground and is used as a substitute for ground beef with great success. Ground turkey also makes tasty sausages. Its perceived health benefits appeal to consumers, especially those seeking substitutes for beef.

Turkey breast meat is often substituted for veal scallops in many recipes, especially those that call for slicing horizontally rather than vertically through the flesh. In lieu of beef or veal, it is often cubed to make stews, ragouts, or blanquettes, and the leg and thigh (*cuisse* in French) is delicious either just roasted or deboned and stuffed before roasting.

DUCK

Although eaten here less often than in Europe, duck is gaining popularity in America. It is a favorite of mine, and I present here a few recipes I enjoy. Fresh duck is hard to find, but I use frozen duck or—when I am lucky—I find the breast meat, called *magret,* for grilling.

BLANC DE VOLAILLE MEDITERRANEE
CHICKEN BREAST MEDITERRANEAN

This recipe is great for a family supper since it so easy to prepare. Sautéed chicken breasts are served on a bed of spaghetti with a colorful and tasty sauce made with mushrooms, tomatoes, olives, and parsley.

8 chicken-breast halves, skinned and deboned
Salt and pepper to taste
2 tbsp. flour
2 tbsp. butter
2 tbsp. peanut oil
2 cloves garlic
1 cup onions, chopped
½ lb. mushrooms, sliced

2 cups tomatoes, peeled and seeded
½ cup white wine
½ cup chicken stock
½ cup black olives, pitted and sliced
⅓ cup parsley, chopped
1 lb. thin spaghetti, cooked al dente

Salt and pepper chicken breasts. Dust lightly in flour. Sauté chicken in butter and oil 3 minutes on each side. Remove chicken and reserve.

Sauté garlic and onions in drippings. Add mushrooms and sauté. Add tomatoes, wine, and stock. Return chicken breasts to skillet. Simmer 5 minutes. Add olives and parsley. Arrange chicken breasts over pasta. Pour sauce over chicken. Serves 8.

POULET ET BOULETTE DE PATE
CHICKEN AND DUMPLINGS

This dish became popular in the South after the Civil War, when many Southerners were destitute, because one chicken could feed a large number of people. The broth from the poaching of the chicken was augmented by a biscuitlike dumpling, thus stretching the dish. Because it is so good, it has become a Southern classic, a comfort food for many.

1 5-lb. baking hen*
2 cups celery, cut into pieces
2 cups onions, cut into pieces
8 sprigs parsley
2 large carrots, cut into pieces
2 qt. water
2 tsp. leaf thyme
1 slice fresh ginger

2 bay leaves
Salt and pepper to taste
2 cups flour, sifted
3 tsp. baking powder
1 tsp. salt
2 medium eggs
$^2/_3$ cup milk

Truss chicken with string so that it is compact. Place in a large stockpot. Surround with celery, onions, parsley, and carrots. Cover with water. Add thyme, ginger, bay leaves, salt, and pepper. Cover and bring to a boil. Reduce heat to simmer. Simmer 30 minutes until chicken is tender.

Remove chicken to a platter. Remove string and allow to cool. Strain cooking liquids. Cool and remove all visible fat. Remove chicken from bones and cut into bite-size pieces, discarding skin.

Combine flour, baking powder, and salt. Blend together eggs and milk. Gently combine the 2 mixtures.

Bring defatted chicken broth to a boil. Reduce to simmer. Drop dumpling mixture by spoonfuls into simmering stock. Cover and simmer for 12 to 15 minutes, until dumplings have doubled in size and are tender. Add chicken and heat 5 minutes, uncovered. Serves 8.

*This dish also can be made with a younger (less than 6 months) chicken, but the older hen (12 or more months old) will have more flavor and produce a richer broth.

POULET AUX AMANDES
ALMOND CHICKEN

Chicken abounds in French cuisine, in recipes using all types of ingredients that complement the subtle flavor of chicken yet add an extra dimension to the dish. This recipe does that by combining the crunchiness and distinct flavor of almonds with the sweet citrus flavor of orange.

½ cup slivered almonds
1 tbsp. butter
3 lb. chicken parts
   (breasts, legs, thighs, or
   wings—your choice)
Salt and pepper to taste

1 tbsp. paprika
3 tbsp. additional butter
1 tbsp. peanut oil
3 oranges, juiced
2 oranges, segmented
1 tbsp. sugar

Sauté almonds in butter until lightly browned. Remove to a dish and reserve.

Salt and pepper chicken parts. Sprinkle with paprika. Sauté chicken in additional butter and peanut oil until brown on all sides. Cover and simmer 20 minutes. Remove chicken to a serving plate and keep warm.

Add the orange juice, orange segments, and sugar to the skillet. Bring to a boil and reduce 2 minutes. Pour over chicken. Garnish with reserved almonds. Serves 8.

POULET AU ROMARIN
ROSEMARY CHICKEN

Rosemary is a wonderful perennial plant that not only fills the garden with beauty and fragrance but also enhances many dishes. I keep huge plants of rosemary in my garden, harvesting as needed or preserving them for drying. I often use this fragrant herb with chicken, as in this recipe.

3 lb. chicken parts,
(breasts, thighs, legs,
wings—your choice)
Salt and pepper to taste
3 tbsp. olive oil

3 tbsp. butter
4 sprigs rosemary
4 cloves garlic
½ cup white wine
4 tbsp. chicken stock

Salt and pepper the chicken parts. Heat olive oil and butter in a large sauté pan. Add rosemary sprigs and garlic cloves. Sauté chicken parts in mixture until brown on both sides, 10 to 15 minutes, turning once. Add wine and bring to a boil. Simmer uncovered, 20 to 30 minutes until chicken is tender. Transfer chicken to a serving platter and keep warm.

Remove and discard rosemary and garlic. Remove excess fat from the pan. Deglaze the pan with chicken stock. Pour over chicken. Serves 8.

POULET AU CITRON
LEMON CHICKEN

Sautéed chicken breasts (supremes) are garnished with a sauce of wine, chicken broth, and lemon juice for another of those recipes that combine chicken and fruit, especially citrus, to achieve a unique flavor. This should be served with a parsleyed rice.

8 chicken breasts, skinned and deboned	**4 tbsp. lemon juice**
Flour for dusting	**6 tbsp. chicken stock**
Salt and pepper to taste	**4 tbsp. parsley, chopped**
2 tbsp. olive oil	**2 tbsp. additional butter**
4 tbsp. butter	**2 lemons, cut into rounds for garnish**

Flatten chicken breasts slightly. Salt and pepper and pass in flour. Sauté supremes in oil and butter 5 to 6 minutes on each side. Transfer to a serving platter and keep warm. Add lemon juice and chicken stock to the pan. Bring to a boil and stir 1 minute. Add parsley and additional butter. Pour over chicken and garnish with lemon slices. Serves 8.

POULET A L'ANANAS
BAKED PINEAPPLE CHICKEN

The flavor of pineapple marries very well with many meats and fowl. This baked-casserole recipe blends onions, pineapple, rosemary, and ginger with chicken parts. This dish will get you many raves.

8 chicken quarters
  (breast-wing or leg-thigh)
2 medium onions, cut into
  rounds
Salt and pepper to taste
1 tsp. dried rosemary
1 tsp. ginger

½ tsp. paprika
1 cup pineapple juice,
  unsweetened
1 cup crushed pineapple,
  unsweetened
2 tbsp. parsley, chopped

Place the chicken pieces in a baking dish just large enough to hold them. Distribute onions over chicken pieces. Sprinkle with salt, pepper, rosemary, ginger, and paprika. Add pineapple juice and crushed pineapple over chicken. Bake at 350 degrees 45 minutes. Garnish with parsley. Serves 8.

PILONS DE POULET A L'ORANGE
CHICKEN LEGS IN ORANGE SAUCE

The classic citrus fruit used to flavor many French recipes of meats and fowl is the orange, and any cookbook on French cooking will feature many "*à l'orange*" recipes. This recipe blends orange juice with curry and other spices to marinate chicken legs and then is joined with cream for a flavorful sauce.

Zest of 2 oranges, finely chopped*
1 tsp. thyme
1 tsp. sage
1 tbsp. curry powder
1 tsp. ginger
8 peppercorns
4 oranges, juiced
16 chicken legs

3 tbsp. butter
2 cups water
2 cloves garlic, chopped
Salt to taste
Zest of 2 additional oranges, cut into thin strips*
2 tsp. cornstarch dissolved in 4 tbsp. cream

Blend together orange zest, thyme, sage, curry, ginger, peppercorns, and orange juice. Pour over chicken legs and marinate 2 hours.

Drain chicken legs, reserving marinade. Sauté legs in butter until brown. Add water, garlic, and salt. Simmer, covered, 40 minutes, turning from time to time. Transfer chicken to serving dish and keep warm.

Deglaze pan with reserved marinade. Strain cooking liquids into a saucepan. Add salt to taste and additional orange-zest strips. Simmer 3 minutes. Add the cornstarch dissolved in cream. Stir until thickened. Pour over chicken legs. Serves 8.

*"Zest" comes from the French term for the colorful skin of citrus fruit that contain very flavorful oils that impart flavor to any dish using it. Only the colorful skin should be used, because the white pith under the skin is bitter. To remove the zest, use a very fine grater or a device called a "zester," which has four or five sharp holes in the end to

scrape against the citrus skin, thus removing only the outer skin. To remove the zest in strips, use a device called a "stripper," which has a singular cutting opening that removes the colorful skin in long strips. Anyone familiar with making cocktails will know the stripper as the gadget that produces lemon twists for drinks.

POULET A L'ESTRAGON
CHICKEN TARRAGON

Tarragon is one of the most popular herbs in French cuisine. It has a rich and robust flavor that marries well with both wine and cream sauces. This recipe combines this herb with apple cider and cream to form a wonderful sauce to complement the chicken.

16 chicken pieces (breasts, thighs, legs—your choice)	½ cup cream
Salt and pepper to taste	2 tbsp. fresh tarragon leaves
6 tbsp. butter	Additional salt and pepper to taste
4 shallots, chopped	2 egg yolks
2 tbsp. Calvados (apple brandy)	½ cup additional cream
2 cups apple cider, dry	Additional fresh tarragon leaves for garnish

Salt and pepper chicken parts. Sauté chicken in butter until brown on all sides. Add shallots, sautéing until wilted. Add Calvados and ignite. Add cider, cream, and tarragon. Salt and pepper to taste. Cover and simmer 30 minutes.

Combine egg yolks and additional cream. Remove chicken to a serving platter and keep warm. Add egg/cream mixture to sauté pan. Simmer 4 or 5 minutes while stirring. Pour sauce over chicken and garnish with additional tarragon. Serves 8.

FRICASSEE DE VOLAILLE A L'ARMAGNAC
FRICASSEE OF BRANDIED CHICKEN

The French term *fricassée* has taken on the meaning in English of a "savory stew," the slow cooking of several ingredients in a flavorful broth that combines their various flavors into a savory meal. This recipe joins brandied chicken and a variety of mushrooms for a true fricassee.

Salt and pepper to taste	½ lb. button mushrooms
3 lb. chicken parts (legs, thighs, and breasts cut in half)	½ lb. crimini mushrooms, sliced
3 tbsp. butter	½ lb. portobello mush rooms, sliced
⅓ cup Armagnac or other brandy*	½ lb. oyster mushrooms, sliced
3 shallots, chopped	3 tbsp. additional butter
3 cloves garlic, chopped	Salt and pepper to taste
1 cup chicken stock fortified with 2 tsp. chicken bouillon crystals	2 tbsp. parsley, chopped

Salt and pepper chicken parts and brown in butter, turning often for 10 minutes. Pour Armagnac into pan and ignite. Add the shallots and garlic and sauté 2 minutes. Blend in the fortified chicken stock, cover, and simmer 30 minutes.

In another skillet sauté the mushrooms in additional butter until they render theirjuices and it evaporates. Salt and pepper to taste and add to the chicken the last 5 minutes. Transfer chicken and mushrooms to a serving platter.

Reduce sauce in skillet until thick. Pour over chicken and mushrooms. Garnish with chopped parsley. Serves 8.

*Armagnac is a brandy distilled from grapes from the Armagnac region of the old region called Gascony, now part of the department of Gers in the southwest part of France below Bordeaux. The flavor of Armagnac is only slightly different than that of Cognac, and any good brandy can substitute.

CURRY DE POULET
CURRIED CHICKEN

This Indian blend of spices (see Seafood Curry, chapter 4), made popular the world over by the English, is especially delicious with chicken, as in this recipe. Chicken braised in curry-flavored chicken stock and served in a chafing dish is great for a buffet. I, however, use only chicken breasts cut into bite-size pieces. Served with rice and a variety of garnishes such as chutney, almonds, raisins, apples, and/or coconut, this dish will please your guests.

2 cloves garlic, chopped
2 large onions, chopped
2 tbsp. butter
1 tbsp. peanut oil
4 tbsp. curry powder
    (see Seafood Curry,
    chapter 4)

3 lb. chicken parts
    (breasts cut in half,
    thighs, legs)
2 tbsp. additional butter
1 tbsp. additional peanut oil
1 cup chicken stock
Salt and pepper to taste
2 bay leaves

Sauté garlic and onions in butter and peanut oil until tender. Add curry and cook another 2 minutes. Transfer onions, garlic, and curry to a bowl and reserve.

Sauté chicken parts in the additional butter and peanut oil 5 minutes, turning from time to time. Add the chicken stock, bay leaves, salt, pepper, and reserved onions, garlic, and curry. Cover and simmer 40 minutes. Transfer to a serving dish. Serves 8.

POULET AUX CHAMPIGNONS
CHICKEN AND MUSHROOMS

This very straightforward recipe for sautéed chicken with mushrooms in a stock broth makes a simple supper when served with boiled rice. I like this recipe because I can prepare it ahead of time and bake it later.

3 lb. chicken pieces (your choice)	3 tbsp. flour
1 large onion, chopped	1 lb. mushrooms, sliced
4 tbsp. butter	1 cup chicken stock
	Salt and pepper to taste

Sauté chicken and onions in butter until browned, about 5 minutes. Sprinkle with flour and cook another minute. Add mushrooms, stock, salt, and pepper. Blend well. Cover and simmer 1 hour until chicken is tender. Serve very hot with rice. Serves 8.

KOTOPOLO ME MANITARIA FYLO
BAKED CHICKEN AND MUSHROOMS IN PHYLLO

This is another of the wonderful Greek recipes provided me by my friend in Boston, John Bokas. Chicken breasts are covered with a mushroom garnish and wrapped in phyllo dough for a crispy and flavorful treat. This is a great prepare-ahead recipe that can be baked at the last minute. Be sure to cover the completed phyllo packages with plastic wrap (so as not to dry them out) and remove from the refrigerator 30 minutes before placing in the oven.

6 tbsp. butter
2 medium onions, chopped
1 lb. mushrooms, chopped
4 tbsp. parsley, chopped
3 cloves garlic, chopped
½ cup finely chopped pecans
3 tbsp. flour
⅔ cup dry vermouth
Salt and pepper to taste

8 chicken breast halves,
  skinned and deboned
3 tbsp. peanut oil
3 tbsp. additional butter
16 sheets phyllo dough*
1 cup plain breadcrumbs
½ cup additional butter,
  melted

Sauté onions in half the butter until soft. Remove from pan and set aside.

Sauté mushrooms in second half of the butter until juices evaporate. Add reserved onions, parsley, garlic, and pecans. Blend in flour and gradually add vermouth, stirring over medium heat until thickened. Season with salt and pepper to taste and set aside.

Sauté chicken breasts in peanut oil and additional butter 2 minutes on each side, until lightly browned. Set aside.

Butter 1 sheet of phyllo dough and sprinkle with 2 tablespoons of breadcrumbs. Cover with a second sheet of phyllo dough and brush with butter. Place a chicken breast at the end of phyllo nearest you. Place ⅛ the mushroom mixture on the chicken breast. Fold sides of phyllo dough over chicken and brush with butter. Roll chicken and phyllo to enclose and brush packages with butter. Place on a baking pan and bake at 350 degrees 35 minutes until golden brown. Serves 8.

*Phyllo dough is available in the frozen-food section of most supermarkets. To use, thaw and carefully unroll onto a flat surface. Cover immediately with a damp towel. Each time you remove a sheet of dough, immediately recover with the damp towel. The dough dries out quickly and becomes brittle if not kept moist.

POULET A LA DUCHESSE
CHICKEN ALMA PEYROUX

This is another of those antique recipes that have been passed on through four generations or more. My mother, whose nickname was "Duchess," learned this unique French manner of frying chicken from my father's grandmother, who probably got it from her mother. The secret is to fry the potatoes in the same oil as the chicken, because the chicken-flavored oil gives the potatoes a special flavor. The steaming with the garlic and parsley gives both chicken and potatoes a wonderful taste. I particularly like the potatoes.

4 lb. chicken parts, skin
  removed (wings, breasts,
  thighs, legs)
Salt and pepper to taste
Peanut oil for frying
2 tbsp. water

3 cloves garlic, chopped
½ cup parsley, chopped
6 lb. potatoes, cut for thick
  French fries
Salt and pepper to taste
2 tbsp. additional water

Salt and pepper skinned chicken pieces. Pan-fry chicken in peanut oil in batches. As chicken is done, place each batch in a Dutch oven on very low heat. Add water, sprinkle some of the garlic and parsley over each batch, and cover.

Fry the potatoes in batches in the same peanut oil until golden. Add potatoes to the Dutch oven with the chicken and sprinkle with remaining garlic and parsley. Salt and pepper the potatoes. Gently toss the chicken and potatoes with the garlic and parsley. Add additional water, cover, and let rest 15 minutes. Transfer to a serving platter. Serves 8.

FOIES DE VOLAILLE A LA MEXICAINE
CHICKEN LIVERS MEXICAN STYLE

As a lover of chicken livers, I was happy to find this recipe: a spicy blend of tomatoes, *Herbes de Provence*, and chili pepper simmered into a sauce joined by sautéed chicken livers and mushrooms. This is exceptionally good over pasta.

2 tbsp. peanut oil	Salt and pepper to taste
2 medium onions, chopped	1 tbsp. flour
3 cloves garlic, chopped	2 lb. chicken livers, cut
1 1-lb. can tomatoes,	into large pieces
chopped	4 tbsp. butter
2 tbsp. tomato paste	2 tbsp. additional peanut oil
2 tbsp. *Herbes de Provence**	½ lb. mushrooms,
1 tsp. chili pepper, seeded	quartered
and chopped	1 cup dry white wine

Sauté onions and garlic in peanut oil 5 minutes. Add tomatoes, bring to a boil, and simmer 5 minutes. Add tomato paste, *Herbes de Provence*, chili pepper, salt, and pepper. Simmer uncovered 20 minutes.

Flour chicken liver pieces. Sauté in butter and additional peanut oil 5 minutes until lightly browned. Transfer livers to paper towel and drain. Add livers, mushrooms, and wine to tomato sauce, bring to a boil, and simmer 5 to 7 minutes. Serve with pasta or rice. Serves 8.

**Herbes de Provence* is the blend of various herbs so common in the department of Provence, France, and also used in many recipes throughout France. A good recipe is 2 tbsp. each of thyme, chervil, tarragon, and marjoram blended with 1 tbsp. each of oregano, rosemary, and summer savory. One or more of these can be omitted as desired. Store in a well-sealed jar.

POULARDE A LA DIJONNAISE
DIJON MUSTARD CHICKEN

Dijon, France, is probably the mustard capital of the world and has given its name to a special blend of mustard that has both a sweet and spicy flavor. Our recipe braises chicken in white wine with thyme and enriches the sauce with cream and Dijon mustard. The sauce is excellent with boiled egg noodles.

3 lb. chicken parts
  (your choice)
Salt and pepper to taste
2 tbsp. butter
2 tbsp. peanut oil

1²/₃ cups white wine
1 tsp. thyme
1¼ cups cream
4 tbsp. Dijon mustard

Salt and pepper chicken parts. Sauté chicken in butter and peanut oil until golden on all sides. Remove chicken and reserve. Pour out excess fat. Deglaze the pan with wine. Add thyme and reserved chicken. Cover the skillet and simmer 30 minutes.

Add cream and simmer 15 minutes. Add mustard, blending well. Serve with boiled noodles or Mustard-Roasted Potatoes (recipe in chapter 7). Serves 8.

POULET AUX EPICES
SPICED CHICKEN

A unique combination of flavors join to create a sauce with which to braise the sautéed chicken parts. Aromatic vegetables, tomatoes, white wine, thyme, and curry are simmered to blend the flavors, and then the sautéed chicken is added for a 20-minute braise. The sweet raisins are a great counterpoint to the spicy curry.

Salt and pepper to taste
3 lb. chicken parts
   (breasts, legs, thighs,
   wings—your choice)
4 tbsp. flour
3 tbsp. butter
1 tbsp. peanut oil
2 medium onions, chopped
2 cloves garlic, chopped

1 large green bell pepper,
   chopped
1 tbsp. curry powder
1 tsp. thyme
1 1-lb. can chopped
   tomatoes and their juice
1/3 cup sweet white wine
Salt and pepper to taste
1/2 cup raisins

Salt and pepper chicken parts. Pass chicken in flour to coat. Sauté chicken in butter and oil until browned on all sides. Remove chicken and set aside.

Sauté onions, garlic, bell pepper, curry, and thyme in pan drippings, stirring for 5 minutes. Add tomatoes and wine. Return chicken to the pan. Salt and pepper to taste. Cover and simmer 20 minutes.

Add the raisins. Serve with potatoes or rice. Serves 8.

TARTE AU POULET
CHICKEN POTPIE

One of my favorite comfort-food recipes is this one for Chicken Potpie. Since acquiring this one many years ago, I have never ceased to enjoy both making and eating it. A melange of colorful and flavorful vegetables is combined with boiled chicken and bound together with a velouté sauce. It is then placed in individual bowls, covered with pastry, and baked. The fragrance when the piecrust is cut is wonderful. I often make these and freeze them for later use.

20 pearl onions
3 medium carrots,
  peeled and diced
2 tbsp. butter
1 tbsp. peanut oil
1 cup red onion, chopped
2 cloves garlic, chopped
1 small green bell pepper,
  diced
4 stalks celery, peeled and
  diced
¼ cup parsley, chopped
2 cups canned button
  mushrooms; reserve liquid

Salt and pepper to taste
2 tsp. thyme
2 tbsp. flour
2 cups chicken stock,
  combined with mushroom
  liquid
⅓ cup milk
4 cups cooked chicken, cut
  into bite-size pieces
1 double recipe Basic Pie
  Dough (see "Desserts"
  chapter for recipe)
1 egg, lightly beaten with
  1 tsp. water

Cut the root end off pearl onions and cut a small cross in the root end. Blanch in boiling water for 2 minutes. Drain, refresh, and slip skins off. Blanch carrots 5 minutes. Drain and refresh and set aside.

Sauté pearl onions in butter and oil until they begin to brown. Add red onion and garlic. Sauté 5 minutes. Add reserved carrots, bell pepper, celery, parsley, and mushrooms. Add salt, pepper, and thyme. Blend in flour. Add stock and milk, blending well. Stir until sauce thickens. Add cooked chicken and blend well. Allow to cool. Distribute mixture into 8 individual serving bowls.

Cut pastry into circles ½-inch larger than the tops of bowls. Cover mixture with pastry, turning excess under and inside bowl. Flute the edges of pastry. Brush with an egg wash. Cut a small hole in the center. Bake at 375 degrees 30 to 35 minutes until pastry has browned. Serves 8.

POULET AUX NOIX
WALNUT CHICKEN

I learned this recipe for Oriental Walnut Chicken 30 years ago in a Chinese cooking class I took from a lovely Chinese lady. I have prepared this many times at home and have taught this in my classes ever since. It never fails to please.

2 lb. chicken breasts, deboned, skinned, and cut into 1½-inch pieces	3 egg whites
	6 tbsp. cornstarch
	1½ cups walnuts, chopped finely
1 tsp. salt	Peanut oil for deep-frying
2 tbsp. dry sherry wine	

Marinate chicken in salt and sherry 20 minutes. Lightly beat egg whites. Blend in the cornstarch. Pass each piece of chicken in the egg/cornstarch mixture. Roll in chopped walnuts. Deep-fry a few pieces at a time until golden. Drain on paper towels. Serves 8.

BOULETTES DE VOLAILLE AU CHOU VERT
POACHED CHICKEN BALLS WITH CABBAGE

Always on the lookout for unique methods of cooking, I was particularly delighted to learn this way of preparing a chicken mousse and forming balls that are then poached in water. Paired with blanched cabbage leaves and garnished with pistachio nuts, the chicken balls become a unique taste experience.

½ cup pistachio nuts
1 egg
2 lb. chicken breast, skinned, deboned, and cut into pieces
Salt and pepper to taste
1 cup cream
1 green cabbage, separated into leaves

¼ cup peanut oil
2 tomatoes, peeled, seeded and diced
2 shallots, chopped
1 tsp. leaf thyme
1 cup white wine
½ cup additional pistachio nuts

Combine pistachio nuts, egg, and chicken-breast pieces in a food-processor bowl. Process until puréed. Add salt and pepper to taste. With the processor running slowly, add cream until blended, then refrigerate.

Blanch cabbage leaves in salted water 1 minute. Drain them and reserve.

With wet hands, form 2-inch balls with the chicken mousse. Drop the chicken balls in simmering water a few at a time. When they rise to the surface, allow to cook 2 minutes. Remove to a plate. Sauté the balls in peanut oil with the tomatoes and shallots 5 minutes. Add the cabbage leaves, thyme, and white wine. Simmer 5 minutes.

Transfer cabbage to a serving platter. Arrange chicken balls over cabbage. Garnish with additional pistachio nuts.

CUISSOT DE DINDE A LA PRINTANIERE
TURKEY LEG WITH SPRINGTIME VEGETABLES

Turkey legs and thighs, the dark meat, are for me the most flavorful part of the bird and are increasingly available in the markets packaged separately. This recipe poaches the browned leg and serves it with springtime vegetables for a variation of traditional baked turkey.

3 cloves garlic, cut in
 quarters
1 2-lb. turkey leg and thigh
1 tbsp. olive oil
1 tbsp. butter
2/3 cup white wine
1 bouquet garni (see Tomato
 and White Bean Soup in
 soups chapter)

Salt and pepper to taste
1 lb. carrots, cut into
 2 or 3 pieces
1 tbsp. butter
1/2 cup chicken stock
1 lb. green peas

Place garlic in slits made in the turkey. Sauté leg in olive oil and butter until brown. Add wine, bouquet garni, salt, and pepper. Cover and simmer 50 minutes.

Sauté the carrots in butter 5 minutes. Add the chicken stock. Cover and simmer 5 minutes. Add the green peas and simmer 5 minutes. Transfer carrots and peas to a serving dish. Place the turkey leg and thigh on the platter.

Remove excess fat from roasting pan. Add the braising liquid from the carrots. Reduce 5 minutes. Pour over turkey and vegetables. Serves 8.

DINDE A LA BOULANGER
BAKED TURKEY LEGS

Tender and moist, these turkey quarters flavored with rosemary, thyme, and bay leaf are a crowd pleaser. The small new potatoes absorb much of the flavor of the herbs and turkey and are delicious. This recipe will feed 8 persons or 6 hungry turkey lovers. Honey-Carmelized Carrots and Garlic is a good accompaniment.

2 thigh/leg portions of turkey	**1 tbsp. additional peanut oil**
Salt and pepper to taste	**1 cup white wine**
2 tbsp. peanut oil	**2 tsp. rosemary leaves**
3 lb. small new potatoes	**2 bay leaves**
3 tbsp. butter	**1 tsp. thyme**

Salt and pepper to taste turkey thigh/legs. Sprinkle with peanut oil. Place in a baking pan. Bake at 350 degrees for 25 minutes.

Sauté potatoes in butter and additional peanut oil 15 minutes, turning frequently. Baste turkey with white wine. Add rosemary, bay leaves, and thyme. Add sautéed potatoes around turkey. Return to the oven. Continue baking another 20 minutes.

Pour the cooking liquid into a measuring cup. Remove excess fat. Serve turkey and potatoes on a serving plate with the sauce on the side. Serves 8.

ESCALOPES DE DINDE AUX ANCHOIS
TURKEY SCALLOPS WITH ANCHOVY

For many years I thought the only way to cook turkey was to bake it, and I never thought about preparing it, except at Thanksgiving and Christmas. I had to go to France to learn the many ways the flesh of our American bird can be prepared. I learned that the breast meat can simulate pork or veal in many dishes, and since then I have added new recipes to my collection. This one reminds me of the classic Veal Viennoise.

4 tbsp. peanut oil
Juice of 3 lemons
1 tsp. oregano
Salt and pepper to taste
8 turkey-breast scallops*
4 tbsp. flour
Salt and pepper to taste
2 eggs

⅓ cup milk
1½ cups breadcrumbs
3 tbsp. parsley, chopped
4 tbsp. additional peanut oil
8 jumbo stuffed olives
8 anchovy filets
3 eggs, hard-boiled
     and sliced

Blend together peanut oil, lemon juice, oregano, salt, and pepper. Marinate turkey scallops in this mixture 1 hour. Drain the scallops and dry on paper towels.

Blend together the flour, salt, and pepper. Beat the eggs and milk in another bowl, then blend together the breadcrumbs and chopped parsley in a third. Pass the turkey scallops in flour, then egg wash, and finally in breadcrumbs. Sauté scallops in additional peanut oil 4 minutes on each side. Remove to a serving plate.

Wrap each olive with an anchovy filet. Place a slice of hard-boiled egg on top of each scallop. Place an anchovy-wrapped olive on top of each egg slice. Serves 8.

*Turkey-breast scallops are best made by slicing a partially frozen turkey breast horizontally with the grain of the flesh. If cut through the breast against the grain of the flesh, the scallops tend to fall apart. I frequently substitute turkey scallops for veal in recipes with great success.

ESCALOPES DE DINDE AUX POMMES
TURKEY SCALLOPS WITH APPLES

This recipe pairs tender scallops of turkey breast with Calvados, a French apple brandy, and with sautéed apples. Apple cider combines with nutmeg and cream to make the garnish sauce for the turkey scallops. Turkey, like pork, has an affinity with many fruits, as this recipe demonstrates.

Salt and pepper to taste
8 turkey-breast scallops
  (see previous recipe)
4 tbsp. butter
4 apples, peeled, cored,
  and cut into slices
2 tbsp. additional butter
2 tbsp. flour

½ cup Calvados
  (apple brandy)
½ cup apple cider
½ cup cream
¼ tsp. nutmeg
Salt and pepper to taste
½ cup walnuts, chopped

Salt and pepper turkey scallops. Sauté in butter 4 minutes on each side. In another skillet sauté apples in additional butter 10 minutes. Pour Calvados over scallops and ignite. Remove scallops to a serving platter and keep warm. Sprinkle flour into skillet and dissolve in pan drippings. Gradually incorporate the apple cider and bring to a boil. Add cream, nutmeg, salt, and pepper. Surround the turkey scallops with the sautéed apples. Sprinkle with walnuts. Pour sauce over turkey. Serves 8.

BLANC DE DINDE FARCI
AUX EPINARDS ET JAMBON
HAM-AND-SPINACH-STUFFED TURKEY BREAST

This treatment of turkey breast is unique and delicious. A deboned turkey breast is stuffed with sautéed spinach, mushrooms, and ham. Wrapped in cheesecloth to help keep its shape, the turkey is poached in an aromatic chicken stock. Unwrapped, placed on a serving platter, and sliced to reveal the spinach and ham, it will get raves.

1 lb. mushrooms, sliced
4 tbsp. butter
3 lb. spinach, blanched,
    drained, and chopped
3 eggs, beaten
1 tsp. thyme
Salt and pepper to taste
1½ cups breadcrumbs
1 7-lb. turkey breast, thawed
1 lb. ham, ½-inch thick and
    cut into 6 x ½-inch strips

3 cups chicken broth
2 cups white wine
1 onion, sliced
2 stalks celery, cut into
    1-inch pieces
2 carrots, peeled and cut
    into 1-inch cylinders
8 peppercorns
2 bay leaves

Sauté mushrooms in butter 5 minutes. Blend together spinach, mushrooms, eggs, thyme, salt, pepper, and breadcrumbs.

Place turkey breast (skin side down) on a cutting board. With a sharp knife, slowly slice against the bones of the rib cage, separating the flesh from bones. Repeat for the second side of the rib cage. Gently remove the rib cage without piercing the skin. Butterfly the flesh and fold out to form an even layer of flesh.

Spread ⅓ of the spinach/mushrooms mixture over the flesh. Place ½ the ham strips over the spinach. Cover with another ⅓ of the spinach mixture. Place remaining ham over and cover with remaining spinach. Bring sides of turkey breast up over the filling. Skewer skin and flesh to hold closed. Wrap turkey roll in 3 layers of cheesecloth, tying ends to form a large sausage. Remove skewers and tie roll with kitchen string.

Place turkey roll, deboned rib cage, chicken broth, wine, onion, celery, carrots, peppercorns, and bay leaves in a roasting pan. Bring to a boil, reduce heat, cover, and simmer 2 hours. Uncover and allow to cool in poaching liquid 1 hour.

Remove turkey roll to a platter and remove cheesecloth. Slice and transfer to a serving dish. Serves 8.

BALLOTINES DE BLANC DE DINDE
ROLLED STUFFED TURKEY TENDERS

The small muscle of the turkey breast, called the "tender," is wonderful for filling and rolling to provide individual servings. This recipe spreads a cream-cheese mixture on the turkey tenders, then rolls them jelly-roll fashion, and wraps each roll with a piece of ham. They are in turn wrapped in a blanched lettuce leaf and plastic wrap. They are then poached in milk in the oven. To serve, they are unwrapped from the plastic and coated with a little of the milk poaching liquid.

8 large lettuce leaves
8 oz. whipped cream cheese
1 tsp. thyme
2 cloves garlic, chopped
Salt and pepper to taste
Juice of 1 lemon
8 turkey tenders, flattened*

8 slices baked or boiled
  ham, the same size as
  the tenders
3 cups milk
Salt and pepper to taste
2 tbsp. butter

Blanch lettuce leaves 1 minute, then refresh in cold water. Drain and set aside.

Blend together cream cheese, thyme, garlic, salt, pepper, and lemon juice. Spread each turkey tender with some of the cream-cheese mixture. Roll tenders to enclose cheese. Wrap each turkey roll in a slice of ham, then wrap in a reserved lettuce leaf. Wrap rolls in a piece of saran wrap. Place rolls in a baking dish. Pour milk over the rolls. Season with salt and pepper to taste. Dot with pieces of butter. Cover loosely with aluminum foil and bake at 350 degrees for 30 minutes.

Remove from oven and remove saran. Place on a serving dish and coat with some of the cooking liquid. Serves 8.

*The breast of a chicken or a turkey is made up of 2 muscles, a larger one called the "supreme" and a much smaller one called the "filet" or "tender." Some markets sell the tenders separately, especially turkey tenders. Large chicken-breast supremes can be substituted but must be pounded until about ½-inch thick.

BLANQUETTE DE DINDE
TURKEY STEW

The classic *blanquette* is the Blanquette de Veau, which is a stew of white veal. Continuing with the theme that turkey is a good substitute for veal, we present this recipe. Cubes of turkey breast are braised with aromatic vegetables and enriched with egg and cream to create a classic white sauce.

2 medium onions, cut into rings	Salt and pepper to taste
3 oz. butter	Additional chicken stock,
2 tbsp. peanut oil	if required
2½ lb. turkey breast and	3 egg yolks
thigh meat, cut into	3 tbsp. flour
1-inch cubes	3 tbsp. cream
2 cups chicken stock	Juice of 1 lemon
2 carrots, peeled and cut	Zest of 1 lemon, cut into
into round slices	thin strips
2 leeks, cut into round slices	

Sauté onions in butter and peanut oil. Add turkey cubes and brown well. Add chicken stock, carrots, leeks, salt, and pepper. Simmer 35 minutes or until turkey is tender, adding additional chicken stock if necessary.

Blend together egg yolks, flour, cream, and lemon juice. Slowly add 1 cup of the cooking liquid to the egg mixture. Pour egg mixture into the pot with the turkey. Simmer 10 minutes until the sauce thickens. Add lemon zest. Serve with boiled rice on the side. Serves 8.

SAUTE DE CANARD AU FENOUIL
SAUTEED DUCK WITH FENNEL

This recipe combines two of my favorite ingredients, duck and fennel. The robust flavor of duck is complemented by the anise taste of fennel and the sweet flavor of onions.

2 tbsp. butter
4 slices bacon, cut into 8 pieces
2 ducks, cut into pieces
  (legs, thighs, breasts, wings)
Salt and pepper to taste
2 large onions, cut into rings
2 cloves garlic, chopped

2 bulbs fennel, cut in half
  and sliced
3 stems savory (or 2 tsp.
  dried savory or 2 tsp.
  thyme)*
½ cup white wine
½ cup chicken stock

Sauté bacon pieces in butter until browned. Remove and reserve. Sauté duck parts in butter/bacon drippings 15 minutes. Remove duck and reserve. Pour out all the fat. Return duck pieces to pan. Salt and pepper to taste. Blend in the onions, garlic, fennel, savory (or thyme), and reserved bacon. Add wine and stock. Cover and simmer 35 minutes.

Remove vegetables and duck to a serving dish. Remove excess fat from pan. Pour remaining sauce over duck. Serves 8.

*Savory, a popular European herb, also is becoming popular in the United States. Savory's flavor is a blend of thyme, mint, and pepper and is used in soups, stews, and vegetables.

CANARD A L'ORANGE
DUCK WITH ORANGE SAUCE

Probably one of the best-known recipes for duck is this one with orange sauce. The sauce is probably as important as the flesh of the bird. Often found on restaurant menus, it is not difficult for the serious cook to prepare at home. The results are well worth the effort.

Zest of 2 oranges in strips
Salt and pepper to taste
2 3-lb. ducks
2 tbsp. butter
1 large carrot, peeled and
  chopped
1 large onion, chopped
1 stalk celery, chopped
¾ cup sugar combined with
  1 tbsp. water

¾ cup white-wine vinegar
2 cups chicken stock
Juice of 2 oranges, strained
4 additional oranges,
  segmented
½ cup Grand Marnier
2 tbsp. additional butter,
  softened and blended
  with 1 tbsp. cornstarch

Blanch orange zest 3 minutes and strain. Salt and pepper the interior of the ducks, close the opening, and prick the skin with a fork. Rub skin with butter. Place in a 475-degree oven 15 minutes.

Remove fat from pan. Distribute carrot, onion, and celery around ducks. Reduce heat to 400 degrees. Bake 40 minutes, turning the ducks frequently.

Heat sugar/water in a pan and caramelize. When amber color, add vinegar off heat. Return to heat and add chicken stock. Reduce by ⅓.

Remove ducks from oven and place in aluminum foil. Return to turned off oven with door ajar. Remove excess fat from the baking pan.

Deglaze pan with the orange juice. Strain into a saucepan. Bring to a boil and whisk in butter/cornstarch mixture. Combine and heat orange segments and Grand Marnier. Place the ducks on a platter. Spoon the sauce over ducks. Garnish with orange slices and blanched orange zest. Serve with remaining sauce on the side. Serves 8.

CANARD AUX CITRONS
CONFITS ET AUX OLIVES
DUCK WITH PRESERVED LEMONS AND OLIVES

This recipe introduces us to a unique product: preserved lemons. They add a special taste to any dish, especially this recipe for duck. See below for a source for preserved lemons or about how to make your own. The olives give a special added flavor and color to the baked duck.

2 3-lb. ducks
Salt and pepper to taste
4 preserved lemons*
3 tbsp. olive oil
1 cup chicken stock

4 additional preserved
lemons, cut into quarters
4 cloves garlic, chopped
1 cup green olives, pitted
1 cup black olives, pitted

Salt and pepper the interior and exterior of the ducks. Place preserved lemons into the cavity of the ducks. Truss ducks with kitchen string. Brown the ducks on all sides in olive oil in a Dutch oven for 15 minutes.

Remove ducks from Dutch oven and discard the fat. Deglaze pot with chicken stock and let reduce on high heat 5 minutes. Return ducks to pot and add the additional preserved lemons and garlic. Cover and simmer 30 minutes.

Add the olives and continue cooking 10 minutes. Transfer ducks to a serving platter and surround with lemons and olives. Strain the cooking liquids and serve on the side. Serves 8.

*Preserved lemons are available in fine food stores and have a unique flavor. To make your own, cut 5 or more lemons in fourths partway through from the blossom end, leaving them attached at the stem end. Place ½ teaspoon kosher salt into each lemon. Place in a large jar. Cover with room-temperature water and a little salt. Close with a lid. These will keep in the refrigerator about 1 month. They can be placed in a hot-water bath for 20 minutes and can be kept for 6 months.

CANARD LAQUE AUX PECHES
PEACH-GLAZED BAKED DUCK

Honey, peach syrup, soy sauce, and vinegar are combined to make a basting sauce that gives the duck a glaze and a sweet and sour flavor. Peaches are heated in peach juice and thickened with cornstarch for a garnish to the beautiful duck.

2 3-lb. ducks
Salt and pepper to taste
2 cloves garlic
6 tbsp. honey
½ cup peach syrup
6 tbsp. soy sauce
4 tbsp. wine vinegar

1 cup water
4 cups canned peach halves
   and their syrup
2 tsp. cornstarch, dissolved
   in 2 tbsp. water
Salt and pepper to taste

Salt and pepper the interior and exterior of ducks. Rub the skin with the garlic cloves. Truss the ducks and place in a baking pan. Bake at 300 degrees 1½ hours. Blend together the honey, peach syrup, soy sauce, vinegar, and water. Brush the ducks with this sauce the last 10 minutes of cooking. Remove ducks and keep warm.

Discard the fats that are in the baking pan. Add the peaches and heat 3 minutes. Add the remaining peach syrup and the dissolved cornstarch. Simmer 1 minute, stirring constantly. Arrange the peaches around the ducks and serve the sauce on the side. Serves 8.

CANETTE A LA CORIANDRE
CORIANDER DUCK WITH RICE

The strong, assertive flavor of duck is complemented with the lemon flavor imparted by the coriander seeds, and the rice pilaf with green peas is the perfect companion to the duck. A flavorful sauce is generated by deglazing the roasting pan with white wine.

2 tsp. coriander*	**2 tbsp. butter**
2 cloves garlic, chopped	**2 cups rice**
4 tbsp. butter	**4 cups water**
Salt and pepper to taste	**Salt and pepper to taste**
2 duck livers	**3 cups green peas**
2 3-lb. ducks	**½ cup white wine**
2 tbsp. olive oil	**½ cup water**
Juice of 2 lemons	**2 tbsp. fresh coriander,**
Salt and pepper to taste	**chopped**
2 medium onions, chopped	

Mix together the coriander, garlic, butter, salt, pepper, and duck livers. Place mixture in the ducks' cavities. Truss the ducks with kitchen string. Place ducks in a baking pan and rub it with olive oil and lemon juice Salt and pepper to taste. Bake the ducks at 400 degrees 50 minutes, basting from time to time with pan juices.

Sauté onions in butter until soft. Add rice and cook until transparent. Add water, salt, and pepper, then cover and simmer 10 minutes. Add green peas and continue cooking another 10 minutes.

Remove ducks from baking pan and set aside. Discard the fat in the baking pan. Deglaze with white wine and water. Place the rice on a serving platter. Cut ducks into serving pieces and place on top of rice. Garnish with fresh coriander (cilantro) and serve sauce on the side. Serves 8.

*Coriander, the seed of the plant we call "cilantro," has a lemon flavor and is used with roasts, fowl, or other foods that cook for a long period of time. The heat of cooking brings out the rich flavor of the spice.

MAGRETS DE CANARD A LA MANGUE
SAUTEED DUCK BREASTS WITH MANGO

On a recent trip to Paris, I experienced this duck-and-mango dish that is one of the best meals I've had. In France the duck breasts *(magret)* usually are large because they come from ducks raised to produce the large livers that are made into *pâté de foie gras*. The duck breasts I have been able to find here are somewhat smaller but are nonetheless flavorful. The combination of the rare, robust duck meat and the sweet mango is a delight.

8 deboned duck breasts
Salt and pepper to taste
2 tsp. peanut oil
1 tbsp. butter
6 mangos, peeled, seeded,
 and cut into bite-size pieces

Salt and pepper to taste
3 tbsp. honey

Salt and pepper duck breasts. Sauté in peanut oil 3 minutes skin side down. Turn and sauté 2 minutes. Remove and set aside.

Add butter to the skillet with the duck drippings. Place mango pieces into the butter and duck fat and toss well. Salt and pepper to taste and add honey, distributing well. Simmer 2 minutes. Remove and set aside.

Slice each duck breast diagonally into ¼-inch slices. Arrange on a serving plate and garnish with sautéed mango. Serves 8.

Vegetables

Of all the categories of foods available to us, vegetables are the most varied and versatile. Too often, they are served merely as poor accompaniments to meats and fish. However, vegetarians discovered a long time ago that there are thousands of ways to cook delicious and original vegetable dishes. Although the recipes here are not intended to be strictly vegetarian, they do lend themselves to becoming the principal dish of a meal or as a complement to meat and fish.

Vegetables are probably the most abused of all the categories of food that we cook. They are frequently cooked beyond recognition, so much so that both color and taste are destroyed. However, there are methods of cooking that will please both the eye and mouth by preserving a vegetable's color and identity and enhancing its flavor.

All vegetables are derived from plants that contain chlorophyll, with the exception of one category: mushrooms and truffles. Chlorophyll-based vegetables are made up of six categories that are identified by the part of the plant from which they come:

Root: beets, carrots, garlic, leeks, onions, potatoes, and turnips
Stem: asparagus, broccoli, celery, and fennel
Leaf: cabbage, endive, lettuce, parsley, and spinach
Flower: artichokes, Brussels sprouts, and cauliflower
Fruit: cucumbers, eggplant, tomatoes, squashes, fruit, and nuts
Seed: beans, corn, and peas

ROOT VEGETABLES

Beets, carrots, garlic, leeks, onion, potatoes, and turnips are the most commonly used root vegetables used in French, Creole, Cajun, Italian, Spanish, and American cooking. Root vegetables whose use is not so widespread include Jerusalem artichokes, kohlrabi, parsnips, rutabagas, celeriac, radishes, etc.

With a few exceptions, root vegetables are most commonly prepared by cooking in cold water with a little salt and sometimes with a small amount of sugar or butter. By starting the cooking in cold water, the vegetable will cook uniformly as the water heats, thus the inside and outside cook evenly. Vegetables should be cut to uniform size so that they will reach the same degree of doneness at the same time.

Sometimes root vegetables are baked or are cooked with dry heat in the oven. Other times they are blanched, as above, and drained as soon as the water comes to a boil; then the final cooking will be done by sautéing in butter or oil. They also can be deep-fried, in which case they should be very dry and placed in very hot oil; doing so seals the vegetable and prevents it from absorbing the oil.

As with all vegetables, root vegetables should not be overcooked. They should be slightly firm and tender and should retain their color and shape.

STEM VEGETABLES

This category of vegetables consists primarily of the edible stem of the plant. They are asparagus, broccoli, celery, and fennel. While broccoli could be classified as a flower vegetable, I classify it as a stem vegetable because a large part of the stem attached to the flower buds is edible and in fact is the tastiest part. Most stem vegetables are best when the stem is peeled, unless the vegetable is very young and fresh. Asparagus is best when the lower two-thirds is peeled with a vegetable peeler. Celery is certainly enhanced by removal of the stringy exterior, and peeling is a must for broccoli stems. I do not think it necessary to peel fennel bulbs.

I find these vegetables best when placed in either boiling salted water or beef or chicken stock and blanched until just barely tender. Drained and refreshed under cold water to stop the cooking and preserve their flavor and color, they can be reheated or cooked further in butter, oil, or chicken broth.

This category of vegetable works well with various sauces from a simple lemon-butter sauce to a Mornay (cheese) sauce or Hollandaise (egg-butter-lemon emulsion).

LEAF VEGETABLES

The most common leaf vegetables are cabbage (both green and red), endive, lettuce, parsley, mustard greens, collards, chard, spinach, watercress, etc. Many—such as cabbage, endive, lettuce, spinach, and watercress—most often appear in salads of one kind or another, yet all are delicious when cooked.

Steaming and braising in a small amount of liquid are the most frequent cooking methods used when cooking leaf vegetables, but they cook well when stir-fried, retaining their color and crispness.

FLOWER VEGETABLES

Artichokes, Brussels sprouts, and cauliflower are the primary flower vegetables that are harvested before they go to seed. The blossom is attached to a stem that can be long or short but is edible. Broccoli can be classified as either a flower vegetable or a stem vegetable.

The artichoke, which is the blossom of a thistle, is prized by the French, the Italians, and the Creoles. The Italians and Creoles are masters of stuffing the vegetable with meats, seafood, or seasoned bread. The French trim the flower to about one-fourth its size and remove the choke to form a container for sauces or other vegetables.

Cauliflower can be boiled or steamed whole or broken into florets and cooked. Serving it with a simple garnish of butter and dill weed or a more elegant sauce makes cauliflower a flavorful addition to a meal. Combined with white sauce and cheese and baked, it becomes a delicious casserole.

Flower vegetables are best cooked by adding to boiling salted water or by steaming.

FRUIT VEGETABLES

Fruit vegetables are many and include those we generally call "fruit." Fruit vegetables frequently are eaten raw or in salads or are cooked as desserts. However, in this chapter we are primarily interested in cooked savory vegetable dishes. This vegetable category includes cucumbers, eggplants, peppers, tomatoes, and squashes (such as vegetable pears and zucchini).

Fruit vegetables are cooked in a variety of ways. They can be boiled, baked, or sautéed, simply seasoned, combined with other vegetables, or stuffed. The French and Creoles are fond of stuffing vegetables like edible containers, while the Italians are masters at combining flavors and spices for memorable dishes.

SEED VEGETABLES

In the last stage of a plant's life, it develops the seeds that will perpetuate the next generation. These seed vegetables are found in many forms on diner's plates: in seedpods (as peas), on the cob (such as corn). A chef sometimes cooks both the pod and seed, as with green beans or snap beens. This category also includes nuts, which are the seeds of a tree or other plant.

This category lends itself to a variety of cooking methods, including boiling, steaming, sautéing, and baking. Sometimes they're just eaten raw.

FUNGUS VEGETABLES

The two nonchlorophyll-based vegetables are mushrooms and truffles. Both grow from underground spores and add great flavor to a meal. Mushrooms grow underground and suddenly pop up to the surface, where they can be harvested. Truffles also grow underground but must be searched for by trained hogs or dogs. Because truffles are rare, they are very expensive and are usually used sparingly to garnish or perfume a dish. Mushrooms, however, come in a multitude of types and are especially delicious when sautéed in butter or combined in ragouts.

ASPERGES GRATINE
GRILLED ASPARAGUS ON TOAST

This queen of green vegetables is delicious when served with grilled cheese on a grilled bread slice. The asparagus makes a wonderful accompaniment to seafood dishes. You can substitute white asparagus for a slight variation.

8 slices bread with a tight crumb
4 tbsp. butter
2 cans asparagus, drained

¼ cup Gruyère cheese, grated
Salt and pepper to taste

Butter both sides of bread slices. Grill bread on both sides until golden. Place on a baking sheet. Arrange asparagus over bread slices. Sprinkle cheese over asparagus. Salt and pepper to taste. Pass under broiler 4 minutes until cheese is lightly browned. Serve as an appetizer or as a side dish to fish.

ARTICHAUTS AU GRATIN
ARTICHOKE AND SWISS CHEESE CASSEROLE

Tender hearts of artichokes are blended with a Mornay sauce (a cheese-based white sauce) and baked with a topping of Swiss cheese and breadcrumbs for a unique casserole. This dish goes well with roasts of meat or chicken.

4 cups canned artichoke hearts, halved, liquid reserved
1 tbsp. lemon juice
4 tbsp. butter
4 tbsp. flour
2 tbsp. onion, grated
1 tbsp. Dijon mustard

Salt and pepper to taste
½ cup reserved artichoke liquid
1½ cups milk, heated
1 large egg, lightly beaten
1 cup Swiss cheese, grated
2 tbsp. breadcrumbs
Paprika for garnish

Place artichoke hearts in a baking dish, cut side down. Set aside artichoke liquid. Sprinkle with lemon juice. Sauté flour in butter 1 minute. Blend in onion, mustard, salt, and pepper. Whisk in artichoke liquid and milk until thickened. Add egg and half the cheese. Pour over artichokes. Distribute remaining cheese over casserole. Sprinkle with breadcrumbs. Garnish with paprika. Bake at 350 degrees for 15 minutes. Serves 8.

FRITTATA CON CARCIOFI E PREZZEMOLO
ARTICHOKE AND PARSLEY OMELET

This Italian omelet was a Friday meal at home when we were kids because of the Roman Catholic prohibition of eating meat on Friday. Although we are French, there was a lot of Italian influence in the home cooking of New Orleans. The ingredients can be varied to substitute or include shrimp, asparagus, ham, or sausage (to your taste).

12 large eggs, beaten
2 cloves garlic, chopped
1 cup parsley, chopped
8 anchovy filets, chopped
½ cup Parmesan cheese

Salt and pepper to taste
2 cups artichoke hearts,
** cut into quarters**
2 tbsp. butter

Combine eggs, garlic, parsley, anchovy, Parmesan cheese, salt, and pepper in a bowl. Add artichoke hearts and blend well.

Melt butter in a 12-inch sauté pan with straight sides until brown. Pour egg/artichoke mixture into the pan. Reduce heat to low and cook about 15 minutes until mixture is set. Place under the broiler about 1 minute until top is browned. Remove from the oven. Place a plate over the sauté pan. Invert pan and plate. Remove pan. Serves 8.

HARICOTS VERTS CREOLE
CREOLE GREEN BEANS

The flavor of green beans is enhanced by the addition of onions, garlic, bacon, ham, and enough chili sauce to coat all the elements in the dish. This would be good with baked ham or turkey.

2 lb. green beans, cut into
  ½-inch pieces
¼ lb. bacon, cut into 1-inch
  pieces

¼ cup green onions, sliced
1 clove garlic, chopped
½ cup prepared chili sauce*
¼ lb. ham, diced

Blanch green beans in salted water 10 minutes until tender-crisp. Drain and refresh in cold water. Drain again and set aside.

Fry bacon until crisp. Remove to paper towels to drain.

Discard all but 1 tablespoon of bacon fat from the skillet and sauté onions in remaining drippings. Add garlic and chili sauce and simmer 5 minutes. Add reserved green beans, bacon, and ham. Toss well and simmer 5 minutes. Transfer to a serving dish. Serves 8.

*For a quick chili-sauce substitute, combine ½ cup catsup, ¼ tsp. garlic powder, ½ tsp. chili powder.

HARICOTS VERTS A LA CREME
GREEN BEANS IN CREAM SAUCE

This dish raises the humble green bean to haute cuisine. I acquired it in Paris at the Cordon Bleu and have taught it in many cooking classes. It is always a hit. Very easy and versatile, it accompanies meat, chicken, and seafood dishes equally well.

2 lb. green beans, cut
  French style
6 tbsp. butter

Salt and pepper to taste
1 cup cream

Blanch beans in salted boiling water 10 to 12 minutes until tender but firm to the bite. Refresh in cold water to stop cooking and preserve color.

Melt butter in a skillet. Toss green beans in butter until coated. Salt and pepper to taste. Add cream and cook rapidly until cream thickens. Turn into a serving dish. Serves 8.

HARICOTS VERTS A L'AIGRE-DOUCE
SWEET AND SOUR GREEN BEANS

Everyone loves the contrast in flavors that comes in a sweet and sour sauce. This recipe combines a unique set of ingredients—mint, pine nuts, raisins, vinegar, cloves, and sugar—to produce a sweet and sour garnish to blanched green beans.

2 lb. small green beans
⅓ cup sugar
¼ cup water
3 tbsp. fresh mint, chopped
3 tbsp. pine nuts

⅓ cup raisins
⅓ cup white-wine vinegar
¼ tsp. powdered cloves
Salt and pepper to taste

Place green beans in boiling water and simmer 15 minutes.

Dissolve sugar in water and heat slowly until it begins to lightly caramelize. Remove from the heat. Add mint, pine nuts, raisins, vinegar, cloves, salt, and pepper.

When beans are cooked, drain and mix with sweet and sour sauce. Transfer to a serving platter. Serves 8.

HARICOTS ROUGES
A LA NOUVELLE ORLEANS
RED BEANS NEW ORLEANS STYLE

A classic Creole recipe is Red Beans and Rice—which, legend has it, was prepared on Mondays, the traditional day for washing clothes in New Orleans. They simmered on the stove without much attention while the wash was being done. The Cajun versions are much heartier and used smoked sausage or pieces of pork instead of ham. Both types are delicious, and red beans still remains my favorite food.

½ lb. ham, diced
2 tbsp. peanut oil
2 large onions, chopped
1 cup celery, chopped
¼ cup parsley, chopped

2 cloves garlic, chopped
2 bay leaves
Salt and pepper to taste
1 lb. red kidney beans
10 cups water

Sauté ham in peanut oil 3 minutes. Add onions and sauté 5 minutes. Incorporate celery, parsley, garlic, bay leaves, salt, and pepper. Blend in beans and toss 1 minute. Add water and bring to a boil. Reduce heat and simmer 3 hours until beans are tender. From time to time, mash a few beans with a large spoon to make the liquid creamy. Serve with boiled rice. Serves 8.

BETTES A L'HARVARD
HARVARD BEETS

One of my favorite root vegetables is the beet. The flavor of cooked fresh beets is distinctly superior to canned, and—except for the time they take—they are easy to prepare. This classic recipe bathes beet slices in a sweet and sour sauce for a colorful and flavorful vegetable.

8 medium fresh beets*
½ cup sugar
2 tsp. cornstarch

½ cup red-wine vinegar
2 tbsp. butter

Place unpeeled beets in cold water to cover. Bring to a boil, then simmer until tender (45 minutes), adding water as necessary. Drain and refresh in cold water. Allow to cool and slip skins off. Slice or cut into quarters and reserve.

Combine sugar, cornstarch, and vinegar in a large saucepan. Bring to a boil and simmer 5 minutes. Add beets and reheat in sauce. Blend in butter and serve. Serves 8.

*Beets also can be cooked in the microwave to save time. Place them in a large dish in a circle. Add 3 tablespoons water. Cover with plastic wrap. Microwave on high about 15 minutes, turning dish several times. Remove plastic wrap, allow to cool, and slip the skins off. Proceed with the recipe.

CHOUX-BROCOLI A LA SAUCE RAIFORT
BROCCOLI WITH HORSERADISH SAUCE

This recipe has been very popular with students in my cooking classes. The broccoli is tender-crisp and retains its bright green color by your refreshing them in cold water after blanching a short time. The sour cream, horseradish, and mustard provide a smooth, spicy sauce as the garnish.

3 lb. broccoli	1 tbsp. Dijon mustard
Salt to taste	6 tbsp. butter
¾ cup sour cream	Salt and pepper to taste
1 tbsp. prepared horseradish	1 egg, hard-boiled and sieved

Separate broccoli into florets, peel stems, and cut into small pieces. Blanch in salted water 2 minutes. Drain and refresh in cold water. Set aside.

Combine sour cream, horseradish, and mustard.

Melt butter in a large pan. Add broccoli, salt, and pepper and toss until hot. Blend sour-cream mixture into broccoli and stir until heated. Transfer to a serving dish. Garnish with hard-boiled egg. Serves 8.

GATEAU DE BROCOLIS
BROCCOLI PIE

Seasoned, blanched broccoli florets and stem pieces are combined with seasoned breadcrumbs and olive oil and simmered slowly. The broccoli is then unmolded onto a serving plate and presented as a pie. The top should be nicely browned.

6 cups broccoli florets
2 cups broccoli stems, peeled
　　and cut into ½-inch pieces
Salt and pepper to taste
6 tbsp. butter, melted
2 tbsp. olive oil

¾ cup seasoned
　　breadcrumbs
3 tbsp. additional olive oil
⅓ cup additional
　　breadcrumbs

Blanch broccoli florets and stem pieces in boiling salted water 3 minutes. Drain and refresh in cold water and drain again. Transfer to a bowl. Add salt, pepper, butter, olive oil, and breadcrumbs, combining all well.

Pour additional olive oil into a 9-inch nonstick skillet. Sprinkle with additional breadcrumbs. Add broccoli mixture and press down. Cover and sauté over low to medium heat 20 minutes. Uncover, raise heat, and cook 5 minutes.

Remove from heat and carefully place a serving platter upside down over skillet. Quickly turn platter and skillet over to unmold broccoli. Remove skillet. Serves 8.

CHOU FARCI A LA FRANÇAISE
FRENCH-STYLE STUFFED CABBAGE

Every nationality seems to have good recipes for stuffed cabbage. This French recipe combines a variety of meats and seasonings and stuffs cabbage leaves into small balls that resemble little cabbage heads. They are served with a bright red tomato sauce that makes a colorful garnish as well as a complementary flavor.

1 large Savoy cabbage*
6 tbsp. butter
3 green apples, chopped
2 cups onions, chopped
2 cloves garlic, chopped
1 lb. ground pork
½ lb. boiled ham, ground
1 lb. chicken breasts, ground
½ tsp. allspice**
½ tsp. thyme
½ tsp. nutmeg

Salt and pepper to taste
2 eggs, beaten
⅓ cup chicken stock
1 cup cubed French bread, moistened with ⅓ cup water
1 cup white wine
8 strips bacon
1 recipe Tomato Sauce for French-Style Stuffed Cabbage (recipe follows)

Remove the core from cabbage and hold cored end under running water. This will cause leaves to separate. Blanch in boiling water a few seconds, then drain.

Sauté apples, onions, and garlic in butter until soft. Add pork, ham, chicken, allspice, thyme, nutmeg, salt, and pepper. Blend eggs and stock, adding to mixture. Incorporate moistened bread into mixture. Remove from heat.

Place a large cabbage leaf on a clean kitchen towel. Spoon 3 or 4 tablespoons of stuffing on leaf. Pull the towel up around cabbage/stuffing to form a ball about the size of a tennis ball. Repeat stuffing and forming, placing cabbage balls in a buttered baking dish. Pour wine over cabbage balls. Lay strips of bacon over cabbage. Cover and bake at 350 degrees 1 hour.

Heat tomato sauce and pour into a serving platter. Arrange stuffed cabbage over sauce. Serves 8.

*Savoy cabbage is a variety of French and Belgian origin that has a more delicate taste than the tight-headed cabbage most often seen in supermarkets. Its leaves are crinkled and attractive, enhancing the appearance of this dish.

**Allspice, thought by many to be a blend of spices, is a berry grown in the Caribbean Islands, especially Jamaica, that has the flavor and aroma of cinnamon, nutmeg, and cloves.

SAUCE TOMATE POUR CHOU FARCI
TOMATO SAUCE FOR
FRENCH-STYLE STUFFED CABBAGE

2 tbsp. butter	1 clove garlic, chopped
2 tbsp. flour	2 tbsp. tomato paste
1 medium onion, chopped	1 cup chicken stock
2 cups crushed tomatoes	Salt and pepper to taste

Sauté flour in butter 1 minute. Add onion and sauté 3 minutes. Add tomatoes, garlic, tomato paste, and chicken stock. Simmer gently 10 minutes. Salt and pepper to taste. Purée in a food processor. Serve with French-Style Stuffed Cabbage. Makes 3 cups.

CHOU VERT ET ROUGE BRAISES
BRAISED GREEN AND RED CABBAGE

Cabbage is so often cooked to death until it resembles mush. This recipe provides a happy alternative, producing a crisp yet tender and colorful side dish that serves well with seafood.

2 cups green cabbage, shredded
2 cups red cabbage, shredded
1 large onion, sliced thinly
1 large green bell pepper,
   sliced thinly
1 cup celery, sliced thinly
¼ cup water
2 tbsp. butter
Salt and pepper to taste

Combine cabbages, onion, bell pepper, and celery. Place in a skillet with water and butter. Salt and pepper to taste. Cover and simmer 10 to 12 minutes. Mixture will be crisp and bright color. Transfer to a serving dish. Serve with seafood dishes. Serves 8.

CHOU ROUGE BRAISE
BRAISED RED CABBAGE

This recipe is an unusual combination of flavors that makes an excellent companion to pork dishes. Layers of blanched cabbage and sautéed apples seasoned with sugar, vinegar, and butter are baked slowly until all the flavors blend together.

1 large red cabbage, shredded
3 tbsp. butter
2 medium onions, cut
   into rounds
2 medium apples, peeled,
   cored, and cut into rounds
1 tbsp. sugar
3 tbsp. red-wine vinegar
Salt and pepper to taste
2 tbsp. additional butter

Blanch the shredded cabbage in boiling salted water 5 minutes. Drain and refresh in cold water, then set aside to drain again.

Sauté onions and apples in butter 5 minutes. Place of the cabbage in a baking dish. Cover with ⅓ of the onion/apple mixture. Sprinkle with some of the sugar, wine, salt, and pepper. Repeat the layering of cabbage, onions/apples, sugar, vinegar, salt, and pepper 2 more times. Dot with additional butter. Cover vegetables with a piece of waxed paper. Cover the baking dish with aluminum foil. Bake at 325 degrees 2 hours. Serves 8.

FLANS AUX CAROTTES
CARROT FLANS

Whenever I can find carrots with the green tops still attached, I quickly buy them and prepare this recipe. With the green tops I know the carrots are fresh and haven't been subjected to long periods of cold storage. Sweet and succulent, they give this recipe a special taste. If I can't find carrots with tops, I look at the stem end to see if they show a little sign of green. As a last resort, I buy packaged carrots, which work well in this recipe.

2 lb. carrots, peeled and cut into 1-inch pieces	**¾ cup milk**
3 tbsp. butter, room temperature	**4 tbsp. cream**
	½ tsp. nutmeg
3 large eggs	**Salt and pepper to taste**
	Parsley for garnish, chopped

Butter 8 ½-cup ovenproof soufflé dishes and set aside.

Boil carrots 30 minutes until soft. Drain and transfer to the bowl of a food processor. Process butter and carrots until puréed. Add eggs, milk, cream, nutmeg, salt, and pepper. Process 30 seconds. Divide carrot purée evenly into soufflé dishes.

Place soufflé dishes in a bain-marie (pan of water). Bake at 350 degrees 30 to 35 minutes until firm. Remove soufflés from bain-marie and let rest 10 minutes. Loosen edges with a knife, invert, and unmold. Garnish with parsley. Serves 8.

Variations:

Broccoli Flans—Substitute 1 lb. cooked broccoli (stems and florets). Bake for 30 minutes.

Parsnip Flans—Substitute 1 lb. cooked parsnips. Bake for 30 minutes.

Cauliflower Flans—Substitute 1 lb. cooked cauliflower. Add 3 oz. shredded Gruyère cheese. Bake 30 minutes.

FRITES BATONNETS DE CAROTTES
FRIED CARROT STICKS

Battered and deep-fried carrot sticks rank alongside battered and deep-fried eggplant, okra, cauliflower, and fennel. The natural sweetness of the carrots is pronounced, and the crunchiness will surprise you. They are wonderful as a side dish to baked meats and fowl.

2 lb. carrots, peeled and
   cut into 3-inch sticks
3 tbsp. salt

6 tbsp. flour
3 large eggs, beaten
Peanut oil for deep-frying

Place carrot sticks in a colander and sprinkle with salt. Allow to rest 2 hours.

Wipe carrots with towels to remove the salt. Toss the carrots in the flour, shaking off the excess. Pass in beaten eggs. Toss carrots in the flour a second time.

Fry in small quantities in hot oil until browned. Remove carrots and drain on paper towels. Keep warm in a low oven until all the carrots are cooked. Serve as an accompaniment to chicken, veal, or pork. Serves 8.

CAROTTES CARAMELISEES MIEL ET AIL
HONEY-CARAMELIZED CARROTS AND GARLIC

There are many recipes for glazing carrots that use sugar, apple jelly, mint jelly, or a host of other ingredients. This recipe is unique in that it glazes the carrots with honey and mixes them with lots of garlic cloves to combine the sweetness of honey and the pungent flavor of garlic. The unpeeled cloves can be squeezed onto bread slices for a unique combination.

4 tbsp. butter	2 lb. carrots, peeled and cut
1 cup water	into ½-inch diagonal rounds
2 tbsp. honey	12 cloves garlic, unpeeled
Salt and pepper to taste	1 tsp. cumin seeds*

Combine the butter, water, honey, salt, and pepper in a large skillet. Bring to a boil. Add the carrots and garlic. Cover and lower heat to moderate. Simmer 30 minutes, stirring from time to time, until water evaporates and the carrots are caramelized.

Sprinkle with cumin seeds. Transfer to a serving platter. Serves 8.

*The seeds of this annual herb, which originated in Egypt, have been used for thousands of years to flavor meats, cheese, sausage, soups, stews, and vegetables, as in this recipe. Cumin is used as a component of curry recipes and chili powder and is popular in Latin American as well as Middle Eastern cuisines.

CHOU-FLEUR EN BECHAMEL AU FOUR
BAKED CAULIFLOWER IN BECHAMEL

Cauliflower is a relative of both cabbage and broccoli but has a distinct and delicate flavor. Introduced into Europe through Italy from Asia, cauliflower has become very popular the world over. The head of cauliflower is the undeveloped flower bud, which is prevented from turning yellow and flowering by tying the surrounding leaves over the head.

2 heads cauliflower, separated into florets	3 tbsp. parsley, chopped
Salt to taste	½ lb. Gruyère cheese, grated
3 tbsp. butter	½ cup additional flour
6 tbsp. flour	3 tbsp. additional butter, softened
2 cups milk	⅓ cup oatmeal flakes
1 cup cooking liquid from boiling cauliflower	½ cup additional Gruyère cheese, grated
2 cups canned corn kernels, drained	⅓ cup sliced almonds

Boil cauliflower florets in salted water 5 minutes. Drain and reserve 1 cup of the cooking liquid.

Dissolve flour in butter in a saucepan. Whisk in the milk gradually. Add the reserved cooking liquid. Bring to a boil and simmer 3 minutes. Add corn, parsley, and cheese. Gently fold in the cauliflower. Turn mixture into a baking casserole.

Combine additional flour and butter. Add the oatmeal flakes, cheese, and almonds. Sprinkle mixture over top. Bake at 375 degrees for 30 minutes. Serves 8.

CHOU-FLEUR GRATINE AU BLEU
CAULIFLOWER WITH BLUE CHEESE

An interesting casserole is prepared by blanching cauliflower florets, combining them with a blue-cheese béchamel sauce in an ovenproof baking dish, garnishing with breadcrumbs, and browning under the broiler. This is particularly good with chicken and turkey.

2 heads cauliflower,	**2 cups milk**
separated into florets	**6 oz. blue cheese**
Salt to taste	**Salt and pepper to taste**
4 tbsp. butter	**2 tbsp. breadcrumbs**
4 tbsp. flour	

Blanch cauliflower in salted boiling water 12 minutes. Drain and place in a baking dish.

Dissolve flour in butter in a saucepan 1 minute. Gradually add milk while stirring. Cook until thickened. Add cheese and stir until melted. Salt and pepper to taste. Pour over cauliflower. Sprinkle with breadcrumbs. Pass under the broiler until the crumbs brown. Serve as soon as possible. Serves 8.

COURONNE DE CHOU-FLEUR
CAULIFLOWER RING MOLD

This recipe is great for a buffet meal and presents beautifully. Puréed cauliflower is combined with butter, eggs, and nutmeg and poured into a ring mold. After a 45-minute stay in the oven, it is unmolded onto a serving plate and garnished with Anchovy Mayonnaise.

2 medium cauliflowers,
  separated into florets,
  stems peeled and cut
  into pieces
6 tbsp. butter
4 large egg yolks

Salt and white pepper to
  taste
¼ tsp. nutmeg
1 recipe Anchovy
  Mayonnaise
  (recipe follows)

Blanch cauliflower florets and stem pieces in boiling salted water 15 minutes. Drain. Process in a food processor until puréed. Add butter, egg yolks, salt, white pepper, and nutmeg. Process until well blended.

Pour into a buttered 6-cup ring mold. Bake at 350 degrees in a water bath (bain-marie) 45 minutes. Unmold onto a serving plate. Serve with Anchovy Mayonnaise. Serves 8.

MAYONNAISE AUX ANCHOIS
ANCHOVY MAYONNAISE

1 cup mayonnaise
6 anchovy filets, chopped

1 tsp. oil from a can
  of anchovies
1 medium shallot, chopped

Blend mayonnaise, anchovy filets, and oil. Add chopped shallots and blend well. Makes 1 cup.

CELERIS D'AMANDES
CELERY AMANDINE

Celery is one of the most underused vegetables. Although incorporated in salads or as an aromatic vegetable when making sauces, it is seldom served warm. This recipe provides a flavorful way to use celery as an accompaniment dish, especially to fish dishes.

4 tbsp. butter
1 cup slivered almonds
6 cups celery, cut into
    diagonal slices
½ cup onions, chopped

1 clove garlic, chopped
½ tsp. ginger root, chopped
½ tsp. sugar
2 cups chicken broth

Sauté almonds in butter until lightly browned. Add celery, onions, garlic, ginger root, and sugar. Toss well ½ minute. Add chicken broth. Cover and simmer 20 minutes, stirring frequently, until celery is tender but still crisp. Transfer to a serving dish. Serves 8.

BEIGNETS DE MAIS
CORN FRITTERS

Although this recipe calls for canned corn, fresh corn can and should be used, when available, for flavor. However, the unavailability of fresh corn should not stop you from enjoying these sweet and tasty fritters that are flavored with Gruyère cheese. These are good with any fried food, whether chicken or shrimp.

2 12-oz. cans corn, drained
4 large eggs, beaten
6 tbsp. butter, melted

½ cup Gruyère cheese,
    grated
Salt and pepper to taste
Peanut oil for frying

Blend together the corn, eggs, butter, cheese, salt, and pepper. Heat oil in a deep pot to 350 degrees. Gently drop the corn mixture by the spoonfuls into the oil. Fry about 4 minutes until browned. Remove with a skimmer to a paper towel. Transfer to a serving platter. Serve as soon as possible. Serves 8.

MAIS AU FOUR
BAKED CORN CASSEROLE

For a quick and easy casserole with lots of flavor, try this casserole of corn. Fresh corn, if available, can certainly be used. The interesting feature here is the topping of crushed potato chips, which add a crispy crust to a puddinglike casserole.

⅓ cup flour	Salt and pepper to taste
4 eggs	4 cups canned corn,
4 tbsp. butter	drained
¾ cup milk	1 cup crushed potato chips

Combine flour, eggs, butter, and milk in a bowl. Add salt and pepper and blend well. Incorporate corn to form a thick batter. Pour into an oven casserole. Sprinkle with potato chips. Bake at 375 degrees for 35 minutes. Serve as soon as possible. Serves 8.

MAIS EN SUMO A LA NASSAU
NASSAU GRITS

This Pensacola specialty goes back 80 years or more, when a Pensacolian named Henry Richardson brought this recipe home from a fishing trip in the Bahamas. Once home, he and his family embellished it and called it Nassau Grits. It became a favorite and found its way into several restaurants. Still found in many restaurants, it serves extremely well with fried fish.

1 lb. bacon	3 cups tomatoes, chopped
2 medium onions, chopped	4½ cups water
2 small bell peppers, chopped	1½ cups grits
1½ cups ham, finely chopped	Salt to taste

Fry bacon, crumble, and reserve. Pour off all but 2 tablespoons of bacon drippings. Sauté onions and bell peppers in drippings. Add ham and cook 3 minutes. Add tomatoes and simmer 1 hour.

Bring water to a boil. Add salt and grits. Simmer until thick and smooth. Combine tomato mixture and grits. Place in a serving dish. Garnish with crumbled bacon. Serves 8.

AUBERGINES AU FROMAGE
EGGPLANT CHEESE CASSEROLE

I have never met an eggplant dish that I did not like. This versatile and beautiful vegetable is popular in Italy, France, and here in the United States. In this recipe the steamed and chopped eggplant is combined with onions and cheese, covered with breadcrumbs, and baked in a casserole dish until browned on top. This casserole complements beef, veal, pork, and chicken and is excellent on a buffet table.

3 medium eggplants,
  peeled and diced
3 large onions, chopped
4 tbsp. butter
1 lb. cheddar cheese, grated
3 eggs, lightly beaten

Salt and pepper to taste
½ cup seasoned bread
  crumbs
4 tbsp. additional butter,
  softened

Steam or microwave diced eggplant until soft. Chop and set aside.

Sauté onions in butter until soft. Combine onions, reserved egg-plant, cheese, and beaten egg, mixing well. Season with salt and pepper and pour into a buttered baking dish. Sprinkle with breadcrumbs and dot with additional butter. Bake in a 350-degree oven 1 hour. Serves 8.

FENOUIL A LA TOMATE
FENNEL AND TOMATOES SAUTE

A very Italian vegetable that also is much beloved by the French, fennel is seen more and more in supermarkets. Here in the United States it is most often used as a salad item, but its mild anise flavor lends itself to all varieties of fish dishes.

1½ lb. fennel bulbs, sliced
  vertically (blossom to stem
  end) into ½-inch slices
3 tbsp. butter
2 cloves garlic, chopped

2 medium onions, chopped
Salt and pepper to taste
2 lb. tomatoes, peeled and
  cut into quarters

Blanch fennel slices in salted water 10 minutes. Drain and set aside.

Sauté garlic and onions in butter 5 minutes. Add fennel slices and toss 1 minute. Add salt, pepper, and tomatoes. Cover and simmer 15 minutes. Serves 8.

FENOUIL A LA TOSCANE
SAUTEED FENNEL TUSCAN STYLE

This crisp aromatic vegetable is known as *fenouil* in France, *finocchio* in Italy, and *hinojo* in Spain. The anise taste of fennel is complemented by Parmesan cheese to make a crisp vegetable side dish for various seafood entrées.

2½ lb. fennel bulbs, cut vertically (blossom to stem end) into ³/₄-inch slices
Salt to taste
2 thin slices of lemon
2 tbsp. olive oil
2 tbsp. butter
Pepper to taste
3 tbsp. Parmesan cheese, grated
Fennel leaves for garnish

Place fennel slices into a stockpot with salt, lemon slices, olive oil, and enough boiling water to cover. Simmer 20 minutes until tender. Drain well.

Melt butter in a baking dish. Add fennel, pepper, and cheese, tossing well. Pass under the broiler until browned. Serve with fennel leaves as a garnish. Serves 8.

POIREAUX GRATINES A LA MOUTARD
BRAISED LEEKS WITH MUSTARD

This very versatile vegetable, much loved by the French as well as many other European countries, is a mild-flavored member of the onion family. Although often used as an aromatic when preparing other foods, it is much prized for itself. This recipe braises 1-inch cylinders of the vegetable, seasons them with brown mustard, butter, and Parmesan cheese, and browns the mixture under the broiler.

3 lb. leeks, top ¾ removed, washed, and cut into 1-inch cylinders	4 tbsp. Parmesan cheese, grated
3 tbsp. brown French mustard (Meaux)	4 tbsp. butter, softened
	Salt and pepper to taste

Blanch leek cylinders in salted water 10 minutes. Drain and transfer to a buttered baking dish.

Blend together the mustard, Parmesan cheese, butter, salt, and pepper. Distribute this mixture over the leeks. Place under the broiler about 6 inches from heat and brown about 10 minutes. Serves 8.

GRATIN DE POIREAU AU CURRY
CURRIED LEEKS AND CHEESE

Mild-flavored leeks are sautéed in butter until tender and garnished with a curried béchamel sauce. A topping of sliced French bread and Gruyère cheese covers the casserole, which is then baked. This is a good combination of flavors to serve with fish dishes.

3 lb. leeks, prepared for cooking*	2 cups milk
3 tbsp. butter	1 tsp. curry powder**
Salt and butter	Salt and pepper to taste
4 tbsp. additional butter	8 slices French bread, cut into ¾-inch rounds
⅓ cup flour	½ lb. Gruyère cheese, grated

Sauté leeks in butter 15 minutes. Salt and pepper leeks and set aside.

Melt the additional butter in a saucepan and incorporate the flour. Gradually add the milk, stirring constantly. Add curry powder, salt, and pepper. Whisk until thickened. Place the leeks into a baking dish. Pour the curry sauce over the leeks. Place the bread slices on top, pushing down lightly into the sauce. Sprinkle the cheese over the bread. Bake at 400 degrees 10 minutes. Serves 8.

*Cut off most of the green top part of the leek and the outer layer of its lower part. Cut off the root, and—starting 6 inches from the root end—cut through to the top. Rotate leek ¼ turn and repeat the cutting so that the top is divided into 4. Wash the leek under running water, removing all visible dirt. Cut the leeks into ½-inch rounds, starting at the root end. Proceed with the recipe.

**Curry powder is a blend of many spices, and there are many blends available, some good, some not. It is wise to use a quality blend such as Madras curry powder, which is a blend of coriander seeds, tumeric, chilies, salt, cumin seeds, fennel seeds, black pepper, garlic, ginger, fenugreek, cinnamon, cloves, anise, and mustard. I find this a mild curry.

CHAMPIGNONS A LA NORMANDE
CREAMED MUSHROOMS NORMANDY STYLE

A large variety of fresh mushrooms is available today in our markets: Paris (button), oyster, portobello, crimini, shitaki, etc. This recipe prepares well with any one of the above kinds or a combination of them. The dish accompanies all kinds of roast meats or veal scallops.

8 tbsp. butter
1 large onion, chopped
2 lb. mushrooms of various kinds, sliced
Juice of 1 lemon
Salt and pepper to taste

3 tbsp. Calvados (apple brandy)*
½ cup parsley, chopped
2 cloves garlic, chopped
1½ cups cream

Sauté onion in butter until it begins to brown. Add the mushrooms, lemon juice, salt, and pepper. Sauté until the mushrooms' juices evaporate (10 minutes). Carefully add the Calvados and ignite. Add parsley, garlic, and cream. Simmer 5 minutes until cream thickens slightly. Transfer to a serving dish. Serves 8.

*Normandy, France, is well known for its dairy and apple products. Calvados is an apple brandy distilled from fermented apple juice (hard cider). Comparable to applejack in the United States, it is often combined with cream, another well-known product from that region, in dishes called "à la Normande."

RAGOUT DES CHAMPIGNONS
MUSHROOM STEW

This recipe is for both mushroom lovers and vegetarians. Prepared as a main course, the mushrooms develop a robust flavor in a velouté sauce with aromatic vegetables.

1 cup onions, chopped
2 cloves garlic, chopped
3 tbsp. butter
2 lb. mixed mushrooms
 (portobello, oysters, crimini,
 chanterelles, etc.) cut into
 bite-size pieces

⅓ cup flour
2 cups veal or beef stock
Salt and pepper to taste
2 tsp. Kitchen Bouquet
2 tbsp. parsley, chopped
2 tbsp. breadcrumbs

Sauté onions and garlic in butter until tender. Add mushrooms and sauté until tender and most of the liquid has evaporated (10 minutes).

Add flour and blend well. Add stock and blend until thickened and smooth. Salt and pepper to taste. Add Kitchen Bouquet for color. Blend in parsley. Divide between 6 individual casseroles. Sprinkle with breadcrumbs. Bake at 350 degrees 10 minutes. Serve immediately. Serves 8.

PORTOBELLO CHAMPIGNON "HAMBURGER"
PORTOBELLO MUSHROOM "HAMBURGER"

There is a wonderful neighborhood restaurant near my home called Madison's that serves a vegetarian version of a hamburger using portobello mushrooms marinated in merlot wine. It is unbelievably delicious. I have tried to simulate the recipe and have added the balsamic dressing.

Salt and pepper to taste
2 tbsp. thyme
4 cloves garlic, crushed
½ cup merlot wine
½ cup olive oil
8 large portobello mushrooms the size of hamburger buns
4 tbsp. balsamic vinegar

Additional salt and pepper to taste
½ cup roasted red bell pepper, peeled and chopped
4 tbsp. additional olive oil
8 hamburger buns, cut side toasted or grilled

Blend together salt, pepper, thyme, garlic, and wine. Whisk in olive oil. Place vinaigrette and mushrooms in a sealable plastic bag. Marinate at room temperature for several hours, turning frequently.

Blend together balsamic vinegar, salt, pepper, and bell pepper. Whisk in additional olive oil. Remove mushrooms from marinade. Combine remaining marinade with balsamic vinaigrette. Simmer 2 to 3 minutes.

Grill or sauté mushrooms 2 or 3 minutes on each side. Place mushrooms on bottom half of buns. Spoon some of the vinaigrette on the top half. Place top half over mushrooms. Serves 8.

DUXELLES DE CHAMPIGNONS
SAUTE OF MUSHROOMS AND ONIONS

Used in many recipes, *duxelles* is a special culinary term designating a flavorful sauté of mushrooms and onions in butter. One can add lemon juice to prevent the mushrooms from turning dark. Spices such as nutmeg, quatre-epices, or curry are an agreeable marriage with duxelles.

1 large onion, chopped
2 shallots, chopped
4 tbsp. butter

2 lb. mushrooms, cleaned
   and chopped
Salt and pepper to taste

Sauté onions and shallots in butter until soft. Add mushrooms, salt, and pepper, blending well. Sauté 15 minutes, stirring often, until there is no liquid remaining in the sauté pan. Yields 2 cups.

CHAMPIGNONS A LA GRECQUE
MUSHROOMS GREEK STYLE

Mushrooms in the Greek style are a wonderful accompaniment to all sorts of meat dishes. Small mushrooms are braised in a seasoned tomato and wine sauce and garnished with chopped parsley.

6 black peppercorns
9 coriander seeds*
2 bay leaves
1 tsp. thyme
6 tbsp. olive oil
6 shallots, chopped

4 medium tomatoes, peeled,
   seeded, and chopped
2 lb. small mushrooms
½ cup white wine
3 tbsp. tomato paste
3 tbsp. parsley, chopped

Place the peppercorns, coriander, bay leaves, and thyme in a piece of cheesecloth and tie with kitchen string to form a bouquet garni. Sauté shallots in olive oil 3 minutes. Add tomatoes, bouquet garni, mushrooms, and wine. Cover and simmer 10 minutes.

Remove the mushrooms to a serving platter. Discard the bouquet garni. Add the tomato paste to the sauce in the pan. Reduce the liquid 5 minutes. Pour over mushrooms. Garnish with chopped parsley. Serves 8.

*Coriander, a small yellowish brown seed of cilantro, has a flavor of lemon peel and sage. For maximum flavor, crush seeds and heat in a skillet a few minutes to release their flavor before adding to a dish.

CROUTES AU CHAMPIGNONS
MUSHROOMS ON GRILLED TOAST

Creamed sautéed mushrooms are seasoned with curry powder and served over grilled bread slices for a great companion to broiled or grilled meats. It also can be served as a first course.

8 slices bread with a tight crumb	**1 lb. mushrooms, sliced**
4 tbsp. butter	**2 cups cream**
1 medium onion, chopped finely	**6 tbsp. cornstarch**
6 tbsp. additional butter	**3 tbsp. water**
Juice of 1 lemon	**1 tsp. curry**
	Salt and pepper to taste
	2 tbsp. parsley, chopped

Butter bread slices on both sides. Grill bread on both sides until golden. Set aside. Sauté onion in additional butter until soft. Add lemon juice and mushrooms. Sauté 5 minutes. Add cream and cook 2 minutes while turning.

Dissolve the cornstarch in water. Add to mushrooms. Stir until sauce thickens. Add curry, salt, and pepper. Divide mushroom mixture over grilled bread slices. Garnish with parsley. Serves 8.

CHAMPIGNONS GRATINEE
GRILLED MUSHROOMS

To accompany roast meats or fowl, try these grilled mushrooms. Sautéed mushrooms are garnished with a mixture of breadcrumbs, ham, parsley, and Parmesan cheese. They are then browned under the broiler to melt the cheese.

2 tbsp. olive oil
2 lb. small mushrooms
  (if large, cut into quarters)
3 tbsp. butter
2 medium onions, chopped
4 cloves garlic, chopped

1 cup breadcrumbs, coarse
2 cups boiled ham, chopped
2 tbsp. parsley, chopped
Salt and pepper to taste
3 tbsp. Parmesan cheese

Sauté mushrooms in olive oil 4 to 5 minutes. Transfer to a baking dish.

Sauté onions and garlic in butter 3 minutes. Add breadcrumbs, ham, parsley, salt, and pepper. Stir well. Pour over mushrooms in baking dish. Sprinkle with Parmesan cheese. Pass under broiler until cheese is browned. Serves 8.

OIGNONS AU FOUR
BAKED ONIONS

Onions of one kind or another find their way into many recipes as the primary aromatic vegetable, supplemented by carrots, celery, and bell pepper. I, however, love to prepare them as a vegetable on their own as in this recipe. Large white or yellow onions are baked with simple seasonings that bring out their natural sweetness.

8 large onions, unpeeled   **Salt and pepper to taste**
4 tsp. butter   **2 tbsp. parsley, chopped**

Cut a small slice off bottom of onions so they will be stable. Cut a small slice off tops of onions. Make 4 small incisions in the top of onion. Place in a baking dish. Top each onion with ½-tsp. of butter.

Bake at 350 degrees for 30 to 45 minutes. Remove an outer skin layer from onions. Place on a serving platter. Salt and pepper to taste. Garnish with parsley. Serves 8.

PETITS OIGNONS GLACES AU MIEL
SMALL ONIONS GLAZED WITH HONEY

Small boiling onions are delicious accompaniments to grilled meats and chicken when they are glazed with sugar and honey and perfumed with springs of rosemary.

3 lb. small boiling   **Salt and pepper to taste**
** onions, peeled**   **1 sprig rosemary**
8 tbsp. butter   **Water to cover onions**
2 tbsp. powdered sugar   **2 tbsp. parsley, chopped**
2 tbsp. honey

Place the onions in a sauté pan with the butter, sugar, and honey. Add salt, pepper, and rosemary. Add water to barely cover. Slowly bring to a boil and simmer 25 minutes until the water evaporates.

Toss the onions to coat with the glaze in the pan and remove to a serving platter. Garnish with chopped parsley. Serves 8.

PAIN PERDU OIGNON ET FROMAGE
ONION AND CHEESE LOST BREAD CASSEROLE

Pain Perdu, or Lost Bread, is usually a breakfast food. It originated as a way to use stale bread, thus its name "lost." Here it is modified by adding onions and cheese to make a savory casserole. It is a wonderful accompaniment to meat or chicken dishes.

2 tbsp. butter, softened	**6 eggs**
8 slices whole wheat bread	**1½ cups cream**
4 tbsp. additional butter, softened	**1½ cups milk**
	1 tsp. dry mustard
¾ lb. Gruyère cheese, grated*	**Salt and pepper to taste**
2 medium onions, chopped	

Butter an 8-cup baking dish. Butter the bread with additional butter. Arrange a layer of bread in the baking dish. Sprinkle with some of the cheese and onions. Repeat layers of bread, cheese, and onions, ending with a layer of cheese.

Beat together eggs, cream, milk, mustard, salt, and pepper. Pour over bread layers. Allow to rest 10 minutes.

Bake at 400 degrees 30 minutes. The bread mixture should be browned and slightly puffed. Serves 8.

*Gruyère cheese is a rich semisoft cheese made from cow's milk in and around the village of Gruyère, Switzerland, on the Gruyère River. Mellow and nutty flavor, it is a preferred cheese in cooking. It melts and browns well, readily combines with other foods, and is the cheese most often used for onion soup or other dishes "au gratin." It is delicious eaten out of hand with fruit. Swiss cheese can be substituted, if necessary, although it lacks the richness of flavor that Gruyère has.

OIGNONS FARCIS A LA PROVENÇALE
STUFFED ONIONS PROVENÇAL STYLE

Although this recipe can be prepared successfully with various types of white or yellow onions, it is the mild and sweet red onion that we fill with a savory meat stuffing. This is an excellent accompaniment to baked chicken or turkey.

8 large red onions, peeled
2 tbsp. olive oil
½ lb. lean ground beef
½ lb. ham, chopped
2 cloves garlic
1 tsp. thyme
½ cup parsley, chopped

2 tbsp. fresh basil, chopped
(or 3 tsp. dried basil)
Salt and pepper to taste
½ cup breadcrumbs, plain
1 large egg, lightly beaten
1 tbsp. additional olive oil

Blanch the onions in salted water 8 minutes. Drain and refresh in cold water. Drain again. Cut ½-inch off the top of each onion and reserve. With a spoon or melon baller, scoop out the center of the onions, leaving a shell about ½-inch thick. Chop the scooped-out centers and set both aside.

Sauté the chopped onions in olive oil 2 minutes. Add the ground beef, chopped ham, garlic, thyme, parsley, basil, salt, and pepper. Sauté 10 minutes. Remove from heat. Incorporate the breadcrumbs and the egg. Fill the reserved onion shells with this mixture, place the reserved tops over the stuffing, and drizzle with additional olive oil. Place in a baking dish and bake at 350 degrees 40 minutes. Serves 8.

FLAN DE LEGUMES
MIXED VEGETABLE FLAN

A variety of aromatic and savory vegetables is precooked and combined with complementary herbs and spices, Gruyère cheese, eggs, and cream. After a 20-bake in a very hot oven, the concoction is transformed into a savory flan that complements seafood dishes very well.

½ lb. carrots, cut into rounds
4 medium onions, cut into
  rings
½ lb. leeks, cut into
  ½-inch slices
1 bulb fennel, cut into slices
½ lb. spinach, stems removed
  and leaves shredded
6 large eggs
4 tbsp. cream

½ tsp. thyme
1 tbsp. parsley, chopped
½ tsp. chervil
1 tsp. chives
Salt and pepper to taste
½ tsp. nutmeg
½ lb. Gruyère cheese,
  grated
1 tbsp. butter

Blanch carrots, onions, leeks, fennel, and spinach in a large pot of salted water for 30 minutes.

Blend together eggs, cream, thyme, parsley, chervil, chives, salt, pepper, and nutmeg. Add Gruyère cheese. Butter a baking dish. Drain vegetables and place in the baking dish. Pour the egg mixture over the vegetables. Bake at 400 degrees 20 minutes. Serves 6.

PECHES EPICS
SPICED PEACHES

Peaches, obviously, are not vegetables; however, I include this dish here because of its virtue as a side item. This recipe can be made with fresh peaches that have been peeled and heated in a simple syrup, but the canned peaches allow this dish to be served at any time of the year. Peaches, obviously, are not vegetables; however, I include this dish here because of its virtue as a side item. It is an excellent accompaniment to various pork dishes and is wonderful with baked chicken or turkey.

4 cups canned peach halves, strained, reserving syrup
Red-wine vinegar
1 cinnamon stick*

1 tsp. peppercorns
½ tsp. mace
½ tsp. allspice
Whole cloves

Measure reserved peach syrup and add half as much red-wine vinegar. Add cinnamon stick, peppercorns, mace, and allspice in a large saucepan. Bring syrup mixture to a boil, then reduce heat to simmer.

Insert 2 cloves into each peach half. Place peaches in simmering syrup. Gently poach peaches 5 minutes. Turn heat off and allow peaches to marinate in syrup for 1 hour. Reheat at serving time. Serves 8.

*Cinnamon, chiefly imported from Indonesia and South Vietnam, is harvested during the rainy season, when the bark of this evergreen tree is more manageable. The bark is peeled off into long quills that we call "stick cinnamon." It is then sold as sticks or is ground into a powder.

POIVRONS, ROUGE, JUANE, ET VERT BRAISE
BRAISED RED, YELLOW, AND GREEN BELL PEPPERS

This colorful, tasty, and easy-to-prepare dish goes extremely well with Grilled Skewered Scallops and Shrimp (in seafood chapter) and Rice Pilaf (in rice chapter). The three colors of the bell peppers and the red tomatoes are appealing to the eyes, and the combination of rosemary, thyme, and vinegar pleases the palate.

4 tbsp. olive oil
2 cloves garlic, chopped
6 bell peppers (red, yellow, and green), cut into 1-inch pieces
2 medium onions, quartered
6 plum tomatoes, quartered
Salt and pepper to taste

1 tbsp. fresh rosemary leaves (or 3 tsp. dried rosemary leaves)
1 tbsp. fresh thyme leaves (or 3 tsp. dried thyme leaves)
2 tbsp. red-wine vinegar

Sauté garlic and peppers in olive oil 5 minutes. Add onions and sauté 5 minutes. Gently add tomatoes and blend well. Add salt, pepper, rosemary, and thyme. Reduce heat and simmer 10 minutes.

Add red-wine vinegar and stir well. Serve hot or cold. Serves 8.

POMMES DE TERRE
AU FOUR A LA MOUTARDE
ROASTED MUSTARD POTATOES

This simple and straightforward potato side dish for various beef, veal, and pork recipes is given a special flavor with the Dijon mustard. It can be varied by standing the potato rounds on their edges rather than layering them. The top edges will become brown and crispy, while the rest of the potato stays moist and tender.

4 oz. butter, melted
3 tbsp. Dijon mustard
Salt and pepper to taste

2 lb. potatoes, peeled and
cut into rounds

Combine butter, mustard, salt, and pepper in a large bowl. Add potatoes and toss well. Arrange potato slices in a baking dish in layers. Bake at 350 degrees 30 minutes. Serve with chicken dishes. Serves 8.

GRATIN A LA PROVENÇALE
BAKED CASSEROLE OF POTATOES

This unique casserole combines potatoes, tomatoes, hard-boiled eggs, anchovy filets, and garlic in layers and bakes them with cream. The result is a flavorful baked-potato dish that complements both meat and seafood entrées.

3 lb. potatoes, peeled and
cut into rounds
1 tbsp. vinegar
2 tbsp. butter, melted
2 cloves garlic, chopped
2 lb. tomatoes, cut into slices
8 eggs, hard-boiled and sliced

1 can anchovy filets, cut
into pieces
Salt and pepper to taste
1 tbsp. parsley, chopped
1 tbsp. chives, chopped
2 cups cream
1 tbsp. parsley, chopped

Boil the potatoes with vinegar in water to cover until tender, about 20 minutes. Drain and cool to room temperature.

Combine butter and garlic in an oval baking dish. Arrange layers of potatoes, slices of tomatoes, and eggs, distributing the anchovies, salt, pepper, parsley, and chives between each layer. Pour cream over vegetables. Bake at 350 degrees for 35 minutes. Sprinkle with additional parsley. Serves 8.

POMMES DE TERRE BOULANGERE
BAKER'S STYLE POTATOES

This very old recipe originated at a time when every household in a village did not have ovens and cooking was done on an open hearth. The cook would prepare the dish and take it to the local bakery, which always had its oven going. Later in the day she would retrieve her dish and bring it home. This simple and delicious recipe can be varied by the use of garlic, crumbled bacon, leeks instead of onions, or the use of herbs such as thyme, rosemary, or sage.

10 medium potatoes, peeled and sliced ½-inch
2 medium onions, sliced
½ cup parsley, chopped

Salt and pepper to taste
8 tbsp. butter, cut into small cubes
1 cup boiling water or stock

Make a layer of potatoes, onions, parsley, salt, and pepper in a baking dish. Repeat a second layer. Dot with butter cubes. Pour boiling water or stock over ingredients. Bake at 400 degrees 30 to 40 minutes until brown and crusty and the water is absorbed. Serves 8.

PAILLASSONS AUX DEUX POMMES
DOORMATS OF TWO APPLES

Paillassons, the fanciful name for this recipe, seems to be derived from the appearance of the shredded potatoes and apples that when sautéed look like doormats. Regardless of what they look like, they are wonderful with fish and pork dishes. A little applesauce alongside makes a nice garnish.

4 cups red potatoes, peeled and grated

2 cups Granny Smith apples, peeled, seeded, and grated

2 cloves garlic, chopped

½ cup parsley, chopped

¼ tsp. nutmeg

Salt and pepper to taste

6 tbsp. peanut oil

Combine grated potatoes and apples. Place in a kitchen towel and squeeze dry. Transfer to a mixing bowl. Add garlic, parsley, nutmeg, salt, and pepper. Divide the mixture into 8 equal portions, shaping into ¾-inch-thick circles. Place into very hot peanut oil, pressing with a spatula. Sauté 7 to 8 minutes and turn on other side. Sauté another 7 to 8 minutes until golden. Transfer to a serving platter. Serves 8.

GATEAU DE POMMES
DE TERRE AU FROMAGE
POTATOES AND CHEESE CAKE

A happy combination of slices of potatoes, Swiss cheese, and onions is slowly cooked in butter to form a cakelike potato dish. When unmolded onto a serving platter and garnished with parsley and chives, it is a sight to behold. This is good with beef and pork recipes.

2 tbsp. butter
3 lb. potatoes, cut into
¼-inch slices
1 cup onions, chopped
Salt and pepper to taste

¾ lb. Baby Swiss cheese,
cut into thin slices
2 tbsp. additional butter
1 tsp. chopped parsley
or chives

Melt butter in a 10-inch nonstick skillet. Remove from the heat. Arrange half the potato slices on the bottom and around the sides in an overlapping fashion. Distribute onions over potatoes. Salt and pepper to taste. Make a layer of the cheese over the onions. Cover with the other half of the potatoes. Cover and cook on low heat for ½-hour.

Uncover and invert the potato cake onto a plate. Add additional butter to the skillet. Slide the cake back into the skillet. Cover and cook another half-hour. Invert the cake onto a serving platter. Garnish with chopped parsley or chives. Serves 8.

CROQUETTES AUX EPINARDS
SPINACH CROQUETTES

These croquettes of spinach are a good complement to chicken dishes. A mixture of spinach, puréed potatoes, onions, garlic, nutmeg, and Gruyère cheese is formed into patties that are then floured and sautéed in peanut oil until they develop a crusty exterior.

1 lb. spinach, stemmed
2 lb. potatoes, peeled
2 tbsp. peanut oil
2 medium onions, chopped
2 cloves garlic, chopped
½ tsp. nutmeg*

2 cups Gruyère cheese, grated
Salt and pepper
Flour for dusting
Peanut oil for deep-frying

Blanch spinach 1 minute. Drain, refresh, and squeeze out all excess moisture. Set aside.

Boil potatoes 20 minutes in salted water. Drain. Pass through a ricer. Set aside.

Sauté onions and garlic in peanut oil 3 minutes. Remove from the heat. Add spinach, mashed potatoes, nutmeg, Gruyère cheese, salt, pepper. Form the mixture into 16 balls and flatten each slightly. Pass the spinach balls in flour. Fry in hot oil 2 minutes until hot and browned. Serves 8.

*Nutmeg is the seed of a peachlike fruit of a tropical tree. The nutmeg is surrounded by a red membrane that is harvested as mace. With its sweet flavor and spicy undertones, it is used in many baked pastries and is excellent with vegetables, especially spinach. The flavor and fragrance are best when freshly ground, so I keep a grater and fresh whole nutmegs handy to add to a dish.

LES EPINARDS A LA VAPEUR
STEAMED SPINACH

The color and flavor of spinach are maintained by steaming the vegetable. The spinach is garnished with olive oil and lemon juice. Fast and straightforward, it serves very well with Trout Amandine.

3 lb. fresh spinach, cleaned
and stemmed
3 cloves garlic, peeled
and sliced

Salt and pepper to taste
3 tbsp. olive oil
2 tbsp. lemon juice

Place spinach in the top of a steamer. Scatter sliced garlic over spinach. Sprinkle with salt and pepper to taste. Place spinach over boiling water and cover. Steam 10 minutes. Remove spinach to a serving plate. Drizzle olive oil over spinach and garlic. Sprinkle lemon juice over serving plate. Serves 8.

EPINARDS AUX RAISINS SECS
SPINACH WITH RAISINS

In this Italian recipe, raisins add sweetness and pine nuts add crunchiness to spinach that is quickly sautéed in olive oil. The dish complements chicken and seafood dishes very well.

½ cup raisins
2 cloves garlic, chopped
½ cup pine nuts
²/₃ cup olive oil

Salt and pepper to taste
3 lb. fresh spinach,
stems removed

Sauté raisins, garlic, and pine nuts in olive oil 1 minute while tossing. Add salt and pepper. Add spinach, tossing in oil 2 or 3 minutes until warm. Transfer to a serving dish. Serves 8.

*Pine nuts are the edible seeds of certain types of pine trees that are imported from Italy and Spain.

MIRLITON FARCI
STUFFED VEGETABLE PEAR

This tropical vegetable probably found its way to New Orleans as early as the seventeenth century through Caribbean immigrants. In Spanish-speaking countries it is called *chayote,* in French-speaking areas it is known as *mirliton,* and in English we refer to it as a "vegetable pear." This vegetable, much loved in New Orleans and southwest Louisiana, has become more readily available in markets around the country, thanks to Frieda's Specialty Vegetable Company.

4 vegetable pears
1 large white onion, chopped
½ cup butter
8 green onions, chopped
2 cloves garlic, chopped
1 lb. crabmeat*

1 cup stale French bread, soaked in ⅓ cup water
2 eggs, lightly beaten
Salt and pepper to taste
½ cup seasoned breadcrumbs

Cut vegetable pears in half. Boil in salted water 20 minutes or until tender. Drain and allow to cool. Remove seed and scoop flesh out, leaving the shell about ¼-inch thick. Chop seed and flesh and set aside.

Sauté white onion in butter 4 minutes. Add green onions, garlic, crabmeat, and chopped vegetable pears. Add soaked French bread and combine well. Blend in beaten eggs. Salt and pepper to taste. Remove from heat.

Stuff vegetable-pear mixture into reserved shells. Sprinkle with breadcrumbs and bake at 350 degrees 5 minutes. Serves 8.

*A crabmeat stuffing in vegetable pears makes a very delicate taste that complements this mild vegetable. In Creole and Cajun homes it is frequently stuffed with boiled shrimp, chopped cooked sausage, chopped ham, or simply with herbs such as thyme or savory.

TOMATES-CERISES SAUTE AU BASILIC
SAUTE OF CHERRY TOMATOES WITH BASIL

This recipe is a delicious and very quick way to prepare a tasty vegetable for a meat, chicken, or seafood companion dish. To avoid overcooking the tomatoes, I combine all the ingredients except the oil and tomatoes in a small bowl ahead of time to be quickly added when I place the tomatoes into the oil.

6 tbsp. olive oil
**2 lb. cherry tomatoes, washed
 and thoroughly dried**
1 tsp. sugar
Salt and pepper to taste

**20 leaves fresh basil, chopped
 (or 1 tbsp. dried basil)**
1 tsp. dried thyme
½ cup parsley, chopped
2 cloves garlic, chopped

Heat olive oil in a large skillet until very hot. Add tomatoes and toss quickly. Add sugar, salt, pepper, basil, thyme, parsley, and garlic. Toss well 2 or 3 times and transfer to a serving platter. Do not overcook the tomatoes. Serves 8.

TOMATES FARCIES AU GRATIN
GRILLED STUFFED TOMATOES

A tasty filling of beef and pork spiced with basil and savory becomes the stuffing for scooped-out tomatoes. A little mozzarella cheese added to the tops becomes browned when run under the broiler.

1 medium onion, chopped
2 cloves garlic, chopped
1 tbsp. olive oil
½ lb. ground beef
½ lb. ground pork
Salt and pepper to taste
½ cup breadcrumbs
2 tbsp. parsley, chopped

2 tbsp. fresh basil (or
  1 tsp. dried basil)
2 tsp. savory*
2 large eggs, lightly beaten
4 large tomatoes, cut in
  half and flesh scooped out
½ lb. mozzarella cheese,
  cut into small cubes

Sauté onion and garlic in olive oil until soft. Add beef and pork and brown. Salt and pepper to taste. Incorporate breadcrumbs, parsley, basil, and savory. Blend in eggs, mixing well.

Fill tomato halves with this stuffing. Place 6 or 7 cubes of mozzarella on each tomato. Transfer to a buttered baking dish. Bake at 350 degrees 20 minutes. Pass under the broiler 2 minutes. Serves 8.

*Savory, of Mediterranean origin, was introduced into England by the Romans and is especially popular in Germany. Savory's flavor, a cross between thyme and mint with a touch of pepper, is used to flavor green or dried beans, other vegetables, and meat dressings. It also is one of the primary ingredients in poultry seasoning.

TOMATE SECHE AU FOUR
OVEN-DRIED TOMATOES

The flavor of Italian plum tomatoes is concentrated by a slow drying process that removes most of the moisture from the tomatoes so they can absorb the olive oil. Although dry, they are still pliable and take on the flavor of the sugar and thyme.

8 medium plum tomatoes   **1 tsp. thyme**
1 tsp. salt   **1 tbsp. olive oil**
1 tsp. sugar

Remove the stem end from tomatoes. Cut in half lengthwise. Arrange the cut side up on an open rack. Combine salt, sugar, and thyme. Sprinkle over tomatoes. Drizzle olive oil over tomatoes. Place rack in the oven. Bake at 250 degrees 4 hours. Serve as a garnish for veal, lamb, or fish. Serves 8.

GRATIN DE NAVETS
AUX HERBES DE PROVENCE
GRILLED TURNIPS WITH HERBS OF PROVENCE

This very old vegetable, which traces its ancestry to times before the Roman civilization, is unfortunately not as popular in the United States as it is in Europe, especially France. This recipe from the south of France layers steamed turnip slices with a cheese sauce flavored with classic Herbes de Provence to make a truly memorable dish.

3 lb. turnips, peeled and cut into ½-inch slices
6 tbsp. butter
½ cup flour
3 cups milk

Salt and pepper to taste
1 tbsp. Herbes de Provence
¾ lb. Gruyère cheese, grated

Steam the turnips 15 minutes until tender. Set aside.

Dissolve flour in butter and cook 2 minutes while stirring. Gradually add the milk and bring to a boil. Add salt, pepper, and ½ the Herbes de Provence. Turn the heat off and add ¾ the cheese while stirring.

Place a layer of steamed turnips in the bottom of a buttered baking dish. Coat with some of the sauce. Repeat the layering of turnips and sauce. Sprinkle the remaining cheese and the Herbes de Provence over the last layer. Place under the broiler for 1 minute until top is brown. Serves 8.

PETITES TIMBALES DE COURGETTES AUX CREVETTES
SMALL ZUCCHINI MOLDS WITH SHRIMP

This very elegant preparation of zucchini and shrimp combines taste and appearance in a side dish. Easier to make than it looks, it can be prepared ahead up to the point of baking, making it simple to serve at a dinner party.

8 small zucchini	1 tbsp. chervil, choped
3 tbsp. butter, softened	(or 1½ tsp. dried chervil)*
Salt and pepper to taste	1½ cups tomato purée
1 lb. headless shrimp,	¾ cup additional cream
boiled and shelled	2 tsp. instant seafood-
¾ cup cream	stock granules
3 large eggs	Salt and pepper to taste

Using a stripper, make grooves in the zucchini lengthwise every ½-inch. Slice crosswise into ½-inch slices. Blanch in salted water for 2 minutes. Drain and refresh in cold water. Dry on paper towels.

Butter 8 ramekins. Cover the bottom of each with slices of zucchini. Arrange additional slices overlapping around the sides. Purée remaining zucchini. Salt and pepper to taste. Dry out in a skillet over medium heat about 3 to 4 minutes.

Reserve 8 large shrimp. Purée the remaining shrimp. Blend together the puréed shrimp and zucchini with cream, eggs, and chervil. Fill the ramekins with the shrimp mixture. Bake in a 400-degree oven in a bain-marie 20 minutes.

Heat together the tomato purée, additional cream, and seafood granules. Boil for 2 minutes. Salt and pepper to taste.

Unmold the ramekins on a serving plate. Place 1 of the reserved shrimp on top of each. Surround with tomato/cream sauce. Serve extra sauce on the side. Serves 8.

*Chervil, believed to a native of southern Russia, made its way to the Mediterranean 300 years before Christ and was brought to England by the Romans. Very popular in France, it is used in cold dishes, soups, salads, and in combination with other green herbs.

COURGETTES A LA MENTHE
MINTED ZUCCHINI

For a colorful and flavorful vegetable dish, try this recipe. The flavors of green-white zucchini, dark green peas, and golden corn are enhanced by the flavors of mint, chives, and butter. This is good with fish and pork dishes.

2 lb. zucchini, sliced
Salt to taste
2 cups frozen green peas
2 cups canned corn kernels

4 sprigs mint
4 tbsp. butter
4 tsp. chives, chopped

Place zucchini in boiling salted water. Add peas, corn, and mint sprigs. Cover and simmer 5 minutes. Drain. Remove mint sprigs and discard. Return vegetables to pot. Add butter and chives, mixing well. Heat on low heat 1 minute. Transfer to a serving plate. Serves 8.

Rice and Pasta

RICE

This ubiquitous grain has a long and prestigious history. Archaeological evidence indicating that rice was cultivated as far back as 2800 B.C. has been found in China, Greece, Persia, and Egypt. Rice migrated to the United States with the early colonization of the Carolinas. In the early eighteenth century it moved into French Louisiana from the Caribbean, where it had accompanied the Spanish in their conquest of Latin and South America. The United States' westward expansion after the Louisiana Purchase, the discovery of gold in California, and the immigration of a large Chinese population to build the railroads—all of these historical events helped spread rice throughout the country. By the turn of the twentieth century, rice was a cash crop on Arkansas, Louisiana, Mississippi, Missouri, Texas, and California.

Although thousands of varieties of rice are grown worldwide, three types are dominant in the United States: long grain, medium grain, and short grain. Long-grain rice is 4 to 5 times as long as it is wide. The grains tend to remain separate and are light and fluffy when cooked. This is the most common form of rice used in general cooking. Medium-grain rice is plump but not round. When cooked, the grains are moister and tenderer than long-grain rice. Short-grain rice is almost round and tends to cling together when cooked.

The white rice we most commonly use is the result of milling, which removes the hulls and bran layers to expose the starchy endosperm. Milled rice whose bran layers are left on is sold as brown rice. Its natural tan color results from the bran layers still on the grain. Cooked brown rice, which has a nutty flavor and a slightly chewy texture, takes longer to cook.

A rule of thumb in cooking white rice is that 1 cup of rice will absorb 2 cups liquid to produce 3 cups of cooked rice. White rice takes about 18 to 20 minutes to cook. The Creole method is to place rice in a large quantity of boiling salted water and simmer 18 minutes. After being drained and washed in hot water, the rice is reheated by steaming over boiling water. Another method of cooking rice is to add 1 cup of rice to 2 cups of liquid. Cover and simmer 18 minutes, then remove from the heat and allow to rest 5 minutes. Fluffed with a fork, the rice is ready to serve. To cook brown rice, use 2 to 2½ cups of liquid for each cup of rice and simmer 45 to 50 minutes to make 3½ to 4 cups. I find rice so easy to cook that I do not use the precooked brands that are available. They are much more expensive and take the same amount of time to prepare.

In the Creole home where I was reared, rice was served at almost every meal. In addition to Red Beans and Rice, Jambalaya, Beef or Veal Stew served with rice, Mother would prepare a rice dessert as well: Rice Pudding. Sometimes we simply ate boiled rice with a generous amount of butter to add some starch to a meal.

I present here a few rice dishes that go well with many of the recipes in this book, as well as some rice dishes that take center stage, such as Chinese Fried Rice and Italian Risotto.

PASTA

Although we have been told that Marco Polo brought pasta from China back to Italy, there is evidence that the Italians were making pasta of various kinds long before Marco Polo was born. Pasta probably originated in China and found its way to Italy through the Arabic countries that traded with Rome and Venice. Catherine de' Medici from Florence, who traveled to France to marry the future King of France, Henri II, and later Marie de' Medici, who became the queen of King Henri IV, brought along expert cooks who delivered to France a sophisticated cuisine that included pasta. From France it spread through the world.

Today pasta has become one of the most popular foods in the United States, and in this chapter I present some of my favorite recipes gathered from studies with Guiliano Bugialli in Florence and Marcella Hazen in Venice, as well as those gathered during a long association with the late Signora Teresa Turci, owner and chef of Turci's Italian Restaurant in New Orleans. From these sources I have collected some great recipes as well as an understanding of pasta cooking.

As Marcella Hazen indicates in her excellent book *The Classic Italian Cookbook*, there is no single cooking process simpler than the boiling of pasta. She instructs us to boil pasta in an abundant quantity of water (4 quarts to 1 lb.), adding 1½ teaspoons of salt when the water reaches the boiling point. Add the pasta all at once, forcing it into the boiling water with a wooden spoon and stirring well to distribute the pasta. Cover the pot to bring to a boil rapidly, then remove cover and keep water at a lively boil. When pasta is al dente, or firm to the bite (the timing of which depends upon the type of pasta being cooked), drain immediately into a colander, shaking vigorously to remove as much water as possible. Transfer to a warm serving bowl. Sauce and serve immediately.

Pasta shapes and sizes come in two basic styles: rolled and extruded. Rolled pastas run the gamut in sizes: full sheets for *manicotti* (muffs) and *ravioli* (small stuffed squares); 2 inches wide for *lasagne;* 1 inch wide for *pappardelle* (broad noodles) and *farfalle* (butterflies); ½-inch wide for *tagliatelle;* ¼-inch wide for *fettucini* (little ribbons); ⅛-inch wide for *linguini* (little tongues); and very, very thin for *capelli d'angelo* (angel hair). Extruded pastas are long and hollow, as in *macaroni* (the basic tubular pasta); long and round, as in *spaghetti* (a length of string); short and hollow, as in *mostaccioli* (small mustaches) and *penne* (quill pens); and come in shapes, such as *conchiglie* (shells), *cresto di galli* (cockscombs), and *pastina* (or "little pasta," tiny shapes used for soups). The choice of size and shape is usually governed by the sauces and other ingredients in the recipe. For example, Baked Lasagne calls for flat pasta for layering; Penne al Limone uses the tubular nature of penne to hold more sauce; Spaghetti a la Ratatouille mixes spaghetti with tomato sauce; and Fettuccine with Shrimp and Lemon Sauce uses fettuccine (or thin spaghetti) for its seafood.

The recipes in this chapter are a few of my favorites; some have been presented on my televisions shows, and some have not. My two favorites are the Penne al Limone and the Spaghetti alla Teresa Turci. I hope you will enjoy them all.

RIZ CREOLE
CREOLE BOILED RICE

There are many ways to cook rice, and every cook seems to have a preferred method. This method, so typical of New Orleans, adds long-grain rice to a large quantity of boiling salted water. Simmer 18 minutes, covered. Wash the rice in hot water and then lightly steam it. This method produces a rice that is not sticky and is free grain for grain.

2 qt. water	**1 cup long-grain rice**
1 tsp. salt	

Bring water and salt to a boil. Add rice, stirring well, and return to the boil. Stir rice a second time. Reduce heat to simmer. Cover and simmer 18 minutes.

Drain into a colander. Refresh rice in hot water. Drain well. Place the colander over a small amount of water in a saucepan. Steam lightly. Serves 4.

PILAF DE RIZ
RICE PILAF

This basic recipe for pilaf can be varied with the addition of other ingredients and spices such as raisins, green onions, pine nuts, almonds, thyme, rosemary, cardamon, etc. Pilaf is a natural accompaniment to lamb, chicken, and fish.

1 cup onion, chopped	**2 cups rice**
1 clove garlic, chopped	**4 cups chicken stock***
2 tbsp. butter	**Salt and pepper to taste**
2 tbsp. parsley, chopped	

Sauté onion and garlic in butter 2 minutes. Add parsley and rice. Sauté until rice becomes slightly browned. Add chicken stock. Salt and pepper to taste. Bring to a boil, cover, and lower heat to simmer. Simmer 18 to 20 minutes until stock is absorbed. Fluff with a fork and serve. Serves 8.

*Because rice absorbs twice its volume of liquid, 1 cup of rice will absorb 2 cups of liquid to produce 3 cups of cooked rice.

RIZ D'OR
GOLDEN RICE

This flavorful and colorful rice recipe is a wonderful side dish for all kinds of seafood dishes, especially Dilled Shrimp Margaret in the seafood chapter.

6 cups chicken stock   **2 tsp. turmeric***
Salt and white pepper to taste   **2 cups rice**

Bring chicken stock, salt, and pepper to a boil. Add turmeric and blend well. Add rice and stir until all grains are floating freely. Return to a boil. Reduce heat to a simmer. Simmer 18 minutes until rice is tender.

Drain in a colander. Rinse lightly with hot water. Transfer to a serving dish. Makes 8 servings.

*Because of its brilliant color, turmeric is used in many preparations (such as mustard, curry powder, and pickles) and is a less expensive substitute for saffron. This native of Asia is the root of a lilylike plant of the ginger family and is grown wherever ginger thrives. Besides its culinary function, it was used in ancient times as a cosmetic, a dye, and a charm against evil spirits.

PILAF DE FOIES DE VOLAILLE
CHICKEN-LIVER PILAF

Because I generally buy whole chickens and cut them into the parts I need for a recipe, I have bonus pieces such as the wings, backs, necks, gizzards, and livers. I use these parts to make stock, excepting the livers, which I freeze until I have enough to make this dish. Sautéed with mushrooms, they become the primary flavors for this rice pilaf.

¼ lb. bacon, cut into
  small pieces
4 tbsp. butter
3 cloves garlic, chopped
1 lb. chicken livers, cut
  into small pieces
½ lb. mushrooms, chopped

1½ cups white wine
1 bouquet garni
1½ cups rice
Salt and pepper to taste
1½ cups chicken stock
4 tbsp. cream
3 tbsp. parsley, chopped

Sauté bacon in sauté pan 3 minutes. Add butter and garlic. Add livers and sauté 5 minutes, turning from time to time. Add mushrooms, wine, bouquet garni, rice, salt, and pepper. Add chicken stock and bring to a boil. Cover and simmer 12 minutes.

Remove cover, raise heat, and stir until rice has absorbed all the liquids. Remove bouquet garni. Add cream and parsley and blend well. Serve as soon as possible. Serves 8.

GRATIN DE RIZ
BAKED RICE CASSEROLE

This unusual rice dish covers a pilaf of a ham, green peas, and saffron-seasoned rice with an egg custard, slices of tomato, and cheese. The custard cooks with the rice, and the tomato and cheese browns to create a special topping. This casserole goes well with seafood dishes as well as roast meats.

2 tbsp. butter	2 eggs
1 medium onion, chopped	2/3 cup cream
1½ cups rice	Salt and pepper to taste
½ tsp. saffron*	3 tomatoes, sliced in
4 cups chicken stock	rounds
½ lb. ham, diced	3 additional slices
2 cups green peas	Gruyère cheese
8 slices Gruyère cheese, chopped	

Sauté onion in butter until transparent. Add rice and sauté 2 minutes. Sprinkle with saffron, blending well. Add chicken stock. Cover and simmer 10 minutes. Add ham and green peas. Simmer 10 minutes.

When all the liquid has been absorbed, make a layer of rice and cheese in a buttered baking dish. Blend together eggs, cream, salt, and pepper. Pour over rice. Place tomato slices over rice and cream. Cover with 3 additional slices of cheese. Bake at 350 degrees 20 minutes. Serves 8.

*Saffron, the flavorful red stigma of the fall-flowering crocus, imparts a beautiful golden color and rich taste to the dish it serves. The stigma of 70,000 crocuses must be harvested by hand to produce 1 pound. Thus, it is probably the most expensive spice in the world.

RIZ AU FINES HERBES
HERB-SEASONED RICE

This straightforward recipe for seasoned rice can accompany almost any meat or fowl recipe.

4 cups chicken stock
Salt and pepper to taste
2 cups rice
½ tsp. thyme

1 bouquet garni of *fines herbes**
⅓ cup parsley, chopped

Bring chicken stock, salt, and pepper to a boil. Add rice, thyme, and bouquet garni. Reduce heat to simmer. Cover and simmer 18 minutes until all the stock is absorbed. Remove from the heat, uncover, and remove the bouquet garni. Fluff rice with a fork. Add parsley and toss well with the rice. Serves 8.

*Fines herbes is a classical garnish in French cookery usually made from chervil, parsley, chives, and tarragon. These are sometimes combined with shallots and garlic and used as an ingredient for chicken, fish, or egg dishes.

RIZ AU CITRON
LEMON RICE

Dry French vermouth and lemon zest give this pilaf-type rice dish a nice zip for serving with all kinds of seafood dishes.

2 tbsp. butter
1¼ cups rice
¼ cup dry vermouth
1¼ cups chicken broth

¾ tsp. salt
White pepper
Zest of 1 lemon, grated
2 tbsp. parsley, chopped

Melt butter in a skillet or saucepan. Add rice and sauté 1 minute. Add vermouth, broth, salt, and pepper. Bring to a boil, reduce heat to a simmer, and cover. Cook 18 minutes. Add lemon zest and parsley, tossing well. Serves 8.

RIZ AUX AMANDE
ALMOND RICE

Turmeric, the spice that gives mustard its bright yellow color, is one of the main ingredients in curry powder. It imparts to this rice dish a wonderful flavor and a bright yellow color. The almonds add a second dimension to the rice. Great with broiled, poached, and fried fish.

4 tbsp. butter
½ tsp. turmeric*
2 cups rice
Salt and pepper to taste

4 cups chicken stock
1 cup slivered almonds, toasted

Melt butter in a stockpot. Add turmeric and blend well. Add rice and stir for 1 minute. Add salt, pepper, and chicken stock, stirring well. Reduce heat to low. Cover and simmer 20 minutes until rice has absorbed all the liquid. Remove from heat. Incorporate almonds while fluffing rice with a fork. Serves 8.

*Turmeric, the root of a lilylike plant of the ginger family and a native of Asia, is now grown in the Caribbean. A very versatile herb, it is used in this recipe to impart both a mild mustard taste and a yellow color. Besides being used in the preparation of many mustards and relishes, it is almost always a primary ingredient in curry powder. It is sometimes called "the poor man's saffron" because of the bright yellow color it bestows.

PAELLA VALENCIANA
SPANISH SAFFRON RICE

Paella is probably Spain's national dish. When I was fortunate enough to visit Madrid, I learned many varieties of the dish, but this classical version is by far my favorite. It is great fun to make a very large Paella and serve in the center of the table, allowing each person to choose those items he or she prefers along with the saffron rice.

3 lb. chicken parts, cut into
    2-inch pieces
½ cup olive oil
¼ lb. ham, diced
¼ lb. chorizo sausage
    (or other spicy sausage)*
1 cup onions, chopped
3 cloves garlic, chopped
2 cups shellfish (mussels,
    clams, oysters, crawfish,
    and/or shrimp)
2 lobster tails and claws,
    cut into 2-inch pieces
    (optional)

3 cups short-grain rice
    (Spanish, Italian,
    or Japanese)
6 cups chicken stock
½ tsp. saffron threads
1 cup green peas
2 bay leaves
Salt and pepper to taste
Lemon wedges
½ cup parsley, chopped

In a 15-inch pan or a very large skillet, brown chicken in olive oil. Remove and set aside.

Add ham, sausage, onions, and garlic to pan and sauté 3 minutes. Add shellfish and lobster and cook 3 minutes. Add rice and coat well with pan drippings 1 minute. Add chicken stock and saffron. Bring to a boil. Add green peas, bay leaves, salt, and pepper. Return chicken to the pan. Place in a 350-degree oven for 20 minutes.

Remove from the oven and cover with foil. Let rest 10 minutes. Remove foil and garnish with lemon slices and parsley. Serves 8.

*Chorizo, the best-known sausage of Spain, is highly seasoned with paprika and garlic and can be found in specialty food stores. However, any spicy sausage can be used in this recipe.

RISOTTO
ITALIAN RICE

Risotto, rice cooked with a broth in the Italian manner, should be tender and creamy, while the individual grains of rice should be distinct. It is best cooked very slowly in a little broth until the broth is absorbed; then add more broth. Although Risotto can be combined with many different ingredients such as mushrooms, seafoods, or asparagus, it is best seasoned with onions, butter, saffron, and Parmesan cheese. Risotto is an Italian comfort food.

1 cup onions, chopped	¼ tsp. saffron threads
4 tbsp. butter	1 tbsp. warm water
1½ cups Italian Arborio rice*	½ cup Parmesan cheese
3 cups chicken stock	2 tbsp. additional butter
Salt and white pepper	

Sauté onions in butter 3 minutes. Add the rice and let it absorb the butter. Add the chicken stock, a little at a time, allowing rice to absorb the stock before adding more. Add salt and pepper to taste. Dissolve saffron threads in water and add to mixture.

When rice has absorbed all the stock, add Parmesan cheese and blend well. Enrich the rice with the additional butter. Rice should be a little creamy. Serves 8.

*Italian Arborio rice is thicker and shorter than American long-grain rice. It takes a little longer to cook but gives the dish its creamy consistency. Arborio rice is available in specialty food stores or in many supermarkets. Japanese short-grain rice or California pearl rice can be substituted. Long-grain rice also can be used, but the dish will not be as creamy as a true Risotto should be.

PILAF A L'ARMENIENNE
ARMENIAN PILAF

This unique recipe combines sautéed fine egg noodles with rice and a variety of flavors we associate with Middle Eastern cooking: basil, mint, and almonds. This pilaf is especially good with lamb dishes.

½ cup fine egg noodles
6 tbsp. butter
2 tbsp. olive oil
4 cups beef or chicken stock
Salt and pepper to taste
½ cup pimento, chopped
1 tbsp. fresh basil leaves, chopped (or 1½ tsp. dried basil leaves)

1 tbsp. fresh mint leaves, chopped (or 1½ tsp. dried mint leaves)
2 cups rice
⅓ cup slivered almonds, toasted
½ cup parsley, chopped

Brown egg noodles in butter and olive oil. Set aside.

Bring the beef or chicken stock to a boil with the salt, pepper, pimento, basil, and mint. Add the rice, almonds, and reserved noodles. Cover and simmer 25 minutes.

Transfer rice mixture into an ovenproof casserole. Cover, leaving the lid slightly ajar. Bake at 350 degrees for 20 minutes. Garnish with chopped parsley. Serves 8.

RIZ SALE A L'ACADIENNE
CAJUN DIRTY RICE

Although the word "dirty" leaves a negative connotation, the richness of flavor given to the dish by the chopped chicken livers and gizzards makes it one of the most popular dishes in Cajun cuisine.

1½ cups rice
1 tbsp. salt
½ lb. chicken livers, chopped
½ lb. chicken gizzards,
   cleaned and chopped
2 tbsp. butter
1 tbsp. peanut oil

1 cup onions, chopped
6 green onions, chopped
2 cloves garlic, chopped
⅓ cup parsley, chopped
2 cups mushrooms,
chopped
Salt and pepper to taste

Boil rice in salted water 18 minutes. Drain and refresh in cold water. Set aside to cool.

Sauté chicken livers and gizzards in butter and peanut oil until browned. Add onions, green onions, garlic, parsley, and mushrooms. Salt and pepper to taste. Cook until all ingredients are tender (10 minutes). Bend in the rice. Continue cooking until rice is hot. Serves 8.

JAMBALAYA A LA CREOLE
CREOLE JAMBALAYA

Jambalaya has become a signature dish in both Creole and Cajun cooking. The dish certainly has its roots in Spain's Paella rice dish, a by-product of the long Spanish domination of Louisiana. The Creole version is usually made with more delicate ingredients such as shrimp and ham—but not exclusively. The Cajun version (recipe follows) is heartier, and its method of cooking differs. The Creole style usually uses leftover cooked rice, and like its Cajun cousin it contains aromatic vegetables, tomatoes, and seasoning.

2 cups onions, chopped
2 cloves garlic, chopped
2 tbsp. butter
1 cup celery, chopped
½ cup green bell pepper, chopped
⅓ cup parsley, chopped
3 whole cloves*
¼ tsp. cayenne pepper

Salt and pepper to taste
1 cup tomatoes, chopped
3 tbsp. tomato paste
1 lb. ham diced
2 lb. boiled shrimp (see Shrimp Remoulade in hors d'oeuvres chapter)
3 cups cooked rice (recipe above in this chapter)

Sauté onions and garlic in butter until onions brown and caramelize. Add celery, green peppers, parsley, cloves, cayenne pepper, black pepper, and salt. Add tomatoes and tomato paste. Incorporate ham and cook 5 minutes. Blend in shrimp and cook another 5 minutes. Fold in cooked rice and toss until heated. Serves 8.

*Cloves are the pink flower buds of a tropical plant that are picked before opening and dried in the sun, where they turn a reddish brown. Used mostly in baking or pickling, cloves are frequently used when a sweet, subtle taste is desired, such as this recipe requires.

JAMBALAYA A L'ACADIENNE
CAJUN JAMBALAYA

As you will notice, Cajun Jambalaya is a heartier version of Creole Jambalaya. While this version is limited to smoked sausage, ham, and chicken, the Cajuns use any number of ingredients, such as duck and game found in the bayous. The cooking of raw rice along with the aromatic vegetables, tomatoes, and a variety of spices is a variation from the Creole style. Whichever style you choose, it will be a good one.

1 lb. smoked sausage, cut into ½-inch pieces
½ lb. ham, diced
4 tbsp. butter
4 tbsp. flour
2 cups onions, chopped
4 cloves garlic, chopped
6 green onions, chopped
1 cup celery, chopped
1 cup green pepper, chopped
2 cups tomatoes, chopped
2 tbsp. tomato paste
1 bay leaf
½ tsp. ground thyme
⅛ tsp. cumin powder
⅛ tsp. ground cloves
⅛ tsp. allspice
⅛ tsp. cayenne pepper
¼ tsp. black pepper
2 cups raw rice
¼ cup parsley, chopped
3 cups beef stock
Salt and pepper to taste
1 cup cooked chicken, chopped

Sauté sausage and ham in butter in a large pot. Remove and set aside.

Blend flour into the drippings and make a light brown roux. Add onions, garlic, green onions, celery, green peppers, tomatoes, and tomato paste. Incorporate bay leaf, thyme, cumin, cloves, allspice, cayenne, and black pepper. Stir in the raw rice and parsley. Add the beef broth and salt to taste. Return sausage and ham along with the chicken to the mixture. Bring to a boil, then lower heat to a simmer. Cover and cook 20 minutes until liquid is absorbed. Serves 8.

RIZ FRIT CHINOISE
CHINESE FRIED RICE

This recipe is one of my favorites from Chinese cuisine. A melange of crispy vegetables is stir-fried with shrimp before combining with precooked rice for a dish that delights both the eye and the taste buds.

2 eggs, beaten
2 tsp. peanut oil
2 tbsp. additional peanut oil
6 green onions, sliced
1 lb. mushrooms, sliced
1 small green bell
  pepper, diced
1 cup celery

$^3/_4$ cup water chestnuts,
  sliced
1 cup bean sprouts
2 cups small boiled shrimp,
  cut in half*
3 tbsp. soy sauce
Salt and pepper to taste
3 cups cooked rice

In a 9-inch skillet, cook the eggs in peanut oil to make a large egg crêpe. Remove to paper towels. Fold egg crêpe over on itself several times. Cut the rolled egg into thin shreds. Set aside.

Pour additional oil into a hot wok and allow to heat very hot. Add and stir-fry, 1 at a time, the green onions, mushrooms, green pepper, celery, water chestnuts, bean sprouts, shrimp, and reserved shredded eggs. Toss ingredients 30 seconds. Add soy sauce, salt, and pepper to taste. Add cooked rice and blend well until hot. Transfer to a serving dish. Serves 8.

*Diced ham or cooked pork can be substituted for the shrimp.

PENNE ALLA BESCIAMELLA
TUBULAR PASTA IN BECHAMEL SAUCE

A flavorful side dish of pasta to accompany Veal Scallopini al Marsala or grilled chicken breasts. The béchamel sauce flavored with Italian ham and cheese fills the tubes of pasta for a lively taste.

1 lb. penne pasta
3 tbsp. butter
1 lb. prosciutto, thinly sliced
3 tbsp. additional butter
2 tbsp. flour

2 cups milk
¼ cup Parmesan cheese
Salt and pepper to taste
3 tbsp. additional
  Parmesan

Cook pasta in boiling salted water until al dente. Drain, combine with half the butter, and set aside.

Sauté prosciutto in additional butter. Blend in flour. Whisk in milk until thickened. Blend in Parmesan cheese. Salt and pepper to taste.

Butter a baking dish. Turn pasta into the dish. Pour sauce over top. Sprinkle with additional Parmesan. Bake in a 350-degree oven until cheese browns, about 10 minutes. Serves 8.

PENNE POMODORO
TUBULAR PASTA WITH TOMATOES

This savory pasta dish creates a light sauce from olive oil, garlic, and the juices that exude from the tomatoes seasoned with red pepper and basil. Refreshing and quick to make, this pasta can accompany both chicken and seafood dishes.

1 lb. penne or rigatoni pasta
4 tbsp. olive oil
4 cloves garlic, crushed
12 plum tomatoes, peeled,
  seeded, and cut into slivers

Salt and pepper to taste
½ tsp. red-pepper flakes
Fresh basil leaves, cut into
  shreds
¼ cup Parmesan cheese

Boil pasta in salted water 12 to 15 minutes until al dente. Sauté garlic in olive oil about 1 minute. Add tomato slivers and sauté 5 minutes. Add salt, pepper, and red pepper, blending well. Drain pasta and combine with the tomato sauce. Add basil. Simmer 5 minutes. Serve with Parmesan cheese on the side. Serves 8.

PATES AU VINAIGRE BALSAMIC
PASTA WITH BALSAMIC VINEGAR

Aged balsamic vinegar has a unique woodsy taste that marries well with tomatoes, garlic, and fresh herbs for a different and refreshing way to serve pasta. This dish is an excellent companion to lamb or chicken.

1 lb. pasta
Salt
2 tbsp. olive oil
12 cloves garlic, cut into
   large chunks
3 tbsp. additional olive oil
1 cup fresh basil, roughly
   chopped
⅓ cup fresh mint,
   roughly chopped

¼ cup fresh oregano,
   roughly chopped*
Salt and pepper to taste
4 cups tomatoes, seeded
   and roughly chopped
1 tbsp. balsamic vinegar
¼ cup Parmesan
   cheese, grated

Boil pasta in salted water until al dente. Drain. Drizzle with olive oil, toss well, and set aside.

Sauté garlic on low heat in additional olive oil. Add basil, mint, and oregano. Salt and pepper to taste. Toss 30 seconds. Blend in pasta and toss well. Incorporate tomatoes and toss well. Heat 1 minute. Add balsamic vinegar. Garnish with Parmesan cheese. Serves 8.

*A perennial of the mint family, oregano is native to the hillsides of the Mediterranean whose name in Greek means "the joy of the mountains." It crossed the Atlantic with the discovery of America and took hold in Mexico. It is probably best known as the primary herb in pizza, but it is used widely in tomato sauces, eggplant dishes, and in stuffings for fish and fowl.

PENNE AL LIMONE
PASTA WITH LEMON CREAM SAUCE

In the summer of 1985 I had the unique experience of studying Italian cooking in Florence, Italy, with Juliano Bugialli. One of the memorable dishes I learned was this tubular pasta, called *penne,* served with an incredible sauce of butter, lemon, and cream. I have since incorporated it into my repertoire and taught it in many cooking classes. This dish serves very well with veal.

1 lb. penne pasta	¼ tsp. nutmeg
6 oz. butter	½ cup Parmesan cheese,
2 cups cream	grated
Zest of 2 lemons, grated	2 tbsp. parsley leaves,
Salt and white pepper	chopped

Boil penne in salted water until al dente. Melt butter in a large skillet. Drain pasta and add to the butter in the skillet. Toss to coat pasta. Add cream, zest, salt, pepper, and nutmeg. Blend well and reduce sauce for 2 minutes. Place pasta on a serving dish and sprinkle with Parmesan. Toss well to distribute cheese and sauce. Garnish with parsley. Serves 8.

GNOCCHI DI PATATE
POTATO GNOCCHI

Potato gnocchi is one of the most interesting of Italian recipes. Although they are primarily made with puréed potatoes, gnocchi are classed and treated as pasta. These light and flavorful dumplings are versatile. The basic recipe for making and serving gnocchi that I present here is simply sauced, but they allow for a variety of sauces, both tomato and cream. I particularly love gnocchi with a cream and Gorgonzola cheese sauce.

2 lb. potatoes, white boiling or baking (do not use new potatoes)
1 cup flour

1 tsp. salt
4 oz. butter, melted
½ cup Parmesan cheese, grated

Microwave the potatoes* until done. Remove skins and, using a ricer, purée into a large bowl. Add most of the flour and salt to form a dough and knead until smooth. Add remaining flour if needed. Divide dough into 8 pieces. Roll each piece into ³/₄-inch cylinders. Cut cylinders into ³/₄-inch lengths. Roll each gnocchi on a grater or against the tines of a fork to make ridges.

Drop gnocchi into a large pot of boiling salted water. When gnocchi rise to the surface, remove with a skimmer and drain. Place on a serving platter. Pour hot melted butter over gnocchi and sprinkle with Parmesan cheese. Toss well. Serves 8.

*Most recipes for gnocchi instruct the cook to boil potatoes until done; however, in this recipe we recommend microwaving potatoes instead. The reason is twofold: first, the potatoes cook more quickly, and secondly, they do not absorb water.

SPAGHETTI A LA RATATOUILLE
SPAGHETTI WITH MEDITERRANEAN VEGETABLES

This recipe, from the Côte d'Azur, combines the classic French recipe for Provencal vegetables and Italian pasta for a happy marriage. All the colors and flavors from the south of France become a refreshing garnish for a boiled pasta that pleases both the eye and mouth.

2 medium eggplants, peeled and cut into bite-size pieces
3 tsp. salt
3 tbsp. olive oil
2 clove garlic, chopped
1 red bell pepper, cut into strips
1 green bell pepper, cut into strips
2 medium zucchini, cut into large dice
4 medium tomatoes, cut into large dice
1 large onion, cut in half and sliced
⅓ tsp. thyme
3 tbsp. parsley, chopped
Salt and pepper to taste
½ cup chicken stock
1 lb. spaghetti

Place the eggplant in a colander and salt well. Let it drain about 1 hour. Rinse in cold water and drain on kitchen towels.

Heat olive oil in a large skillet. Add garlic and sauté 30 seconds. Add eggplant, peppers, zucchini, tomatoes, onion, thyme, parsley, salt, and pepper, blending all well. Add chicken stock, cover, and simmer 40 minutes, stirring from time to time and adding additional water if necessary.

Boil pasta in salted water until al dente. Drain and add to the vegetable mixture. Toss well. Transfer to a serving platter. Serves 8.

LASAGNE AUX FRUITS DE MER
SEAFOOD LASAGNE

Next to my recipe for Crab Pie, this recipe for Seafood Lasagne is probably the most requested by students and viewers of my cooking shows. A combination of crustaceans, shellfish, and artichoke hearts in a savory tomato sauce is layered with lasagne pasta and covered with mozzarella cheese. A garnish of anchovies and a 30-minute stay in the oven produces a memorable meal.

1 lb. lasagne pasta
1 tbsp. butter
3 cups Tomato Sauce for
  Lasagne (recipe follows)
1 cup oysters, poached
1 cup shrimp, boiled
  and shelled
1 cup dark crab claw meat

10 artichoke hearts,
  quartered
3 tbsp. parsley, chopped
Salt and pepper to taste
½ lb. mozzarella cheese,
  sliced
12 anchovy filets

Boil lasagne pasta in salted water until al dente. Drain and return to pot with warm water to keep from sticking together.

Butter a lasagne baking dish (9 x 13-inch). Cover bottom with a thin layer of sauce. Place a layer of lasagne over sauce drying each piece on towels. Blend together the remaining sauce, oysters, shrimp, crabmeat, artichokes, and parsley. Salt and pepper to taste. Alternate layers of tomato/seafood and lasagne, ending with sauce. Cover with mozzarella cheese and place half the anchovy filets diagonally over the cheese. Arrange the second half of the anchovy filets diagonally in the opposite direction. Bake at 350 degrees 30 minutes. Serves 8.

SAUCE TOMATE DE LASAGNE
TOMATO SAUCE FOR LASAGNE

1 cup onions, chopped
½ cup carrots, chopped
½ cup celery, chopped
3 tbsp. olive oil
2 cups tomatoes, peeled,
  seeded, and chopped

2 tsp. capers
Salt and pepper to taste
½ tsp. Italian seasoning
  (a blend of oregano,
  rosemary, savory, thyme,
  marjoram, sage, and basil)

Sauté onions, carrots, and celery in olive oil until soft. Add tomatoes, capers, salt, pepper, and Italian seasonings. Simmer 15 minutes. Cool to room temperature. Process in a food processor until puréed. Makes 3 cups or more.

LASAGNE CON MELANZANE
ALLA THERESA TURCI
EGGPLANT LASAGNE THERESA TURCI

Over the years I have presented several recipes I acquired from the late Madam Theresa Turci, who operated the finest Italian restaurant I have ever experienced. Madam Turci closed her restaurant on Fridays because it was a Roman Catholic day of fasting and back then few Catholics ate meat on Fridays. I was privileged to be invited to her home on Fridays, when she would prepare meatless meals such as this eggplant lasagne.

1 lb. lasagne pasta
2 tbsp. olive oil
5 lb. eggplants, peeled and cut into round slices ¼-inch thick
Salt to taste
½ cup additional olive oil

1 recipe Tomato Sauce for Lasagne (see preceding recipe)
1 recipe Salsa Balsamella (recipe follows)
½ cup Parmesan cheese, grated

Boil lasagne pasta in boiling salted water until al dente. Drain and toss with olive oil to prevent sticking together.

Place eggplant slices in a colander and sprinkle with salt. Allow to drain 20 minutes. Rinse off salt and dry slices on towels. Fry eggplant slices in additional olive oil until lightly brown. Drain on paper towels.

Oil a rectangular lasagne baking dish (9 x 13 inches). Spread a thin layer of tomato sauce in the baking dish. Make a layer of lasagne on bottom and sides of the baking dish. Spread another layer of tomato sauce over pasta. Place a layer of eggplant over tomato sauce. Cover with a thin layer of Balsamella Sauce. Repeat layering lasagne, tomato sauce, eggplant, and Balsamella until the dish is full, ending with Balsamella. Sprinkle with Parmesan cheese. Bake at 350 degrees 25 minutes. Allow to rest 10 minutes.

Cut into 8 portions. Remove with a wide spatula. Serve with remaining tomato sauce and Parmesan cheese on the side. Serves 8.

SALSA BALSAMELLA
Basic White Sauce

6 tbsp. butter
6 tbsp. flour
3 cups milk

½ tsp. salt
¼ tsp. white pepper

Melt butter in a saucepan. Stir in flour and cook 1 minute. Add milk. Whisk until mixture comes to a boil and thickens. Add salt and pepper to taste. Makes 3 cups.

FETTUCCINI AUX CREVETTES ET SAUCE CITRON
FETTUCCINI WITH SHRIMP IN LEMON SAUCE

Looking for a good recipe for shrimp and pasta, I combined elements of several recipes from my collection and produced a rich and tasty shrimp in a lemon-cream sauce that is served over boiled fettuccine pasta. It was delicious and got many compliments, so I know you will enjoy this. Although this dish is a main course, it can be served in smaller portions as a first course.

1 lb. fettuccine pasta
2 tbsp. butter
½ cup green onions, chopped
4 tbsp. additional butter
1½ lb. medium shrimp,
   shelled, and deveined
1½ cup half-and-half cream

Grated zest of 2 lemons
Salt and white pepper
   to taste
1 large tomato, peeled,
   seeded, and chopped
1 tbsp. chopped parsley

Boil fettuccine until al dente. Drain in a colander and toss with butter. Place colander over simmering water and keep warm.

Sauté green onions in additional butter until soft. Add shrimp and sauté 4 minutes. Remove from pan with a slotted spoon and reserve. Add cream, lemon zest, salt, and white pepper. Bring to a simmer for 2 minutes. Add chopped tomatoes and parsley. Simmer 1 minute longer. Serve over boiled fettuccine. Serves 8.

SPAGHETTI ALLA TERESA TURCI
SPAGHETTI WITH MEATBALLS,
CHICKEN, AND MUSHROOMS

The late Ettorie and Teresa Turci operated the finest Italian restaurant in New Orleans during the first part of the twentieth century. The specialty of the house was this extremely popular recipe. I was privileged to know Signora Turci and with the help of her granddaughter (my sister-in-law) and some correspondence of her daughter Virgina, I have been able to reconstruct this recipe and preserve a tradition.

1 recipe for Turci Sauce
Bolognese (recipe follows)
2 cups small (1-inch) Meatballs
(recipe follows)
2 cups boiled chicken breast
meat, cut into slivers

2 cups sliced mushrooms,
sautéed in butter
1 lb. spaghetti, boiled
al dente
½ cup grated Parmesan
cheese

Combine the Turci Sauce Bolognese and the meatballs and simmer for 10 minutes. Add the chicken and mushrooms and heat 5 minutes.

Place spaghetti in a serving dish. Add 1 cup of the Bolognese sauce and toss well. Transfer the meatballs, chicken, mushrooms, and Bolognese sauce into a serving bowl.

To serve, place a serving of pasta into a soup bowl. Ladle meatballs, chicken, mushrooms, and sauce over spaghetti. Sprinkle with Parmesan cheese. Serves 8.

SALSA BOLOGNESE ALLA TURCI
TURCI SAUCE BOLOGNESE

Although this meat sauce was specifically designed as an element of the recipe for Spaghetti alla Teresa Turci, it is excellent served on any pasta shape desired.

1 tbsp. olive oil
½ lb. ground beef
½ lb. chicken gizzards, ground
⅓ lb. pork, ground
⅓ cup additional olive oil
1 cup ham and ham fat, diced
1 cup onions, finely chopped
1 cup celery, finely chopped
1 clove garlic, finely chopped
2 cups tomato paste
2 cups chicken stock
Salt and pepper to taste

Sauté beef, chicken gizzards, and pork in olive oil until well browned. Transfer to a bowl and reserve.

Add additional olive oil to skillet and sauté ham and ham fat 2 minutes. Add onions, celery, and garlic. Sauté until vegetables are soft and onions begin to caramelize. Add tomato paste and blend well. Gradually blend in chicken stock. Salt and pepper to taste. Add the reserved beef, gizzards, and pork. Cover and simmer 1½ hours. Add additional chicken broth if necessary.

Use this sauce as the base for Spaghetti alla Teresa Turci or as the sauce for Pasta alla Bolognese. Yield about 10 cups.

POLPETTE DE MANZO
MEATBALLS

1½ lb. ground beef
1 medium egg, lightly beaten
2 tbsp. chopped parsley
Salt and pepper to taste
½ tsp. oregano

¾ cup stale bread, soaked
  in ⅓ cup water
Flour for dusting
2 cups peanut oil for
  deep-frying

Combine beef, beaten egg, parsley, salt, pepper, oregano, and soaked bread, blending well. Shape mixture into small ¾-inch meatballs. Dust lightly with flour and fry in ½-inch hot oil until browned. Do not overcook. Remove to paper towels and drain. Add to the Spaghetti alla Teresa Turci recipe as instructed.

An alternate method is to omit the flouring of the meatballs and place them on a oiled baking pan. Bake at 350 degrees 20 to 25 minutes until brown. Add to the recipe as required. Yields about 40 small balls.

Desserts

The final touch to an elegant meal, its last course, is the dessert. The term "dessert" comes from the French verb *desservir*, meaning "to clear the table." It first appears in 1600 A.D., and a study of the history of dining in France indicates that the table was cleared so that elaborate preparations could be displayed and consumed at the end of a meal. Today desserts are less elaborate but are no less delicious, and the table is still cleared away before the presentation of the grand finale.

It is interesting to observe that in various cuisines desserts are more common than in others. The French have probably developed more and varied kinds of sweets than any other cuisine, and anyone traveling to France marvels at the beauty and variety of pastries and desserts available in pastry shops, restaurants, and homes. The Italians tend to have their desserts in pastry and coffee shops, and most Italian meals, especially in the homes, end with cheese and fresh fruit. But Italian cuisine has many delicious desserts that are prepared and served most often on special occasions and at Sunday meals. Spanish customs lean to simple desserts: fruit and cheese, flans, and ice creams. Spaniards tend to eat sweets and pastries as snacks in between meals and as part of a Sunday dinner. Oriental cuisines, especially Chinese and Japanese, have very few desserts and occasionally serve fresh fruit at the end of a meal. The United States, with its variety of ethnic backgrounds, has taken from these other cultures and has developed a love of all kinds of sweets. Desserts come in all shapes and sizes: fresh fruit, creams and custards, puddings, cakes, pies, and in various combinations thereof.

The more elaborate desserts I leave to the professional chef and baker. In this volume I present some of my favorite desserts that are both straightforward and delicious. Many of the best desserts that have become classics were created out of the need not to waste leftover food; one example is the classic Bread Pudding, which the country French housewife made to used leftover stale French bread. Because she always had eggs and milk, she combined them with a little sugar and—*voilà*—created a classic. The Creoles and Cajuns adapted the foods of the old country upon their arrival in south Louisiana and added a Whiskey Sauce to embellish their bread pudding.

Many desserts in this chapter are combinations of various fresh fruits with a crunchy pastry topping, as in Peach Crumble. Some serve fresh fruits over fried bread, as in French Toast with Apples. Others combine eggs, milk, and sugar to produce French pancakes, as in Crêpe Mold or Pineapple Filled Crêpes. Pie dough is filled with pecans for Pecan and Cream Cheese Pie or Sweet Potato and Pecan Pie. One of my favorites is Fried Milk, which hails from Spain. Delicious and easy to prepare, it will get you compliments. Rice plays an interesting role in some of these desserts, such as Rice Pudding, Rice Cake, and Rice and Almond Tart. All three are desserts you will make again and again.

I have tried to present desserts that taste delicious, are easy to prepare, and that have brought me many compliments over the years. I hope you find them as rewarding as I do and include some of them in your personal recipe file.

POUDING AU PAIN
PEYROUX SAUCE WHISKEY
BREAD PUDDING PEYROUX WITH WHISKEY SAUCE

This Creole-style bread pudding is one of the two most popular desserts in my repertoire. The other is Rice Pudding, whose recipe follows. The secret to this recipe is to use a small amount of bread in relation to the other ingredients. The result is a light bread pudding with an egg-custard quality.

6 cups milk	1 tbsp. vanilla*
3 cups French bread, cut into 1-inch cubes	1 cup dried fruit, chopped (optional)
½ cup butter	1 cup pecans, toasted and chopped (optional)
3 large eggs, lightly beaten	
½ cup sugar	1 tsp. nutmeg
½ tsp. salt	1 recipe Whiskey Sauce

Generously butter the bottom and sides of a baking dish (10 x 12 x 2 inches) and arrange the French bread cubes over the bottom.

Bring milk just up to a boil and remove from heat. Combine eggs, sugar, salt, and vanilla and incorporate with the milk. Add the dried fruit and nuts if desired. Pour over the bread cubes in the baking dish. Sprinkle the top with nutmeg.

Place the baking dish in a larger pan, with water halfway up the sides of the baking dish. Bake at 350 degrees 1 hour and 15 minutes. Remove from oven and cool to room temperature. Serve with the following whiskey sauce. Serves 8.

*Vanilla extract is the product of a tropical orchid whose seed pods are dried and sold as vanilla beans or combined with alcohol to form vanilla extract. The long, slender, 6- to 8-inch vanilla beans contain thousands of very small seeds that impart the strongest flavor and can be used for maximum flavor or when you do not want to use alcohol-based extract. The beans come from Madagascar, Tahiti, Mexico, and Indonesia, with slight variations in flavor.

SAUCE WHISKEY
WHISKEY SAUCE

2 medium eggs, lightly beaten   **2 4-oz. sticks butter**
1½ cups confectioner's sugar   **½ cup bourbon whiskey**

Combine eggs and sugar in a bowl until well blended. Melt butter in a double boiler. Add egg/sugar mixture to butter. Whisk slowly until sauce thickens. Remove from heat and pour into a bowl. Allow to cool to room temperature. Slowly whisk in the whiskey. Serve with bread pudding. Makess 2½ cups.

Note: Rum can be substituted for the whiskey for an equally delicious rum sauce. For a nonalcoholic sauce, substitute ⅓ cup lemon juice and 1 tbsp. grated lemon zest.

PUDDING AU RIZ
RICE PUDDING

The second of the two most popular desserts I prepare is this custard rice pudding. The secret to this recipe is the small quantity of rice. Do not increase this amount because it will produce a thick and heavy pudding rather than a light and delicate one.

½ cup rice   **5 large eggs**
6 cups milk   **1 cup sugar**
1 tsp. salt   **2 tsp. vanilla**
2 cups additional milk   **½ tsp. nutmeg**

Blend together rice, milk, and salt in the top of a double boiler. Cover and cook 1 hour, stirring occasionally until rice is tender.

Combine milk, eggs, sugar, and vanilla in a large bowl. When rice is cooked, blend with the egg mixture. Pour into a 3-quart ovenproof bowl or soufflé bowl. Set the bowl in a larger baking pan with 1 inch water. Sprinkle with nutmeg. Bake uncovered at 325 degrees for 1 hour.

Remove to a wire rack and allow to cool. Refrigerate for 3 hours. Serves 8.

LECHE FRITA
FRIED MILK

"Unique" is the word for this dessert. It is a Spanish classic found in almost every restaurant in Spain. Milk and sugar are flavored with orange and thickened with cornstarch. Allowed to cool and firm, it is then cut into squares, covered with breadcrumbs, and then deep-fried. Garnished with sugar and cinnamon (or with orange marmalade), it becomes an unforgettable experience.

½ cup cornstarch, dissolved in 1 cup milk
2 cups additional milk
½ cup sugar
Zest of 1 orange, grated*
2 tsp. vanilla
1 tsp. orange extract

2 large eggs, lightly beaten
1 cup plain breadcrumbs
⅓ cup peanut oil
2 tbsp. butter
2 tbsp. sugar, combined with 1 tsp. cinnamon
¾ cup orange marmalade

Combine cornstarch/milk mixture, additional milk, and sugar. Bring to a boil on high heat, stirring. Add orange zest and continue stirring until thick. Remove from heat. Add vanilla and orange extract. Pour into an 8-inch square pan and refrigerate until firm.

With a knife dipped in hot water, cut congealed mixture into 2 x 3 rectangles. Remove, and dip in egg, and coat with breadcrumbs.

Fry rectangles in oil and butter 2 minutes on each side. Remove to a serving platter. Serve with sugar and cinnamon or orange marmalade. Serves 8.

*The colorful outer skin of citrus fruit such as lemons, oranges, and grapefruit is called *zeste* in French. The zest is removed into small thin strips with a device called a "zester" into small, thin strips. Longer and wider strips are removed with another device called a "stripper." In all cases, the zest should not contain any appreciable amount of white pith under the outer skin, which is bitter. The zest contains a very flavorful and fragrant citrus oil that imparts the desired flavor to the dish.

POIRES AGENAISES
POACHED PEARS AND PRUNES

Because Agen, a city in the southwest of France between Bordeaux and Toulouse, is well known for growing and drying plums to make prunes, many dishes that contain prunes are called *Agenaises* (in the style of Agen). This is true of this dessert, which pairs prunes with pears in seasoned syrup. They are delicious.

1 lb. large pitted prunes
1 cup water
1 cup red Bordeaux wine
1 tbsp. sugar
¾ cup additional water

¾ cup additional sugar
⅓ cup lemon juice
1 tsp. vanilla
3 lb. small pears, peeled
   and cored

Marinate prunes in water and Bordeaux overnight. Add sugar and simmer 1 minute. Make a syrup of additional water, additional sugar, lemon juice, and vanilla. Place pears into syrup and simmer slowly until tender (ten minutes). Allow to cool. Blend together the prunes, pears, and their syrups. Serve at room temperature. Serves 8.

POIRES ROTIES AU MIEL
BAKED PEARS WITH HONEY

The fresh taste of pear is highlighted by lemon juice, confectioner's sugar, and honey for a quick and simple dessert. Pears are very popular in France and find their way to the table in early winter as desserts of all kinds.

4 lb. pears, peeled, seeded, and sliced
Juice of 1 lemon
2 tbsp. butter
6 tbsp. confectioner's sugar
6 tbsp. honey

Juice of 2 additional lemons
6 tbsp. additional butter
¾ cup cream, lightly beaten
⅓ cup pear brandy (or ⅓ cup strawberry syrup*)

Combine pears and lemon juice to prevent darkening. Butter a baking dish. Arrange a layer of pears in the baking dish. Sprinkle with part of the confectioner's sugar. Pour some of the honey over pears. Drizzle some of the lemon juice over fruit. Repeat layers of pears, sugar, honey, and lemon juice. Dot with additional butter. Bake at 400 degrees 15 minutes.

Combine lightly beaten cream and pear brandy (or strawberry syrup). Pour over pears. Return to oven 5 minutes. Serves 8.

*Strawberry syrup can be made by boiling 3 or 4 crushed strawberries with ½ cup confectioner's sugar until thickened. It can be strained or not, as you desire.

CRUMBLE AU PECHES
PEACH CRUMBLE

Colorful and flavorful early-summer fruits are combined with brown sugar, topped with a mixture of flour, sugar, and butter, and baked to make a delicious casserole of fruit with a crunchy topping.

2 tbsp. butter, softened
8 peaches, peeled, seeded, and sliced
2 cups blackberries
1 cup cherries, pitted
Juice of 1 lemon
¼ cup brown sugar

3 cups flour
¾ cup additional brown sugar
1 pinch salt
8 oz. additional butter, softened

Butter a baking dish (8 cups). Combine peaches, blackberries, cherries, lemon juice, and sugar in the dish.

Combine flour, additional brown sugar, salt, and butter until the mixture forms pea-shaped pieces. Cover the fruit with the flour mixture. Bake at 475 degrees 35 to 40 minutes, until top is brown. Cool and serve at room temperature. Serves 8.

MOUSSES DE PECHES AU MIEL
HONEY PEACH MOUSSE

Simplicity itself is this peach mousse. Puréed peaches sweetened with honey are combined with stiffly beaten cream and fill individual bowls for a light and airy dessert. A simple garnish of three or four raspberries, strawberries, blueberries, or other fruit completes this elegant dessert.

10 peaches, peeled, seeded, and cut into pieces
Juice of 1 lemon
2 tsp. vanilla

6 tbsp. honey
1½ cups cream, very cold, beaten until stiff

Purée peaches with lemon juice in a food processor. Combine purée with vanilla and honey. Gently fold in the beaten cream. Pour into individual bowls. Refrigerate at least 1 hour. Serves 8.

SABAYON AUX NECTARINES
BAKED NECTARINES IN WINE SAUCE

Sabayon is a custard made by whisking egg yolks, sugar, and wine slowly over moderate heat. The classic Italian sabayon is one made with sweet Marsala wine and eaten as a dessert. In this French recipe the sabayon is flavored with sweet white wine and becomes a topping for sweetened nectarines.

8 nectarines, cut into slices
6 tbsp. confectioner's sugar
3 tbsp. butter
6 egg yolks

8 tbsp. brown sugar
1¼ cups sweet white wine
Mint leaves for a garnish

Arrange nectarine slices in a baking dish. Sprinkle with confectioner's sugar. Dot with butter. Bake at 350 degrees for 10 minutes.

Combine egg yolks and brown sugar in the top of a double boiler. Incorporate wine gradually while whisking. Whisk constantly for 15 minutes until thickened. Pour over nectarines. Pass under the broiler a few minutes. Garnish with mint leaves. Serve immediately. Serves 8.

DELICIEUX GATEAU AUX POIRES
DELICIOUS PEAR CAKE

Pears are probably my most favorite fruit, and whenever I find a recipe for pears it automatically goes into my file. I found this one on one of my trips to France, and it has become a regular at home. A basic cake batter flavored with cinnamon is the base for pear halves placed on top. This cake is as handsome and as delicious as the name implies.

4 eggs
1⅓ cups powdered sugar
8 oz. butter, softened
1¾ cups flour
1 tsp. baking powder*
1 tsp. cinnamon

1 tsp. vanilla
6 pears, peeled, cut in
half, and seeded**
1 tsp. additional butter
1 tbsp. additional
powdered sugar

Whisk together eggs and powdered sugar until light and creamy. Incorporate softened butter. Blend together flour, baking powder, and cinnamon. Gradually blend into egg mixture. Add vanilla, blending well.

Butter a cake pan or deep pie dish with additional butter. Pour batter into the buttered cake pan or pie dish. Arrange pear halves over batter, narrow ends inward. Sprinkle with additional powdered sugar. Bake at 350 degrees 1 hour. Allow to cool before unmolding or cutting. Serves 8.

*Baking powder is a combination of sodium bicarbonate (baking soda), cream of tartar, or sodium aluminum sulfate and cornstarch. When combined with moisture and heat, it reacts to create carbon dioxide, thereby causing the ingredients in the recipe to expand or rise. Cream of tartar (potassium acid tartarte) is a by-product of wine making and is used as a stabilizer. Cream of tartar is often added to beaten egg whites to stabilize the volume beaten into the eggs.

**Try other fruits such as peaches, plums, or prunes soaked in wine.

GATEAU MOELLEUX AU CITRON
VELVETY LEMON CAKE

If you like the flavor of lemon, this recipe is for you. A basic yellow cake is flavored with lemon syrup and rum and then garnished with candied lemon slices. The slow simmering of lemon slices in a simple syrup tenderizes them and makes them easy to eat.

½ cup sugar
3 eggs, room temperature
1½ cups flour, sifted
4 tbsp. butter, softened
2 tsp. baking powder
Zest of 2 lemons, grated
4 lemons, juiced

⅓ cup additional sugar
3 tbsp. rum*
1 cup sugar
1¼ cup water
6 additional lemons, sliced
    thinly in rounds

Blend together sugar and eggs until pale yellow. Fold in the flour. Add butter, baking powder, and zest. Pour batter into a buttered and floured 9-inch cake pan. Bake at 350 degrees for 25 to 30 minutes. Remove cake from the oven. Cool and remove from the pan.

Bring lemon juice and additional sugar to a boil for 2 minutes. Remove from heat. Add rum. Moisten cake with the lemon/rum syrup.

Dissolve the final cup of sugar in water. Bring to a simmer and add lemon slices. Poach until they become transparent, 15 to 20 minutes. Drain the sliced lemons. Cut enough lemon slices in half to place around the sides of the cake, cut side down. Arrange remaining whole slices around top outer edge of cake in an overlapping manner. Serves 8.

*Rum is an alcoholic beverage made from distilled, fermented sugarcane juices or molasses. Dark rum has a richer and more pronounced rum flavor than light rum, and the decision to use either is based upon your desire for a lighter or stronger rum flavor.

GATEAU AU FROMAGE ALMA
CHEESECAKE ALMA

This recipe was a specialty of my mother. I have no idea where she found this recipe, but she prepared this relatively light cheesecake for years. I have adopted it and serve it frequently when I have dinner parties.

4 medium eggs
1 cup sugar
3 large Philadelphia
  cream cheeses, softened
7 tbsp. milk
¼ cup butter, softened

20 graham crackers,
  crushed
¾ cup additional sugar
2 tsp. vanilla
2 cups sour cream

Blend together eggs, sugar, cheese, and milk. Combine graham crackers, butter, additional sugar, and vanilla. Line a 9-inch cake pan with crumb mixture. Pour cheese mixture over crumbs. Bake at 300 degrees for 45 minutes.

Turn oven off, leaving cake in the oven 30 minutes. Remove from oven and let stand 30 minutes. Spread sour cream over top of cake. Bake at 350 degrees for 10 minutes. Cool and then refrigerate. Serves 8.

GATEAU DE RIZ
RICE CAKE

This recipe is a happy blend of two popular Creole recipes: Egg Custard with Carmel, and Rice Pudding. White raisins and orange juice and zest contribute additional flavors. This recipe is delicious and presents well.

1 qt. milk
1 cup rice
⅔ cup sugar
½ cup white raisins soaked
   in ¼ cup orange juice
1 tbsp. orange and lemon zest

2 cups cream
3 large eggs, lightly beaten
½ cup sugar
3 tbsp. water
1 recipe English Cream
   (recipe follows)

In a large pot, blend together milk, rice, sugar, raisins, orange juice, and zests. Heat to a simmer. Cook over low heat, stirring frequently, until thick, about 40 minutes. Cool to room temperature. Add cream and eggs.

Heat sugar and water in a nonstick skillet until a light caramel color. Pour into a 9½ x 5½ x 3-inch loaf pan. Pour rice mixture into mold over caramel. Place in a bain-marie. Bake at 350 degrees for 60 minutes. Cool, then refrigerate until firm. Unmold, slice, and serve with a Creme Anglaise Sauce. Serves 8.

CREME ANGLAISE
ENGLISH CREAM

This sauce is excellent served over fruit.

6 egg yolks
½ cup sugar, extra
   finely granulated
1 cup milk

1 cup half-and-half cream
½ cup cream
1 tsp. vanilla

Whisk egg yolks and sugar together until light, fluffy, and pale yellow. Bring milk, half-and-half, and cream just up to a boil. Slowly add the egg/sugar mixture while stirring with a wooden spoon. Stir over low to medium heat until sauce thickens and coats the back of a wooden spoon. Remove from heat and stir in the vanilla. Yields 3 cups.

PAIN PERDU AUX POMMES
FRENCH TOAST WITH APPLES

Pain Perdu, or "Lost Bread," is a popular breakfast dish wherein slices of French bread are soaked in beaten egg, fried, and served with syrup, honey, or preserves. This recipe takes the breakfast item and turns it into a delightful dessert garnished with spiced apples and brandy.

½ cup honey
1 cup confectioner's sugar
4 tbsp. butter
6 apples, peeled, cored, and
    cut into medium slices
½ tsp. nutmeg, grated
8 slices egg bread,
    ½-inch thick

⅓ cup Calvados
    (apple brandy)
3 eggs, beaten
1 cup milk
8 tbsp. additional butter

Heat honey, sugar, and butter slowly in a sauté pan until blended. Add the apple slices and the nutmeg. Simmer until tender and golden.

Sprinkle bread slices with Calvados. Combine beaten eggs and milk. Pass each slice of bread in egg/milk mixture. Sauté bread slices in additional butter until brown on both sides. Place bread on a serving platter.

Arrange the apple slices on top in a circle. This dessert can be served hot or at room temperature. Serves 8.

POMMES DOREES
BRONZED APPLES

Another of the many simple French recipes, this one combines apples with sautéed bread cubes. Garnished with whipped cream, it becomes an elegant dessert.

6 apples, peeled, seeded, and cut into ½-inch cubes
8 tbsp. light brown sugar
4 tbsp. butter
Juice of 1 lemon

4 tbsp. additional butter
8 slices thick bread, cut into ½-inch cubes
½ cup whipped cream

Combine apples and brown sugar, mixing thoroughly. Sauté in butter until tender and browned. Transfer to a platter. Sprinkle with lemon juice.

Melt additional butter in the same skillet. Sauté bread cubes until golden. Return the reserved apples to the skillet. Mix well. Transfer to a serving platter. Garnish with whipped cream. Serves 8.

CLAFOUTIS AUX CERISES
A LA CREME D'AMANDES
ALMOND CHERRY COUNTRY PUDDING

A truly unique French dessert is *clafoutis,* which is as simple a dessert as you can make. A seasoned pancake batter is poured over fresh fruit and baked at high heat. This cherry clafoutis is flavored with almonds for a happy marriage of tastes.

1½ lb. cherries, pitted
1 tbsp. butter
3 eggs lightly beaten
1 cup confectioner's sugar
½ cup flour, sifted
¼ tsp. salt

½ cup almonds
1 tbsp. cream
1¼ cups milk
3 drops almond extract
2 tbsp. additional confectioner's sugar

Butter an oval baking dish (2 quarts). Scatter cherries in baking dish and set aside.

Beat eggs and sugar until smooth. Process flour, salt, and almonds in a food processor until almonds are powdered. Add to egg/sugar mixture. Add cream, milk, and almond extract. Pour over cherries. Bake at 350 degrees 35 minutes until browned. Remove from oven and cool to room temperature.

Sprinkle additional confectioner's sugar over clafoutis. Serve room temperature or cold. Serves 8.

CLAFOUTIS AU POMMES A LA NORMANDE
APPLE CUSTARD TART FROM NORMANDY

Normandy, on the English Channel coast, is known for its abundant dairy products and apple production. Much of this fruit is made into a signature product, Calvados, a brandy made from apples. Both the fruit and the brandy find their way into the cooking of the region, as in this recipe.

6 apples, peeled, seeded, and sliced
6 tbsp. butter, melted
3 eggs, lightly beaten
½ cup brown sugar
4 tbsp. flour

Zest of a large lemon
3 tsp. Calvados (apple brandy)
1 cup milk
½ cup additional brown sugar

Arrange apples slices in a deep pie dish. Pour melted butter over apples. Bake at 500 degrees for 3 minutes. Remove and lower oven temperature to 400 degrees.

Combine eggs, sugar, flour, lemon zest, Calvados, and milk. Pour over apples. Return to the oven and bake 20 minutes.

Sprinkle additional sugar over clafoutis. Bake another 5 minutes. Cool to room temperature. Serve room temperature or cold. Serves 8.

CREPES GRAND-MERE
GRANDMOTHER'S FRENCH PANCAKES

One of the simplest of all classic French desserts is *crêpes,* or French pancakes. I can still see my great-grandmother making them on a wood-burning stove and simply sprinkling them with sugar before rolling them up. This basic recipe can be prepared and served as simply as she did or, as will be seen in the following recipes, can be turned into glamorous desserts.

1 cup flour, sifted	**2 tbsp. butter, melted**
1 tbsp. sugar	**1 tsp. additional butter**
¼ tsp. salt	**½ cup additional sugar**
3 large eggs	**(optional)**
2 cups milk	

Blend together flour, sugar, salt, eggs, milk, and butter. Strain and allow to rest 30 minutes.

Using a 6-inch crêpe pan or small skillet, heat 1 tsp. of butter until very hot and pour out. Pour about 3 tablespoons of batter into crêpe pan, turning to coat the bottom, and cook about 1 minute. Turn pancake over and cook the other side about ½-minute. Slide out of the pan onto a plate. Repeat crêpe making until all the batter is used.

Proceed with a specific recipe that requires crêpes or serve them grandmother's style by turning pancake over so that the first-cooked side is facing down. Sprinkle 1 tsp. sugar over crêpe. Roll jelly-roll fashion. Place on a serving platter over a pot of simmering water. Cover loosely with foil. Makes 16 crêpes.

CREPE SOUFFLES AU COULIS D'ABRICOT
SOUFFLED CREPES WITH APRICOT SAUCE

This attention-getting dessert is easy to prepare and delicious to eat. Whipped egg whites are incorporated into a classic Creme Anglaise, which is a filling for a folded crêpe. When baked, the heat causes the whipped egg whites to expand, thus causing a soufflé. When garnished with apricot sauce, it becomes an elegant dessert.

1 cup milk	**1 recipe Crêpes**
½ 1 vanilla bean	**Grand-mère**
4 large egg yolks	**(preceding recipe,**
½ cup sugar	**omitting sugar)**
2 tbsp. flour	**1 recipe Apricot Sauce**
4 large egg whites	**(recipe follows)**

Scald milk with the ½-vanilla bean. Blend together egg yolks and sugar until sugar dissolves. Whisk in flour and gradually incorporate the hot milk. Return to heat and bring to a boil while stirring. Remove vanilla bean and cool mixture completely.

Whip egg whites until firm and fold into filling mixture.

Butter a cookie sheet and place crêpes on the sheet. Spoon some filling on each crêpe. Fold crêpe in half over the filling. Bake at 450 degrees about 7 minutes, until crêpes puff. Serve with apricot sauce. Serves 8.

SAUCE ABRICOT
APRICOT SAUCE

The beautiful orange color of the puréed apricots is a natural contrast to the light colors of crêpes and soufflé. The flavor is heavenly.

1 lb. can of apricot halves	**3 tbsp. lemon juice**
in heavy syrup	

Drain apricots, reserving 3 tablespoons of syrup. Purée apricots, reserved syrup, and lemon juice. Chill. Makes about 1 cup.

TIMBALE DE CREPES
CREPE MOLD

This unusual recipe produces a fantastic crêpe mold by bathing each crêpe in an orange-and-lemon-flavored sauce and stacking them in a springform pan. The mold is baked for a short while and unmolded. A garnish of powdered sugar completes the dessert.

3 eggs
1 cup flour
1 tsp. sugar
¼ tsp. salt
1 cup milk
3 tbsp. butter, melted
3 egg yolks
⅓ cup sugar
1 tbsp. cornstarch

1 cup milk, scalded
1 tbsp. orange zest,
  finely chopped
½ tbsp. lemon zest,
  finely chopped
Juice of 1 orange
Juice of ½ lemon
2 oz. Cointreau liquor
⅓ cup powdered sugar

Whisk together the eggs, flour, sugar, and salt. Blend in the milk. Let rest 1 hour. Add the melted butter. Make as many 9-inch crêpes as the batter allows. Set aside.

Whisk together the egg yolks, sugar, and cornstarch. Add the scalded milk. Incorporate the orange and lemon zests. Bring the mixture to a boil while stirring. Add the orange and lemon juices and Cointreau liquor. Heat until boiling and thickened.

Butter a 9-inch springform pan. Pass each crêpe in the egg/milk mixture. Place crêpes in spring form pan 1 on top of the other. Bake at 400 degrees for 10 minutes. Unmold and sprinkle with powdered sugar. Serves 8.

CREPES GEORGETTE
PINEAPPLE-FILLED CREPES

I learned this delicious dessert at Le Cordon Bleu in 1976. Pineapple and pastry cream are the filling for rolled crêpes that are heated in the oven. This rich and elegant dessert will get you raves.

1 recipe Pastry Cream
  (recipe follows)
1 cup crushed pineapple

1 recipe crêpes
  (see previous
  Crêpe Mold recipe)

Blend together Creme Patisserie and pineapple. Place 3 tablespoons of mixture on each crêpe. Roll crêpe. Place in an ovenproof platter. Heat for 5 minutes at 350 degrees. Serves 8.

CREME PATISSERIE
PASTRY CREAM

Try this basic recipe of pastry cream as a dessert in itself.

1 cup milk
1 tsp. vanilla
3 eggs

1 cup sugar
⅓ cup flour
3 tbsp. butter

Heat milk and vanilla. Beat eggs and sugar until pale yellow. Fold in flour and beat until it forms a ribbon. Gradually add milk. Whisk over medium heat until thick. Blend in butter. Pour into a bowl. Film with a little butter to prevent a crust. Makes 2½ cups.

TOURTE AUX POMMES AUX RAISINS
SEC A LA CANNELLE
DEEP-DISH APPLE RAISIN CINNAMON TART

For a happy variation on apple pie, try this deep-dish tart. A layer of almonds, sugar, cinnamon, and raisins is followed by a layer of apples, then another layer of almonds, sugar, cinnamon, and raisins—all baked in a piecrust.

1 double recipe pie dough (recipe above)
3 lb. apples, peeled, cored, and quartered
2/3 cup sugar
1/2 cup water
Juice of 1 lemon
Zest of 1 lemon
1/3 cup almonds, sliced
1/3 cup almond powder
1 tsp. cinnamon
1/2 cup additional sugar
1/2 cup raisins soaked in 4 tbsp. rum
1 egg, diluted with 1 tsp. water

Roll 2/3 of pie dough until 1/4-inch thick. Line a deep tart pan with the dough. Cover with aluminum foil. Fill with dried beans or rice. Bake at 250 degrees 10 minutes. Remove foil with beans or rice. Set partially cooked pie dough aside.

Cook apples in sugar, water, lemon juice, and zest 10 minutes. Blend together the 2 almonds, cinnamon, additional sugar, and raisins. Sprinkle half the almond mixture over the bottom of partially cooked pie shell. Arrange apples over the mixture. Cover with remaining almond mixture.

Roll remaining pie dough 1/4-inch thick. Cover tart with dough. Garnish with pastry cutouts. Brush with egg wash. Bake at 350 degrees 25 minutes. Cool 1 hour. Serves 8.

TARTE AUX FRAISES
STRAWBERRY TART

This is the classic French strawberry tart one sees in pastry shops all over France. It combines a rich pastry cream with the fresh taste of glazed strawberries in a flaky pie dough for a taste sensation you will never forget. This will get you raves at your next dinner party.

1 recipe Basic Pie Dough (recipe follows)

2 cups dried beans (white, red, or navy, to act as a weight)

1 recipe Pastry Cream (recipe above)

2 pt. fresh strawberries, hulled*

¾ cup raspberry or red-currant jam

Line a 9-inch tart pan with removable bottom with pie dough. Prick bottom with a fork. Line pie dough with aluminum foil. Fill with dried beans. Bake at 350 degrees for 10 minutes. Remove foil and beans and discard. Return to the oven and bake 10 to 12 minutes until golden. Remove from oven and allow to cool.

Fill baked tart with pastry cream and spread evenly. Arrange strawberries closely over pastry cream, stem ends down and pointed ends up. Heat jam until melted and allow to cool slightly. Using a soft pastry brush, glaze the strawberries with the jam. Serves 8.

*Other fruits, poached pears, figs, cooked apple slices, peaches, nectarines, seedless grapes, etc., can be substituted with great success.

PATE BRISEE
Basic Pie Dough

The food processor has made the making of pie dough very simple. The secret, however, is to have all the ingredients very cold and to not let the butter and solid shortening melt.

2 cups flour
½ tsp. salt
4 oz. butter, cold

3 tbsp. cold, solid
shortening (Crisco)
¼ cup cold water

Using your fingers, blend together flour, salt, butter, and shortening until it resembles small peas. Gradually add water until dough forms a ball (this can be done in a food processor). Wrap in plastic wrap and chill 30 minutes. Roll dough as required in the recipe. This recipe makes dough for a 9- or 10-inch tart or pie pan. Doubling the recipe provides dough for a top crust as well as for pastry cutouts or decorations.

PATE DE PECANE ET FROMAGE A LA CREME
PECAN AND CREAM CHEESE PIE

The late Leon Soniat, author of *La Bouche Creole*, taught this recipe in his cooking classes in New Orleans. The cream cheese counteracts the cloying sweetness of the corn syrup and provides a smooth richness to this pecan classic. Leon's book, whose title is translated as "The Creole Taste," is one of the best personal volumes on Creole cookery. I highly recommend it.

8 oz. cream cheese
1 egg
4 tbsp. sugar
1 tsp. vanilla
¾ cup corn syrup
1 tsp. additional vanilla
3 additional eggs

2 tbsp. additional sugar
1 9-inch Basic Pie Dough
  (recipe above)
¾ cup pecans, chopped
1 cup additional pecan
  halves

Blend together cream cheese, egg, sugar, and vanilla until smooth. In another bowl, blend corn syrup, additional vanilla, eggs, and sugar. Pour cream cheese mixture into pie shell. Cover with chopped pecans. Pour corn-syrup mixture over pecans. Garnish top with pecan halves. Bake at 375 degrees for 35 minutes. Remove from oven and cool to room temperature. Serves 8.

TOURTE DE PATATES DOUCES ET PACANES
SWEET POTATO AND PECAN PIE

This Cajun recipe combines two Cajun favorites, sweet potato pie and pecan pie, and what a happy marriage it is. The sweetness of the potatoes complemented by aromatic spices is joined with the crunchy pecans in a piecrust. The aroma while baking is almost as good at its taste.

2 medium sweet potatoes
2 eggs
½ cup butter, softened
1 cup light brown sugar
2 tsp. combination of equal parts cinnamon, ginger, nutmeg, allspice, and cloves
½ tsp. salt

1 tsp. vanilla
1 cup half-and-half cream
1 cup pecans, chopped
1 cup pecan halves
1 9-inch pie shell
1 cup sweetened whipped cream (optional)

Boil sweet potatoes* until tender. Drain and refresh in cold water to cool. Peel sweet potato and mash 2 cups of pulp. Blend together sweet-potato pulp, eggs, butter, and sugar. Add combined spices, salt, vanilla, and cream. Fold in chopped pecans. Pour into pie shell. Garnish top with pecan halves. Bake at 350 degrees for 50 to 60 minutes. Cool. Top with sweetened whipped cream, if desired. Serves 8.

*Sweet potatoes can be microwaved instead of boiled, or 2 cups of canned mashed sweet potatoes can be substituted.

TARTE ANTILLES
RICE AND ALMOND TART

Almond rice custard in a pie shell is probably the best description for this dessert. After the ingredients for the rice custard are prepared and placed in a pie shell, whole almonds are pressed partway into the custard with the pointed ends up. The rich, creamy taste of rice custard is complemented by the cooked almonds to make a unique dessert.

3 cups milk
⅔ cup rice (raw)
⅓ cup sugar
3 tbsp. butter, cut into
  small pieces
4 egg yolks, lightly beaten
3 oz. almonds, finely chopped
1 9-inch Basic Pie Dough
  (recipe above)

2 cups dried beans
1 egg, lightly beaten
3 tbsp. additional butter,
  melted
3 oz. additional almonds,
  whole

Bring milk to a boil. Add rice and simmer 20 minutes until milk is absorbed. Combine cooked rice, sugar, and butter. Add egg yolks and chopped almonds to rice mixture.

Prick bottom of pie shell with a fork. Line with aluminum foil and fill with dried beans. Bake 15 minutes at 350 degrees. Remove foil with beans and discard.

Pour almond/rice mixture into pie shell. Combine egg and melted butter. Pour over rice. Insert whole almonds, pointed ends up, halfway into the rice mixture. Bake at 425 degrees for 20 minutes. Cool to room temperature. Serves 8.

TARTE AU RIZ A LA COMPOTE DE POMMES
RICE AND APPLE PIE

Here is another unusual combination of flavors. Rice cooked with sugar, milk, and vanilla is combined with sautéed apples and rum-soaked raisins for a pie filling.

½ cup raisins
3 tbsp. rum
1¼ cups milk
½ cup confectioner's sugar
2 tsp. vanilla
⅓ cup short-grain rice
2 apples, peeled,
   cored and chopped

1 tbsp. butter
2 tbsp. sugar
1 recipe Basic Pie Dough
   (recipe above)
2 tbsp. cream
1 large egg

Place raisins and rum in a bowl to soak and set aside.

Bring the milk, confectioner's sugar, and vanilla to a boil. Add the rice and blend well. Lower heat and simmer 30 minutes. When rice is cooked, allow to cool.

Sauté apples in butter with the sugar until soft.

Roll dough ¼-inch thick and place in a tart pan or pie dish. Combine rice, apples, cream, egg, and the raisins and rum. Pour into the tart pan. Bake at 400 degrees 30 minutes.

Unmold tart and allow to come to room temperature. Serves 8.

Index

Basic White Sauce, 279
Bayley, William, 28
Bean curd, 102
Bean sprouts, 101
Beans: Creole Green Beans, 208; Garbanzos beans, 58; Green Bean and Tuna Salad, 52; Green Bean Salad, 51; Green Beans in Cream Sauce, 208; Red and White Bean Salad, 55; Red Bean Salad, 54; Red Beans New Orleans Style, 210; A Salad from Tuscany, 57; Smothered Crawfish with Beans, 114; Sweet and Sour Green Beans, 209; Tomato and White Bean Soup, 68; White Bean and Shrimp Salad, 56
Beef: Beef Nuggets in Wine Sauce, 129; Beef Stew, 128; Beef Stroganoff, 130; Beer-Braised Beef, 131; Boiled Brisket of Beef with Horseradish Sauce, 132; Brisket of Beef, 132; Carbonade, 131; Corned-Beef Turnover, 139; Horseradish Sauce, 133; Macaroni and Meat Pie, 137; Meat Loaf, 134; Meatballs, 282; Meatballs in Lemon Sauce, 138; Pastitsio, 137; Spaghetti with Meatballs, Chicken, and Mushrooms, 280; Stuffed Cabbage Leaves Greek Style, 136; Sweet and Sour Small Beef Balls, 31
Beef extract, 130
Beets: Harvard Beets, 210; Red and Yellow Salad, 40
Bercaw, Doe, 23
Bezout, Chef Phillipe, 100
Bisque, Shrimp, 78

Boiled Brisket of Beef with Horseradish Sauce, 132
Bokas, John, 178
Bouchées, 104
Bovril, 130
Braised Green and Red Cabbage, 214
Braised Leeks with Mustard, 226
Braised Red Cabbage, 215
Braised Red, Yellow and Green Bell Peppers, 239
Braised Veal Rounds New Orleans Style, 140
Braised Veal Shanks with Rice, 141
Breaded Veal with Parmesan Cheese Turci, 146
Breads: Bread Pudding Peyroux with Whiskey Sauce, 286; French Toast with Apples, 298; Fruits of the Sea in Bread Boats, 118; Hardtack (Sea Biscuit), 48; Onion and Cheese Lost Bread Casserole, 235; Sautéed Breadcrumbs, 120
Broccoli: Broccoli Pie, 212; Broccoli Soup Amandine, 82; Broccoli with Horseradish Sauce, 211
Bronzed Apples, 299
Bugialli, Guiliano, 150, 255
Butter, Clarified, 95

Cabbage: Braised Green and Red Cabbage, 214; Braised Red Cabbage, 215; French-style Stuffed Cabbage, 213; Marinated Red Cabbage Salad, 43; Poached Chicken Balls with Cabbage, 186; Stuffed Cabbage Leaves Greek Style, 136; Sweet and Sour Cabbage Salad, 44; Cab-